MAKING CHOICES FOR MULTICULTURAL EDUCATION

Five Approaches to Race, Class, and Gender

Christine E. Sleeter
University of Wisconsin—Parkside

Carl A. Grant
University of Wisconsin—Madison

Merrill, an imprint of
Macmillan Publishing Company
New York

Collier Macmillan Canada, Inc.
Toronto

Maxwell Macmillan International Publishing Company
New York   Oxford   Singapore   Sydney

Macmillan Publishing Company
866 Third Avenue, New York, New York 10022

Macmillan Publishing Company is
part of the Maxwell Communication
Group of Companies.

Maxwell Macmillan Canada, Inc.
1200 Eglinton Avenue East
Suite 200
Don Mills, Ontario M3C 3N1

This book was set in Bookman.

Administrative Editor: David Faherty
Production Coordinator: Linda Hillis Bayma
Art Coordinator: Lorraine Woost
Cover Designer: Jolie Muren

Photo Credits: All photos copyrighted by individuals or companies listed.
Bell & Howell, p. 2; Joanne Meldrum, p. 174; Merrill Publishing/photographs
by Jean Greenwald, p. 206; and Bruce Johnson, pp. 74, 104, 136; David
Strickler, p. 34.

Library of Congress Catalog Card Number: 87-63313
International Standard Book Number: 0-675-20804-1
Printed in the United States of America
    5 6 7 8 9—92

PREFACE

O ur primary reason for writing *Making Choices for Multicul-tural Education: Five Approaches to Race, Class, and Gender* was to offer to the educational community a way of thinking about race, language, culture, class, gender, and disability in teaching. This book grew out of a chain of inquiry to investigate multicultural education, how it is defined, how it is taught in school, its conceptual base, and reasons for its development. We realized that when people use the term *multicultural education*, they mean different things. Some people think only about racial or cultural diversity, while others conceptualize gender, social class, and additional forms of diversity. At the same time, many people who discuss gender equity share concerns similar to those of multicultural education advocates, but ignore race and culture or give them only passing attention. The same can be said of those who address social class and disability.

Based on our knowledge of the literature addressing race, culture, language, gender, social class, and disability, we sensed that there were overarching issues common to all these, and at the same time different approaches to addressing these forms of human diversity in the classroom. Therefore, we decided to examine the educational literature to determine these different approaches. We reviewed over 200 articles and 60 books written on multicultural education and reported this information in three journal articles.[1] Perhaps we should have stopped there, but we continued to investigate each of the approaches to multicultural education we discovered. (Like the saying goes, once you get a tiger by the tail, it's hard to let go.)

This investigation, we believe, is thorough, although perhaps not exhaustive. We did this as more than just an intellectual exercise. We believe that educators need to be very clear about what multicultural, nonsexist, mainstream education means to them. What goals does an educator actually have in mind? What target student population? What vision of society? What ideas about how to achieve a better society? What assumptions about learning? No single set of answers is embraced by the majority of educators who are concerned with race, language, culture, gender, social class, and disability. But it is important for you, the reader, to be clear about your own beliefs in order to achieve effectively what you are attempting to achieve. We have also taken the liberty, after sharing what we have learned about each of the approaches, to explain the one we like best. We hope you don't see that as being arrogant, for that is not our intention. Instead, after much debate and soul searching, we decided that you might like to know which approach we prefer. Why? Because even as objective as we have tried to be in writing the first six chapters, we know that what people say and how they see the world is shaped by their ideology, background, and vision of the world. Also, we know that the colleagues and students we work with are self-thinking people and not easily persuaded, and most are capable of making up their own minds.

Finally, we are very proud of *Making Choices for Multicultural Education: Five Approaches to Race, Class, and Gender* because we believe that it makes a vital contribution to the fields of multicultural education, nonsexist education, and mainstreaming at an important time in their development. Enjoy the fruit of our labor, and if you are inclined, let us know what you think, for your thoughts will help us to grow as we continue to swing the tiger by the tail.

---

[1]C. A. Grant & C. E. Sleeter, The literature on multicultural education: Review and analysis, *Educational Review*, *37* (1985): 97–118; C. A. Grant, C. E. Sleeter, & J. E. Anderson, The literature on multicultural education: Review and analysis, Part II, *Educational Studies*, *12* (1986): 47–71; C. E. Sleeter & C. A. Grant, An analysis of multicultural education in the U.S.A., *Harvard Educational Review*, *57* (1987): 421–444.

ACKNOWLEDGMENTS

For us, the writing of this book was a lonely process. It reflects our own collaborative thinking, but relatively little direct input from others. While our thinking has grown as a result of our interaction with colleagues over the years, and this growth is certainly reflected in this book, only a few individuals have contributed directly to its production.

Grace Thomsen is thanked for her very useful and insightful contribution of information and ideas related to language-minority students. Our own students have read and responded to drafts of chapters, providing helpful feedback and perspectives on the value, readability, and comprehensibility of the book. Specifically, they are graduate and undergraduate students at the University of Wisconsin—Parkside who were enrolled in "Living in a Multicultural Society" and in "Multicultural Education" and students at the University of Wisconsin—Madison who took the graduate seminar "Multicultural Education." The following reviewers are acknowledged for their helpful suggestions and enthusiastic reception of this book: Gilbert Cuevas, University of Miami; Patricia J. Larke, Texas A&M University; Samuel A. Perez, University of Oregon; and Joseph Ponterotto, University of Nebraska. And finally, we thank Janet Dewane, who patiently worked through our sloppy handwriting, arrows, and inserts to produce a final manuscript.

CONTENTS

CHAPTER **7**

CHAPTER 1

Illusions of Progress:
Business as Usual

Picture the following class: Out of 30 students (15 girls and 15 boys), 21 are White, five are Black, three are Hispanic, and one is Asian. Two of the Black students, one Hispanic student, and four White students come from families who live below the poverty line, while another four white students are from upper-income homes. These social class distinctions are not readily visible, however, since most of the students are clad in jeans and cotton shirts or T-shirts, but a glance at their home addresses and at the free-lunch roster suggests their social class backgrounds. The students' families vary widely: Whereas only two come from homes in which the father works and the mother stays home, seven are from single-parent families (four of which live below the poverty line), and both parents of the remaining 21 students hold or have recently held jobs at least part-time. Most of the students grew up speaking English, but two of the Hispanic students speak Spanish at home, and one White student speaks French at home. The students' academic skills vary widely: Two spend part of the day in a learning disabilities class, one in a class for the mentally retarded, one in a gifted program, and one in a speech therapy program.

How does a teacher teach such a wide variety of students? What sort of curriculum is taught? Are all students taught the same curriculum? What teaching strategies are used? How are students grouped for instruction—or are they grouped at all? How are they seated? You may find two conflicting images forming in your head, one depicting how you believe a teacher *should* teach these students, the other depicting how most teachers really *do* teach them.

Where does one find this class of students? We based our hypothetical class on statistics describing the composition of public schools in the United States in the early 1980s (*Digest of Educational Statistics,* 1985–1986; U.S. Department of Commerce, Bureau of the Census, 1986). Actually, student composition varies widely across the country, even within the same city or the same school. But given the diversity of America's students, schools, and classrooms, the same questions persist: How do teachers actually teach their students, and how should students be taught?

These are the central questions this book addresses. We recognize, however, that schools do not exist in a vacuum. They are, instead, quite closely connected to the society they serve. Therefore, when considering what kind of education would best serve America's diverse student population, we also need to consider the nature of the society in which schools exist. This chapter will first briefly discuss the nature of society in the 1980s as it relates to race, language, culture, gender, social class, and handicap, then synthesize recent research to provide a portrait of how teachers actually teach America's diverse student population. Finally, it will provide the framework used in subsequent chapters to address alternative approaches to teaching.

SOCIETY TODAY

Some people may think that sexism, racism, and bias against the handicapped are no longer major societal problems. We see increasing numbers of White women and Black men as mayors of large cities, growing Hispanic political clout, a Black sit-com on television leading the way to first place in the ratings war, and another sit-com with a blind person as the leading character. One can think of additional illustrations of progress in the 1980s: Hands Across America raised millions of dollars to fight poverty and homelessness; women and minorities as astronauts are no longer big news; the U.S. Supreme Court has its first female member (further diversifying it since the addition of its first Black member); and a Vietnamese refugee was recognized as Teacher of the Year and congratulated personally by the president for her achievement. In addition, a quick glance at a cover story in *Time* would suggest that America still opens its arms to new groups of immigrants, welcoming culturally diverse new citizens in its Ellis Island tradition.

But these indications of progress obscure the larger picture. In spite of such examples (which often involve only small numbers of people), there is considerable evidence that U.S. society is still very stratified on the basis of race, gender, and disability. In fact, stratification based on social class is a prominent feature of U.S. society and one that social policy in the last 3 decades has made little sustained attempt to change.

When considering racism in society, Americans often cite improved racial attitudes as a sign of progress. Indeed, attitudes have improved somewhat. One study reports that White attitudes toward Blacks are much less negative than they were 3½ decades ago (Taylor, Sheatsley, & Greely, 1978). A 1978 survey conducted by the *New York Times* and CBS, designed to replicate the study conducted by the Advisory Commission on Civil Disorder in 1968, summarizes the recent new attitude of Whites very appropriately, however: Although Whites have better attitudes about race relations and improved understanding, they lack the will to take the bitter medicine that the remedies for racism require (Herbers, 1978). Additionally, in a study analyzing racial attitudes toward residential integration, Bobo, Schuman, and Steeh (1986) found that

> there is evidence of a steady progressive trend toward acceptance
> of the goal of residential integration and toward support for enforce-
> ment of blacks' housing rights. These chances are lent further cre-
> dence by expressed white willingness to take part in integrated living
> situations that involve more than a token black presence. On the other
> hand, support for enforcing blacks' rights to free residential choice is
> well below that for the principle itself. Indeed, respondents proved to
> be quite willing to endorse the principle and express reluctance to en-
> force it. (p. 165)

The last 3 decades may have brought about improved White attitudes and improved access to facilities such as schools, but Blacks, Hispanics, and Native Americans are still distinctly subordinate economically and politically. For example, in 1983, although the average educational attainment of Blacks was only slightly below that of Whites (12.2 years and 12.6 years, respectively), the income of Black families was a little less than 60% of that of White families and had improved little in over a decade. Hispanics with at least a high school diploma were more than twice as likely as Whites to be living in poverty in 1983, and Blacks, more than three times as likely (U.S. Department of Commerce, Bureau of the Census, 1985). As Table 1–1 shows, education does not pay off equally for members of different racial groups: Being White has measurable economic and employment advantages.

TABLE 1-1   *Family income and unemployment rate in 1984*

Years of Schooling Completed	Family Income, by Education Level of Householder			Unemployment Rate		
	White	Black	Hispanic	White	Black	Hispanic
8 years	17,002	12,164	16,219	—	—	—
High school: 4 years	26,541	18,427	23,429	7.4%	18.3%	9.7%
College: 4 years or more	43,642	32,057	37,339	2.5%	6.3%	3.6%

Source: U.S. Department of Commerce, Bureau of the Census, *Statistical Abstract of the United States* (107th ed.), 1987.

People of color continue disproportionately to experience poverty and unemployment. As Figure 1-1 shows, the poverty rate among Blacks has never been substantially better than 30%, nor has the poverty rate among Hispanics been better than 22%, even though the poverty rate among Whites has hovered around 10% (U.S. Department of Commerce, Bureau of the Census, 1985). The gap in unemployment has not improved, either: Whites continue to have greatest access to available jobs. The unemployment rate for Blacks has remained about twice that for Whites since World War II (U.S. Department of Commerce, Bureau of Statistics, 1979), and the unemployment gap between Black and White youth has widened. Mare and Winship (1984), after studying racial inequality and joblessness among Black youth, observed that this gap is widening because Black youth are both staying in school longer and joining the military in greater numbers and thus no longer have a "head start" in the labor market for unskilled or semiskilled jobs. Their study suggests that "worsening labor force statistics for Black youths do not denote increasing racial inequality, but rather persistent racial inequalities previously hidden by race differences in other aspects of young adulthood" (p. 54).

As a result of differential access to jobs, housing, and health institutions, other estimates of quality of life vary according to race. In 1983, for example, while 14% of all Whites were not covered by some form of health insurance, 21.8% of all Blacks and 29.1% of all Hispanics were not covered (U.S. Department of Commerce, Bureau of the Census, 1986). Moreover, Whites can enjoy a longer life expectancy than Blacks, and as life expectancy for the general population increases, a racial gap persists (see Figure 1-2).

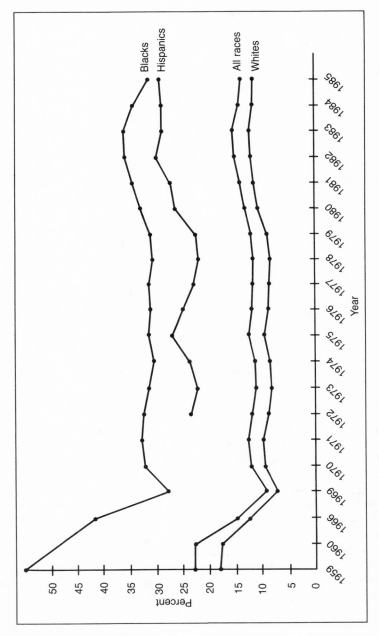

FIGURE 1–1 U.S. poverty rate: Percent of families below poverty line (Source: U.S. Department of Commerce, Bureau of the Census, Current Population Reports, series P-60, Nos. 138 and 145; U.S. Bureau of the Census, *Statistical Abstract of the United States* [107th ed.], 1987.)

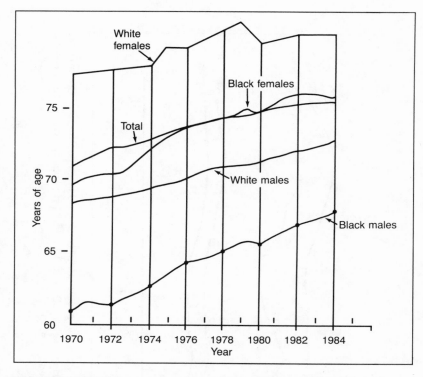

FIGURE 1–2 *Life expectancy at birth (Source: U.S.* Department of Commerce, Bureau of the Census, *Statistical Abstract
of the United States* [107th ed.], 1987.)

People of color are also more likely than Whites to be imprisoned.
For example, in 1983, although Blacks made up only about 12% of the
total population and Whites made up 83% of the total population, 39.1%
of all jail inmates were Black, while 58.2% were White (U.S. Department
of Commerce, Bureau of the Census, 1987). In 1984, 42.8% of all death
sentences went to Blacks (U.S. Department of Commerce, Bureau of
the Census, 1986).

People of color are also still locked out of much of the political
system, even though increasing numbers of big-city mayors are men
of color. Since 1971 there has been only one Black U.S. senator, and
in 1987, there was none; the number of other senators of color has
fluctuated between two and three. Between 1971 and 1986, the number
of Black congresspersons increased from 12 to 23, but 23 still consti-
tuted only 5.3% of the House, a significant underrepresentation for the

12% of Americans who were Black. Less than 3% of the House in 1986 was Hispanic (11 Hispanic members); Hispanic representation had grown over a decade but still underrepresented the 6% of Americans who were Hispanic (*Congressional Quarterly Weekly Report*, 1986). There were two Asian senators and four Asian members of the House (personal communication, Congressman Robert Matsui's office, June 8, 1987). The *Congressional Quarterly Weekly Report* office informed us that data are not kept on representation of Native Americans in Congress. The year 1984 had the first Black presidential candidate, but his white constituency was small and his support of the Democratic nominee was considered a liability by many Whites.

Women, too, are still distinctly subordinate, both economically and politically, in spite of recent gains. Women are participating in the labor market in ever-growing numbers. However, the earnings of full-time working women are only about 70% the earnings of full-time working White men. This wage gap has fluctuated over the last 3 decades and appears to be shrinking currently as women enter male-dominated fields (Table 1–2). This gap is true of men and women who have attained the same levels of education (Treiman & Hartman, 1981). A number of studies have examined human capital factors (e.g., work experience, evidence of work commitment) that might explain this differential; but taken together, Treiman and Hartman report that these "factors usually account for less than a quarter and never more than half of the observed earnings differences" (p. 42). One major institutional factor perpetuating this situation is that "women are concen-

TABLE 1–2   *The wage gap over time*

For every dollar earned by a full-time working man, a full-time working woman earned:

1955	63.9¢	1977	58.9¢
1959	61.3¢	1979	59.6¢
1960	60.8¢	1980	60.2¢
1962	59.5¢	1981	59.2¢
1965	60.0¢	1982	61.7¢
1967	57.8¢	1983	63.8¢
1970	59.4¢	1984	67.8¢
1972	57.9¢	1985	68.2¢
1973	56.6¢	1986	69.2¢
1975	58.8¢		

Source: U.S. Bureau of Labor Statistics, *Employment Earnings*, monthly.

trated in low-paying occupations and, within occupations, in low-paying firms" (p. 42). Although women are making substantial inroads into some high-paying traditionally male occupations, such as law, over 85% of female workers in 1982 were concentrated in low-paying "pink-collar" ghettos, such as clerical work, nursing, teaching, day care, health services, and domestic service (U.S. Department of Commerce, Bureau of the Census, 1983). And even in 1984, the jobs paying the most were still dominated by men (see Figure 1–3).

As women increasingly become heads of households, this persistent wage gap contributes heavily to the growing pauperization of women and children. In 1984, while the average married-couple family earned $29,612 and the average unmarried male earned $23,325, the average unmarried female earned only $12,803 (U.S. Department of Commerce, Bureau of the Census, 1987). Currently, about half of all female-headed households live below the poverty line. This situation heavily affects children: Women are given custody of children in about 90% of divorce cases and often must attempt to support the family on a low-wage budget. As a result, about 21% of American children in 1985 were living in poverty, a proportion that had risen over time, as Figure 1–4 indicates (U.S. Department of Commerce, Bureau of the Census, 1987).

The influx of women into the labor market is taking another toll on women as well: Because housework and child care continue to be regarded as women's responsibilities, most husbands do not assume

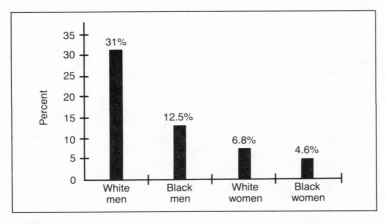

FIGURE 1–3 *Who gets the high pay jobs? Persons earning incomes over $25,000 in U.S., 1984 (Source:* U.S. Department of Commerce, Bureau of the Census, *Statistical Abstract of the United States* [107th ed.], 1987.)

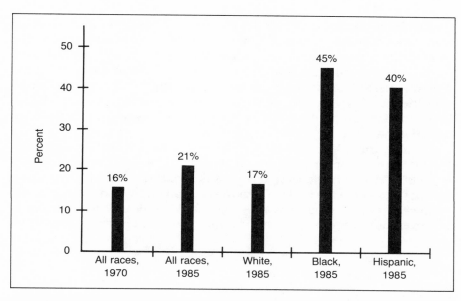

FIGURE 1–4 *Children in U.S. schools who live below the poverty line (Source:* U.S. Department of Commerce, Bureau of the Census, *Statistical Abstract of the United States* [107th ed.], 1987.)

an equal share of these roles, and married women who hold jobs are finding themselves with less and less leisure time (Pleck, Staines, & Lang, 1980; Stafford, 1980).

The political position of women has improved somewhat, but is still no better than their economic position. Although greatly increasing numbers of women have been elected to local and state offices, women still constitute only a small minority of officeholders at the state level, and an even smaller minority at the national level. Only about 14% of the state legislators in 1985 were women, as were 5.3% of the members of the House and 2% of all U.S. senators. In 1986, furthermore, only two of the women in Congress were of color (*Congressional Quarterly Weekly Report*, 1986). Only one or two states at a time have a female governor. While 1984 saw the first woman nominated by a major political party for vice president, she needed to make herself acceptable to the public by emphasizing that she had fulfilled traditional roles of wife and mother in addition to pursuing a career.

The United States is a distinctly social class-stratified society. Although debates about racism and sexism have always existed, and in the last two decades have been quite plentiful, Americans have devoted much less attention to social class stratification. Yet there are tremendous inequities in the distribution of wealth. In 1978, the top 20% of the population earned 41.5% of the total income and controlled 76% of the total national wealth, while the bottom 20% earned 5.2% of the total income and controlled 0.2% of the total national wealth (Parenti, 1978). Furthermore, inequity in wealth distribution has grown over the past few years. As Figure 1–5 shows, the middle class shrank between 1978 and 1986, and the lower class grew over twice as much as the upper class.

Since the 1960s, the poverty rate has risen continuously (U.S. Department of Commerce, Bureau of the Census, 1985), reaching 15% by 1986. Although the United States is a relatively wealthy nation, it has not been able to rid itself of poverty. Many may find it tempting to blame the poor for poverty, arguing that they do not want to work. However, our economy sustains an unemployment rate that rarely falls

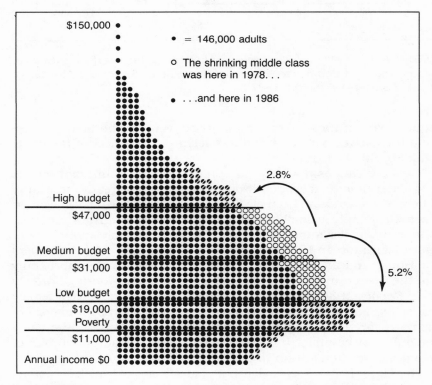

FIGURE 1–5 *The shrinking middle class: 1978–1986 (Source:* S. J. Rose, *The American Profile Poster.* New York: Pantheon Books, a Division of Random House, Inc. 1986. Reprinted by permission.)

below 7%. This means that there are not enough jobs to go around, and 7% of Americans actively seeking work are unable to find it; this figure does not include those who have given up and stopped looking. Furthermore, many of the poor are employed, but are paid very low wages.

Harrington (1984) believes that there is a growing gap between rich and poor in the United States and that the middle class today is shrinking as a result of changes in the economic structure:

> People who, twenty or even ten years ago, were secure in their
> jobs and communities now live somewhere between poverty and semi-
> affluence, walking the edge of an economic precipice. Their problems
> will be ameliorated, but far from ended, by economic recovery, if this
> really does come. For they, or people like them, are likely to face down-
> ward social mobility for twenty or thirty years, unless this country
> turns around. These are not, then, the instant "new poor" that the me-
> dia discovered in that winter of American discontent, 1982–83. (p. 64)

In spite of the popular belief that anyone who desires it can attain wealth through individual effort, Jencks et al. (1972) found occupation to be predicted largely by educational attainment, which in turn is predicted mainly by family socioeconomic background. In other words, children tend to grow up to occupy the same social class position as their parents. Even among those with the same level of education, the children of wealthy parents are much more likely to attain high-paying jobs than are children of lower- or middle-class parents (Rumberger, 1983). In addition, those controlling the greatest proportion of wealth tend to have the most political power. As Parenti (1978) points out, those who are most likely to sit on state and local boards, boards for colleges and universities, and boards of corporations are from the upper socioeconomic classes.

Finally, disabled people constitute a subordinate group, although statistics are not kept on them nearly as much as on other groups. Historically, public concern for their welfare has risen and fallen. In the last 2 decades, concern has risen, but if history is an accurate guide, that concern will wane. Although federal and state laws have recently been passed to protect the rights of the disabled, and although support services have been expanded, handicapped people as a group are still overrepresented in the ranks of the poor, although they are somewhat invisible as an impoverished group, since statistics on their employment and income are not widely kept and published.

Nevertheless, there are some patterns. Most disabled adults are either unemployed or employed part-time, and earnings are often below the poverty level. For example, Hasazi, Gordon, and Roe (1985) followed up on 459 youths exiting special education programs in Vermont. Their employment rate was only 54%. In a similar follow-up study in Colorado, Mithaug, Horiuchi, and Fanning (1985) found an employment rate of 69%, but almost half of those employed were earning less that $3.00 per hour. In 1984, only 27.4% of the disabled were employed full-time, a decrease of two percentage points since 1972. Of those employed, the poverty rate is 26% (Habeck, Galvid, Frey, Chadderden, & Tate, 1985). Unemployment and poverty are particularly severe among disabled people of color, who face double discrimination in the job market.

Disabled people often lack the access to facilities and opportunities that most citizens enjoy. For example, although mentally retarded people are no longer automatically institutionalized in most states, increasing numbers have been institutionalized in some states in the last few years (Gearheart, 1980). Zoning laws restrict where homes for deinstitutionalized retarded people can be built. Blind, deaf, and physically impaired people have legal rights to public facilities, but in practice find it difficult or impossible to get around in many buildings, communicate with public service workers, or use certain public channels of communication. The disabled also bear stereotypes of incompetence. As Gliedman and Roth (1980) have noted, public images of the disabled emphasize limitations, and the disabled have no counterimage, such as "Black is beautiful," to offset these. Many disabled people also must depend on others to articulate their concerns. Siegel (1986) has pointed out that the physically disabled represent "an extremely vocal and powerful lobby," whereas the mentally retarded and emotionally disabled are less able to express their own interests persuasively and assertively (p. 50).

BUSINESS AS USUAL

Before we discuss approaches that teachers can take to deal constructively with race, class, gender, and handicap, it is important to describe what often occurs in many classrooms and schools. School, it has been observed, reflects society. Just as a few improvements in society may give an incomplete or inaccurate view of progress in reducing racism, sexism, class bias, and bias against the handicapped, a few improvements in our schools are similarly misleading. In many schools, one can readily observe students of color and White students socializing; girls in classes such as woodshop and autoshop, once considered the exclusive domain of the boys; boys in home economics classes, once considered no-man's-land; Spanish spoken in mathematics classes; and students in wheelchairs attending proms and participating in many other school events. Also, the cheering squad, band, and sports teams often reflect the diversity of the student body. Moreover, it is not unusual in integrated schools for the president of the student council to be a person of color and for the queen's court to include a girl of color.

Furthermore, many teachers and school administrators support equal opportunity and access to all courses and activities for all students enrolled in the school: They support events that recognize the contributions of people of color and women; many welcome mainstreamed special education students into their classes; most work to eliminate sexist behavior in the classroom; and virtually all support having students from different social class backgrounds attend the same school. Also, many teachers examine their curriculum materials for bias and try to avoid using those that are obviously biased.

These examples suggest that success for all students is the order of business in classrooms and schools. However, to the discerning observer, much has been left out. Like the society we described earlier, schools are beset with problems related to race, class, gender, and handicap.

Our description of "business as usual" is based on several studies published during the 1980s in which researchers observed what actually takes place in the schools. We will describe the main patterns that emerge. We acknowledge that schools and classrooms vary, although those that vary significantly are usually few and far between. But we invite you to compare this description with schools you may be familiar with. We have organized this description into five categories: how teachers teach, what teachers teach, how students are grouped, other patterns, and student culture.

How Teachers Teach

Many studies have found strong similarities in how teachers teach (Cuban, 1984; Everhart, 1983; Goodlad, 1984; Grant & Sleeter, 1986). Cuban (1984) summarizes these well, drawing on his own research. He separates the elementary and secondary levels, acknowledging a greater diversity among elementary teachers than among secondary teachers. Cuban reports that in elementary classrooms, he

> came to expect a number of regularities. Almost half of the teachers (43 percent) put up a daily schedule on the blackboard. If it were time for reading, the teachers would work with one group and assign the same seatwork or varied tasks to the rest of the class. If it were math, social studies, science, or language arts generally the teacher

would work from a text with the entire class answering questions from it or either from dittoed sheets or workbooks. (p. 220)

Both Cuban, in his study of 6 school districts, and Goodlad (1984), in his study of 13 elementary–middle–high school feeder systems, found many elementary teachers to deviate from this pattern by individualizing instruction, using learning centers, and using small groups. However, the majority favored teacher-centered, large-group instruction in which all students worked on the same tasks and much of the work depended on the textbook, dittoed sheets, or workbooks.

At the secondary level there is much more uniformity. Cuban describes the main pattern as "rows of tablet-arm chairs facing a teacher who is talking, asking, listening to student answers, and supervising the entire class for most of the period—a time that is occasionally punctuated by a student report, a panel, or a film" (p. 222). Cuban found labs in science classes to offer the main variation from this pattern in academic courses; Goodlad added that vocational, physical education, and art classes involve more varied activities and much more hands-on learning.

These patterns have several implications for student diversity. One implication is that students whose learning style diverges from predominant teaching styles are at a disadvantage. For example, Shade (1982) argues that Black students suffer academically in schools because their learning style tends to be oriented toward cooperation, content about people, discussion and hands-on work, and whole-to-part learning, which conflicts with the independent, task-oriented, reading-oriented, part-to-whole style that most teachers employ with most students. As another example, Deyhle (1985) found young Navajo students to interpret tests as games, in contrast to White students, who viewed them as serious business, a result of different home socialization. Whereas White children learn early to display knowledge publicly for evaluation, Navajo children learn that serious learning is private and therefore do not exert their best effort when tested. Furthermore, Goodlad notes that the activities used in nonacademic areas, such as industrial arts, attract students who prefer active involvement in learning. This may help lure lower-class and minority students, more than middle-class White students, into these areas and away from academics.

A second implication is that students whose skills deviate from those of the majority present a problem for the classroom teacher, because most teachers individualize very little. The main solution schools have used has been to place such students in remedial or special education classes or to track them. This has created additional problems.

Clearly, this uniformity in teaching procedures conflicts with the mainstreaming movement. In a study of one junior high school, we found that regular education teachers modified their procedures only minimally for mainstreamed students, and they expected everybody else to learn at the same rate, through the same instructional procedures and materials (Grant & Sleeter, 1986). It seems that regular and special educators often find themselves in conflict over the intent of PL 94-142: Many regular educators view special education as a place to put students whose skills deviate significantly from the majority, while special education teachers are trying to move students from special education back into the mainstream and wish to see regular education teachers become more flexible in how they teach.

Similarly, many bilingual education teachers find themselves in conflict with "regular" classroom teachers over the specific needs of limited English proficiency (LEP) students. Although sent to other classrooms for reading, mathematics, or other instruction, LEP students are often "mainstreamed" in art, music, and physical education. Unfortunately, some teachers refuse to alter their standard approaches to meet the needs of these students.

A third implication is that much instruction given in classrooms is uninteresting and alienating for many students. In our study of a junior high school, the word students used most often to describe instruction was *boring.* Goodlad (1984) describes classrooms as emotionally flat. Students who do not readily identify with schooling, with their teachers, or with the content being taught tend to become turned off and disengaged. This seems particularly true when the content is unrelated to the students' experiential background. Everhart (1983) describes an incident in a junior high classroom in which students were filling in a worksheet after reading about Switzerland in their textbook; Not having been to Switzerland, and not having been provided experiences to develop visual, aural, or tactile imagery about Switzerland, the students discussed the weekend football game while completing an assignment that to them was merely verbal gymnastics.

All this is not to say that there are not some excellent and dynamic teachers, because there are. But much of the usual classroom instruction discourages some students, turns off others, and fails to engage the minds of many. And those who tend to become turned off, disengaged, or frustrated are disproportionately lower-class students and students of color. (Students mainstreamed from special education may also become frustrated and disengaged, but they usually have the support and help of a special education teacher.)

There is another instructional problem that occurs in some classrooms. Research has found many teachers to interact with, call on, praise, and intellectually challenge students who are White, male, and middle class more than other students in the same classroom and to reprimand Black male students the most (Jackson & Cosca, 1974; Sadker & Sadker, 1982). Teachers are usually unaware that they are doing this, but it can benefit members of advantaged social groups when it occurs.

What Teachers Teach

Goodlad's (1984) study of 38 schools nationwide provides a comprehensive view of what teachers today are teaching. We will not provide extensive description, but rather note salient findings. The main finding was school-to-school uniformity, especially at the secondary level. Goodlad summarized two subject areas as follows: "Overall, the impression that emerged from the analysis of English and language arts was one of great curricular similarity from school to school. This impression comes through even more strongly for mathematics" (p. 208). He found that teachers in both subject areas emphasized the acquisition of skills, often apart from context or real-life use. Social studies and science at the elementary level varied considerably from classroom to classroom, often being grounded in students' experiential background. For example, primary-grade social studies usually revolved around the family and neighborhood. At the secondary level, however, content in these areas became increasingly alike and increasingly removed from student experience. More variation was found in what was taught in the arts and vocational areas. Goodlad also found heavy emphasis on rote learning: Although teachers often said they were developing higher-level thinking skills, their tests overwhelmingly emphasized regurgitation of memorized material.

Curricula emphasize the White wealthy male experience, although less so today than 20 years ago. Analyses of curricular materials in use today find the following patterns. Blacks, especially Black males, are included much more than they used to be, although they are often added on in a supplementary fashion; Hispanic Americans, Asian-Americans, and contemporary Native Americans are still barely visible in the curriculum. White females appear much more than they used to, although they, too, are often added on to existing male-dominated curricula; females of color are still largely omitted; and whereas many White females are shown in nonstereotypical roles, males still occupy traditional male roles. Social class is rarely studied, and perspectives of the middle and upper classes predominate. In the last 10 years, more books and stories have appeared with handicapped main characters, but there are still few materials with handicapped support characters or with handicapped main characters in a story about something other than what it is like to be handicapped (Anyon, 1979; Butterfield, Demos, Grant, Moy, & Perez, 1979; Grant & Grant, 1981; Rupley, Garcia, & Longnion, 1981; Scott, 1981). Furthermore, there seems to be more cultural diversity in curricular materials than in the actual content teachers teach. For example, although several teachers use culturally pluralistic and nonsexist materials, most of them do not refer very often to people of color or women when talking or lecturing (Grant & Sleeter, 1986). Thus, what teachers teach when doing "business as usual" includes people of color somewhat and in a supplementary way, but Whites still predominate; it includes White females, but males still dominate; it includes handicapped people sporadically; and it virtually excludes the working- or lower-class experience.

The curriculum responds most actively to diversity when there are non-English-speaking students. Since the Supreme Court decision in *Lau v. Nichols* (1974), schools have been required to provide help in learning English as well as instruction in the child's language while the child is learning English. Under business as usual, this seems to mean providing bilingual or English as a Second Language (ESL) instruction for as short a time as possible until minimal English proficiency is achieved. For example, Guthrie (1985) studied a Chinese-English bilingual program in California. She found that the Chinese community wanted its children to learn the Chinese language and culture, whereas the school system expected bilingual education to work toward as rapid a transition to English as possible. Debates at the federal level during the 1980s support the school system's expectation: Debates revolve around how to teach English most effectively, not how to promote bilingualism. (Interestingly, however, business as usual does encourage college-bound English-speaking students to acquire minimal competence in a second, usually Western European, language.)

So far, our description suggests that all students of a given grade level are taught much the same thing, regardless of geographic region, student interest, or ethnic background, except in the case of non-English-speaking students. This is only partially correct. There does appear to be a standard curriculum that most teachers use as a guide. It is not codified in a national curriculum guide; rather, it is codified into standardized achievement tests and text materials, which are more alike than different for any given subject area. Teachers tend to use the content of text materials and standardized tests as the basis for what they teach. They then modify this material to fit the average skill level of a class and, to a much lesser degree, student interest and experiential background. For example, consider the teachers in the junior high studied by Grant and Sleeter (1986). When asked how they decided what to teach, most teachers reported starting with an idea of what students at that grade level should know in that subject area, then adjusting forward or backward to most students' current level of mastery. In this case, students were behind grade level in most areas, so teachers either retreated to earlier material or watered down grade level material to make it simpler. Student interest rarely affected what these teachers taught.

Goodlad's (1984) study of 38 schools supports this. The main variation he found in content was between tracks or ability groups. Teachers beefed up or watered down content in response to student skill level. Student interest played at most a minor role in determining the curriculum. Geographic locale played no role. Student ethnic background played a minor role. Since track or ability group plays the main role in determining how teachers vary both instruction and content, we turn next to how students are grouped.

How Students Are Grouped

Within school districts, students are grouped in various ways: by school, by ability group or track, by special education need, and by interest (in the form of electives). We will discuss aspects of grouping under business as usual that relate to race, social class, gender, and handicap.

First, although schools are supposed to be racially desegregated, they do not need to be desegregated on the basis of social class. It is quite common for schools to serve primarily or solely upper-class, middle-class, working-class, or lower-class students. And schools serving different social classes are not alike. They differ somewhat in the availability of resources, such as computers (Campbell, 1984), and in the salaries they are able to offer. They differ strikingly in curriculum and instruction. For example, based on observations in five schools, Anyon (1981) reported differences that are virtually the same as those we will describe between tracks.

Racial desegregation is also less a reality than many of us would like to believe, particularly for language-minority students. While the segregation of Black students has decreased, the segregation of Hispanic students has increased (Orfield, 1986). The majority of Hispanic students attend schools that are predominantly minority. This increased segregation of Hispanic students interferes with their acquisition of English-language competence (Garcia, 1986) and is related to higher high school dropout rates. In addition, the schools that Hispanic students attend are largely inferior, reporting the highest dropout rates, lowest achievement rates, and greatest problems with teacher turnover, overcrowding, and gangs (Kyle, Lane, Sween, & Triana, 1986). As Orum and Vincent (1984) put it, "Hispanics now have the dubious distinction of being not only the most undereducated group of American children, but also the mostly highly segregated" (p. 26).

A second important kind of grouping is ability grouping, pervasive in elementary schools, and tracking, which is a pervasive feature of high schools in the major academic areas. Based on a review of research on the effects of tracking, Oakes (1985) reports that although many people assume that ability grouping and tracking are best for most students, the evidence points clearly to the conclusion that "no group of students has been found to benefit consistently from being in a homogeneous group," and those in the middle and lower groups are often affected negatively (p. 7). Her own investigation of 25 secondary schools across the country in the late 1970s found considerable tracking being used. In multiracial schools, upper-track classes were disproportionately White, lower-track classes disproportionately minority and lower-class. Upper-track students tended to receive the following: at least 80% of class time spent on instruction, considerable homework, more varied teaching activities, clear instruction, higher-level thinking skills, and exposure to content that would gain them access to college. Lower-track students, on the other hand, received about 67% of class time spent on instruction, half (or less) the homework of upper-track students, varied materials but very routinized instructional activities, less clarity in instruction, emphasis on rote memory, and content oriented around everyday life skills (which may seem practical but which also blocks access to college). Most upper-track students reported enthusiasm for school and feelings of personal competence, whereas lower-track students were often turned off to school and felt academically incompetent. These are the same sorts of differences Anyon found between upper-class and working-class schools.

These studies clearly show that students are being grouped partly on the basis of race and social class and then taught differently. Upper-track and upper-class students are offered more instructional time, more challenge, interesting and effective instruction, opportunities to think, and preparation for college. Lower-track and lower-class students tend to receive routine and dull instruction, less challenge, memory work, and little or no preparation for college. Middle groups receive something in between. Although people often say that these groupings meet students' instructional needs and provide opportunity for advancement, lower groups are for the most part being turned off to school and are not being pushed to catch up, making the groups more and more different as they proceed through school. For this reason, schools have been very accurately described as a sorting machine, slotting the young for a stratified labor market (Spring, 1976).

A third problem is the proportionately smaller numbers of female students in upper-level mathematics and science courses and in computer courses. It appears that although girls may take almost as many mathematics and science courses as boys, they often avoid the more difficult courses, which greatly hinders access to mathematics and science majors in college (Fennema, 1984).

A fourth aspect of grouping is special education, which in many ways fits into the tracking system, although less so for the physically, visually, and hearing impaired than for other categories. Gifted classes are disproportionately White, whereas classes for the mentally retarded and emotionally disturbed are disproportionately minority (DBS Corporation, 1982). Learning disability classes appear to be shifting from protective areas for White middle-class failing children to remedial classes for students previously classified as retarded or slow (Sleeter, 1986). The nature of content and to some extent instruction parallels distinctions between upper and lower tracks. However, special education teachers often do a better job than most other teachers of adapting instruction to students' learning styles, skill levels, and interests and often act as advocates and helpers for their students, helping to get them through the school system to graduation (Grant & Sleeter, 1986).

A fifth aspect of grouping is vocational classes, which at the secondary level group students somewhat by interest. Even here, however, we find grouping roughly following social class, race, and gender lines. For example, Oakes (1985) found a distinct racial difference in vocational courses: Home economics and general industrial arts were by far the main vocational courses in White schools, while courses preparing students for specific blue-collar and clerical occupations were common in nonwhite and racially mixed schools. In spite of Title IX (an education amendment of 1972 to forbid schools from restricting access to courses and school activities based upon sex), one is also likely to find a gender difference, with home economics and clerical courses dominated by girls and industrial arts courses dominated by boys (DBS Corporation, 1982). Although enrollments in vocational courses depend largely on student choice, researchers find that other factors strongly affect what students choose. Those factors include availability of courses at their school, how comfortable students feel with the gender composition that is usually in a given course, how useful students think the course will be in helping them attain what they consider is a realistic (although not necessarily desirable) future occupation, and the quality of guidance and encouragement they receive (Grant & Sleeter, 1986; Oakes, 1985; Valli, 1986).

A sixth aspect of grouping at the secondary level is bilingual education or English as a Second Language. Many bilingual programs at the secondary level are seen by local administrators as remedial in nature, designed primarily for the limited English proficiency student who needs to "catch up" or minimally develop "survival" English skills. In addition, many programs segregate language-minority students within the school, making it more difficult for them to interact with Anglo students in English or to receive exposure to the curriculum that Anglo students are being taught. In some states where graduation requirements have recently been raised, bilingual and ESL classes are not counted for graduation. With the institution of minimum competency testing (in English), many language-minority students face the possibility of not receiving a high school diploma or of receiving "attendance diplomas" that will close opportunities for postsecondary education (Fernandez & Velez, 1985).

All of this suggests that when schools operate according to business as usual, students are grouped in ways that roughly parallel race, class, and gender lines and then are taught in ways that help channel them into roles currently occupied by members of their race, class, and gender groups. Grouping is usually based on tests, teacher judgment, grades, and student choice, but as ethnographic studies of schools are revealing, all these processes are often linked in subtle but strong ways to race, social class, and gender.

Other Patterns

Additional patterns in schools tend to mirror and help reproduce prevailing race, social class, and gender patterns. Viewing school systems from top to bottom, one finds the following staffing patterns: Superintendents are overwhelmingly White males; women and men of color in administration tend to be elementary school principals, central office staff, or administrators charged with duties related to Title IX, desegregation, and so forth; over 90% of teachers are White, and this percentage is increasing; over 80% of elementary school teachers are female; mathematics, science, and industrial arts teachers are predominantly male, whereas foreign language, English, and home economics teachers tend to be female; people of color are often custodians and aides; and over 90% of secretaries are women. These patterns offer distinct role models and authority relationships for students.

In addition, the growing lack of minorities in teaching and administration means that fewer teachers are likely to identify with and advocate concerns particular to minority students. Furthermore, the preponderance of men in decision-making positions sometimes hinders attention to concerns of female students, while the preponderance of women at the elementary school level makes it difficult for many boys to identify with school and its requirements.

Extracurricular activities can also mirror existing societal patterns and reinforce segregation patterns, although this varies from school to school. However, the following patterns are not uncommon. Middle- and upper-class students often dominate the activities, especially activities that are academically oriented; in racially mixed schools, especially if Whites are clearly in the majority, Whites tend to dominate. When this occurs, other students often feel unwelcome in activities. Students of color may dominate some of the sports; sometimes, sports are race/class divided, with golf or swimming, for example, predominantly White and basketball predominantly Black (Rist, 1979). Boys' sports often receive a larger share of the budget than girls' sports and may receive better coaches, better playing schedules, and so forth. Probably the greatest change in extracurricular activities in the past several decades has been the development of girls' sports; the challenge now seems to be to make them qualitatively equal to boys' sports.

Student Culture

The preceding discussion has centered on what schools do. But students do not respond to schools in a mechanical fashion. Researchers are increasingly aware of how student cultures develop that often help reproduce existing social patterns, make it difficult to change student behavior, and reaffirm to teachers that their own behavior toward students is correct. Often, great gaps exist between how teachers and students perceive each others and themselves.

Everhart (1983), for example, studied boys in a White working-class junior high school. The boys entered school uncertain about occupational goals, but familiar mainly with working-class jobs and ways of life. The teachers perceived the students as academically average or below and as probably headed for working-class jobs. Classroom instruction was teacher dominated, rarely individualized, and routine, emphasizing memorization of predigested material. To an observer, it was immediately apparent that students spent quite a bit of time goofing off and were investing only as much effort in classwork as they needed to get by. But on closer examination, Everhart found the students actively engaged in creating a culture that would help make school livable. The students saw school as analogous to the work world, and the school offered much on which to base this analogy: It was clearly dominated by authority figures with whom the students could not identify; the work was routine and unrelated to the students' daily lives; most of their time was structured; and they were rewarded for accomplishing prescribed pieces of work. Without consciously connecting their interpretion of school to the labor market or their future life chances, they attempted to control whatever fragments of time they could and build relationships with each other. To the teachers, the students' behavior reaffirmed that the students were not interested in academic work and were incapable of managing substantive decisions, so there was no point in challenging them. The teachers seemed unaware that the student culture was generated partly in response to what they offered the students; and the low level of academic work, accepted by both teachers and students, helped ensure the students a working-class future.

Gaskell (1985) offers a similar portrait of working-class girls in clerical courses. The girls chose the courses for several reasons: These courses offered more hands-on learning than did college-preparation courses and were therefore more fun; the students were treated more like adults than were academic students; and the courses would help the girls secure a secretarial job before settling down to raise a family. Many of the girls did not particularly like secretarial work, but given the world they grew up in, this looked like a viable alternative. In school, they developed a culture that rejected academics (academic kids being viewed as somewhat childish rather than mature). Their culture centered around building social relationships with each other and drew on traditional patterns of femininity for guidance in how to control bosses, handle male workers, make boring work fun, and so forth. To the outside observer, it seemed that these girls were predisposed to be traditional women, that they chose secretarial work because they liked it, and that the school had nothing to do with these things. From the inside, it was found that the girls developed their secretarial culture as a way of trying to make the best of what they saw as limited career options, cope with male co-workers, and attain some status for themselves in relationship to middle-class, college-bound students.

Student culture has relevance to "business as usual," because it helps shape many of the decisions students make about school and because it develops as much from within the school as from outside the school. Many teachers believe that all or most of their students' values and beliefs are generated only from outside; students who fail, turn off, drop out, or choose low-ability or vocational classes are doing so in spite of the school's attempt to give all an equal chance. These teachers often blame the students' home culture or society in general.

Although society and home certainly cannot be discounted, they do not determine student behavior. In a very real sense, students determine it as they make sense of the school experience they confront every day. All the patterns described here as business as usual present students with experiences that vary somewhat according to student race, social class, and gender, among other factors; the experiences that students have outside the school give them frameworks that also vary by race, social class, and gender, and students use these frameworks to interpret school life. There has always been a gap between teachers and students, resulting at least from age and role and often compounded by differences in cultural background. Some teachers bridge this gap and grasp the student culture fairly well; many do not and interpret student behavior as part of the natural order of things that teachers need to control but do not help produce. As the teaching staff in the United States becomes increasingly older and increasingly White, it is quite possible that the gap between teachers and students, and especially lower-class and minority students, will widen to become a chasm in many schools.

APPROACHES TO MULTICULTURAL EDUCATION

The problems we have just described have existed for a long time and have been recognized and contested by many educators. In fact, the progress that we noted has come about largely through the efforts of educators, working in conjunction with community and social movements, to make schools, along with other social institutions, fairer.

The reforms that educators have advocated bear different names, but are directed toward common practices. Some of the more common names are multicultural education, nonsexist education, human relations, multiethnic education, ethnic studies, sex equity, bilingual/ bicultural education, and mainstreaming. Multicultural education has emerged as an umbrella concept that deals with race, culture, language, social class, gender, and handicap. Although many educators still apply it only to race, it is the term most frequently extended to include additional forms of diversity. For that reason, we will use the term *multicultural education* to refer to educational practices directed toward race, culture, language, social class, gender, and handicap, although in selecting it we do not imply that race is the primary form of social inequality that needs to be addressed. We see racism, classism, and sexism as equally important, with handicap categories having been created partly as a result of these.

Educators have not advocated a single, unified plan for approaching multicultural education. Responding to somewhat different issues in different schools, employing different conceptual views of school and society, and holding somewhat different visions of the good society, educators over the years have constructed different approaches to multicultural education.

Gibson in 1976 reviewed advocacy literature in multicultural education, identifying four approaches and suggesting a fifth. The four approaches she identified were education of the culturally different, or benevolent multiculturalism, which seeks to incorporate culturally different students more effectively into mainstream culture and society; education about cultural differences, which teaches all students about cultural differences in an effort to promote better cross-cultural understanding; education for cultural pluralism, which seeks to preserve ethnic cultures and increase the power of ethnic minority groups; and bicultural education, which seeks to prepare students to operate successfully in two different cultures. She proposed, as an alternative, "multicultural education as the normal human experience," which teaches students to function in multiple-cultural contexts, ethnic or otherwise (such as regional).

Pratte's (1983) typology of approaches was similar. He identified the following four approaches: restricted multicultural education, which seeks to remediate deficiencies in culturally different students and teach majority students to tolerate minorities; modified restricted multicultural education, which seeks to promote full school services for all groups and promote equality among groups within the school; unrestricted multicultural education, which seeks to remediate ethnocentrism in all students by teaching them to identify with a plurality of cultural groups; and modified unrestricted multicultural education, which seeks to prepare all students for active citizenship in a racially diverse society.

Combined, these two typologies distinguish fairly well among approaches to multicultural education, but have some limitations, the main one being that neither author fleshed out the theory undergirding each approach. (Each approach occupied a page or less in a journal.) A second limitation is that both typologies were applied only to race and missed or glossed over distinctions related to gender and social class. A third limitation is that the two typologies did not quite capture the range of practices we have observed in schools. Finally, a fourth limitation is that they tended to focus on issues related to cultural diversity more than social inequality.

Based on our own work as teachers, an administrator, and ethnographic researchers, as well as on extensive reviews of the literature on multicultural education (Grant & Sleeter, 1985; Grant, Sleeter, &

Anderson, 1986; Sleeter & Grant, 1987), we constructed our own typology of approaches to multicultural education. We will briefly introduce these approaches.

During the 1960s, in efforts to desegregate schools, many White educators "discovered" students of color and saw them as culturally deprived. This view was contested vigorously by those who argued that these students were different, not deficient, and that their cultural differences should be accepted by the school. This view has been paralleled by many special educators who argue that handicapped students' differences should be accepted and built on. The approach that emerged—Teaching the Exceptional and the Culturally Different—focuses on adapting instruction to student differences for the purpose of helping these students more effectively succeed in the mainstream. This corresponds to Gibson's first approach and Pratte's first and second.

During about the same period, but building on the post–World War II Intercultural Education Movement, other educators argued that love, respect, and more effective communication should be developed in school to bring people who differ closer together. This developed into the Human Relations approach, which corresponds to Gibson's second approach. It has often been applied to race, gender, and handicap.

The 1960s also saw the emergence of more assertive approaches to change the mainstream of America rather than trying to fit people into it. Ethnic studies, women's studies, and, to a lesser extent, labor studies were developed in an effort to focus attention on specific groups, raise consciousness regarding that group's oppression, and mobilize for social action. This was a portion of Pratte's second approach.

The Multicultural Education approach emerged during the early 1970s and has developed as some educators have grown disenchanted with earlier approaches and as others have begun conceptualizing more complete and complex plans for reforming education. This approach links race, language, culture, gender, handicap, and, to a lesser extent, social class, working toward making the entire school celebrate human diversity and equal opportunity. Both Gibson and Pratte described it as their third approach, and we have subsumed Gibson's fourth and fifth approaches under it.

Finally, the 1970s and 1980s have seen the development of a fifth approach, which we are calling Education That Is Multicultural and Social Reconstructionist. This approach extends the Multicultural Education approach into the realm of social action and focuses at least as much on challenging social stratification as on celebrating human diversity and equal opportunity. Pratte's fourth approach leaned in this direction.

PLAN OF SUBSEQUENT CHAPTERS

Our reviews of the literature on multicultural education led us to an important observation: The existing literature on these various approaches is fragmented and in many cases conceptually weak. Much of it simply prescribes what teachers should do, offering short and sometimes simplistic reasons. Furthermore, books and articles that are well conceptualized and well researched tend to present their approaches as if they were the only approaches.

The chapters that follow offer two major features to correct these shortcomings. First, they explicate the five approaches and allow the reader to compare them. A critique of each approach is offered in this regard. The reader is invited to think through the goals, assumptions, and practices of each approach to determine which makes the most sense.

Second, each approach is developed here in some depth. The first part of each chapter discusses each approach's goals, assumptions, and theoretical base. This provides a clearer picture of what the approach is attempting to do and why, as well as guidance for developing strategies to implement it. Next, recommended practices are summarized, followed by one or two vignettes that illustrate the approach in action. Then the approach is critiqued from the vantage points of other approaches. Finally, a table summarizing the main goals, target audience, and recommended practices is presented, enabling the reader to see the main ideas of the approach at a glance. We invite the reader to think through carefully about which approach makes the most sense. We are not without our own opinion on this. After presenting each approach in what we hope is an unbiased manner, we will argue (in our last chapter) why we feel that one approach is preferable to the other four.

REFERENCES

Anyon, J. (1979). Ideology and United States history textbooks. *Harvard Educational Review, 49,* 361–386.

Anyon, J. (1981). Elementary schooling and distinctions of social class. *Interchange, 12,* 118–132.

Bobo, L., Schuman, H., & Steeh, C. (1986). Changing racial attitudes toward residential integration. In J. Goering (Ed.), *Housing desegregation and federal policy* (pp. 153–169). Chapel Hill: University of North Carolina Press.

Butterfield, R. A., Demos, E., Grant, G. W., Moy, P., & Perez, A. (1979). Multicultural analysis of a popular basal reading series in the International Year of the Child. *Journal of Negro Education, 48*, 382–389.

Campbell, P. (1984). The computer revolution: Guess who's left out? *Interracial Books for Children Bulletin, 15*, 3–6.

Congressional Quarterly Weekly Report. (1986, 8 Nov.).

Cuban, L. (1984). *How teachers taught.* New York: Longman.

DBS Corporation. (1982). Elementary and secondary schools survey. Unpublished paper prepared for the U.S. Office of Civil Rights, Washington, DC: U.S. Department of Education.

Deyhle, D. (1985). Testing among Navajo and Anglo students: Another consideration of cultural bias. *Journal of Educational Equity and Leadership, 5*, 119–131.

Digest of Educational Statistics. (1985–1986). U.S. Department of Education, Office of Educational Research and Improvement.

Everhart, R. (1983). *Reading, writing, and resistance.* Boston: Routledge & Kegan Paul.

Fennema, E. (1984). Girls, women, and mathematics. In E. Fennema and M. I. Ayer (Eds), *Women and education* (pp. 137–164). Berkeley: McCutchan.

Fernandez, R. R., & Velez, W. (1985). Race, color, and language in the changing public schools. In L. Maldonado & J. Moore (Eds.), *Urban ethnicity in the United States: New immigrants and old minorities* (pp. 123–144). Beverly Hills, CA: Sage.

Garcia, E.E. (1986). Bilingual development and the education of bilingual children during early childhood. *American Journal of Education, 95*, 96–121.

Gaskell, J. (1985). Course enrollment in the high school: The perspective of working-class females. *Sociology of Education, 58*, 48–59.

Gearheart, B. (1980). *Special education for the '80s.* Columbus, OH: Merrill.

Gibson, M. A. (1976). Approaches to multicultural education in the United States: Some concepts and assumptions. *Anthropology and Education Quarterly, 7*, 7–18.

Gliedman, J., & Roth, W. (1980). *The unexpected minority.* New York: Harcourt Brace Jovanovich.

Goodlad, J. I. (1984). *A place called school.* New York: McGraw-Hill.

Grant, C. A. & Grant, G. W. (1981). The multicultural evaluation of some second and third grade textbook readers—A survey analysis. *Journal of Negro Education, 50*, 63–74.

Grant, C. A., & Sleeter, C. E. (1985). The literature on multicultural education: Review and analysis. *Educational Review, 37*, 97–118.

Grant, C. A., & Sleeter, C. E. (1986). *After the school bell rings.* Barcombe, England: Falmer Press.

Grant, C. A., Sleeter, C. E., & Anderson, J. E. (1986). The literature on multicultural education: Review and analysis, Part II. *Educational Studies, 12*, 47–71.

Guthrie, G. P. (1985). *A school divided.* Hillside, NJ: Lawrence Erlbaum Associates.

Habeck, R. V., Galvid, D. E., Frey, W. D., Chadderden, L. M., & Tate, D.G. (1985). Economics and equity in employment of people with disabilities: International policies and practices. *Proceedings from the Symposium,* East Lansing, MI: University Center for International Rehabilitation.

Harrington, M. (1984). *The new American poverty.* New York: Holt, Rinehart Winston.

Hasazi, S., Gordon, L., and Roe, C. (1985). Factors associated with the employment status of handicapped youth exiting high school from 1979 to 1983. *Exceptional Children, 51*, 455–469.

Herbers, J. (1978, February 26). Decade after Kerner report: Division of races persists. *New York Times*, p. 1[+].

Jackson, G., & Cosca, C. (1974). The inequality of educational opportunity in the Southwest: An observational study of ethnically mixed classrooms. *American Educational Research Journal, 11*, 219-229.

Jencks, C., Smith, M., Acland, H., Bane, M. J., Cohen, D., Gintis, H., Heyns, B., & Michelson, S. (1972). *Inequality: A reassessment of the effect of family and schooling in America.* New York: Harper & Row.

Kyle, C. L., Jr., Lane, J., Sween, A., & Triana, A. (1986). *We have a choice: Students at risk of leaving Chicago public schools.* Chicago: DePaul University Center for Research on Hispanics.

Mare, R. D. & Winship, C. (1984). The paradox of lessening racial inequality and joblessness among black youth: Enrollment, enlistment, and employment, 1964–1981. *American Sociological Review, 49*, 39–55.

Mithaug, D. E., Horiuchi, C. N., & Fanning, P. N. (1985). A report on the Colorado statewide follow-up survey of special education students. *Exceptional Children, 51*, 397–404.

Oakes, J. (1985). *Keeping track: How schools structure inequality.* New Haven: Yale University Press.

Orfield, G. (1986). Hispanic education: Challenges, research, and policies. *American Journal of Education, 95*, 1–25.

Orum, L., & Vincent, A. (1984). Selected statistics in the education of Hispanics. Washington, DC: National Council of La Raza.

Parenti, M. (1978). *Power and the powerless.* New York: St. Martin's Press.

Pleck, J. H., Staines, G. L., & Lang, L. (1980, March). Conflicts between work and family life. *Monthly Labor Review*, 29–32.

Pratte, R. (1983). Multicultural education: Four normative arguments. *Educational Theory, 33*, 21–32.

Rist, R. C. (1979). *Desegregated schooling: Portraits of an American experiment.* New York: Academic Press.

Rumberger, R. W. (1983). The influence of family background on education, earnings, and wealth. *Social Forces, 3,* 755–773.

Rupley, W. H., Garcia, J., & Longnion, B. (1981). Sex role portrayal in reading materials: Implications for the 1980s. *The Reading Teacher, 34,* 786–791.

Sadker, M., & Sadker, A. (1982). *Sex equity handbook for schools.* New York: Longman.

Scott, K. P. (1981). Whatever happened to Jane and Dick? Sexism in texts reexamined. *Peabody Journal of Education, 58,* 135–140.

Shade, B. J. (1982). Afro-American cognitive style: A variable in school success? *Review of Educational Research, 52,* 219–244.

Siegel, S. (1986). *The right to work: Public policy and the employment of the handicapped.* Unpublished doctoral dissertation, San Francisco State University and University of California, Berkeley.

Sleeter, C. E. (1986). Learning disabilities: The social construction of a special education category. *Exceptional Children, 53,* 46–54.

Sleeter, C. E., & Grant, C.A. (1987). An analysis of multicultural education in the U.S.A. *Harvard Educational Review, 57,* 421–444.

Spring, J. (1976). *The sorting machine: National education policy since 1945.* New York: McKay.

Stafford, E. P. (1980, December). Women's use of time converging with men's. *Monthly Labor Review, 103,* 57–58.

Taylor, D. G., Sheatsley, P. B., & Greely, A. M. (1978). Attitudes toward racial integration. *Scientific American, 238,* pp. 42–49.

Treiman, D. J., & Hartman, H. I. (1981). *Women, work, and wages: Equal pay for jobs of equal value.* Washington, DC: National Academy Press.

U.S. Department of Commerce, Bureau of Statistics. (1979). *The social and economic status of the black population in the United States: An historical view, 1890–1978.* Washington, DC: Government Printing Office.

U.S. Department of Commerce, Bureau of the Census. (1983). *Statistical Abstract of the United States* (103rd ed.). Washington, DC: Government Printing Office.

U.S. Department of Commerce, Bureau of the Census. (1985). *Statistical Abstract of the United States* (105th ed.). Washington, DC: Government Printing Office.

U.S. Department of Commerce, Bureau of the Census. (1986). *Statistical Abstract of the United States* (106th ed.). Washington, DC: Government Printing Office.

U.S. Department of Commerce, Bureau of the Census. (1987). *Statistical Abstract of the United States* (107th ed.). Washington, DC: Government Printing Office.

Valli, L. (1986). *Becoming clerical workers.* Boston: Routledge & Kegan Paul.

CHAPTER 2

Teaching the Exceptional and the Culturally Different

P sychologists, and even our own experiences, tell us that we are often threatened by, do not understand, or want to change those who differ from ourselves. In our classrooms, we often find students who do not look like us, talk like us, think like us, or know what we know. Students may have grown up in neighborhoods unlike our own. Some may not behave as we were taught to behave. Some may not show much interest in learning things we personally value. Some, because of hearing impairments, visual impairments, reading difficulties, and so forth, may not have acquired knowledge that we take for granted. However, as teachers, we very often want to make our students become more like us.

GOALS

Many teachers see themselves as responsible for helping students fit into the mainstream of American society. They believe that those students who do not readily fit because of cultural background, language, learning style, or learning ability require teaching strategies that remediate deficiencies or build bridges between the student and the school. To these teachers, multicultural education means teaching the exceptional or the culturally different so that they can better meet the traditional demands of the school and American life.

Proponents of this approach believe that American society is essentially fine as it currently exists and that, as Table 2–1 shows, the main goal of schooling is to assimilate the young into it (see page 67). This means that students should become equipped with the cognitive skills, concepts, information, language, and values required by American society to hold a job and function within its existing institutions and culture. The poor, the unemployed, and the alienated members of society are believed to suffer primarily from a lack of the right skills, values, and knowledge.

The main goal of this approach is to incorporate those who are not White, those who do not speak English, those who are from lower-class homes, those who have emigrated from other nations, and the disabled into the mainstream by helping them acquire these knowledge resources. Under this approach, special and usually temporary modifications are made in schooling to facilitate these students' transition to the mainstream culture that White, middle-class children are learning.

This approach is based on the human capital theory of society and its implications for our understanding of what normal human development is. After presenting these implications, we will discuss two quite different orientations that teachers use to interpret student differences: one that views differences as deficiencies, and the other that views them simply as differences.

THE HUMAN CAPITAL THEORY AND THE "NORMAL" PERSON

The human capital theory holds that education is a form of investment in that the individual acquires skills and knowledge that can be converted into an income when used to get a job. You probably have been told that you should go to school so that you can get a good job and that the more time and energy you invest in school, the better the job you will get. In a technological society such as ours, what counts as capital is "the knowledge and skills required to take on and use efficiently the superior techniques of production" (Schultz, 1977, p. 322). This means that schools should teach skills and attitudes appropriate for working at a very wide range of jobs, as well as for consuming products. This approach assumes that opportunities open up to individuals at a level commensurate with the level of education they have acquired and that the more individuals develop their human capital through education, the better their life circumstances, our economy, and society in general will be. It suggests that the poor are poor mainly because they have not developed their human capital. The more they acquire the knowledge and skills needed by society, the better their opportunities for success. Theoretically, then, poverty and discrimination result largely from insufficient opportunity for people of color, the poor, the handicapped, and women to acquire the needed knowledge and skills.

Those who exemplify the values, skills, and abilities that mainstream society requires become the standard for determining what constitutes normal development. For example, think of a person who is successful in today's society, such as a lawyer or a businessperson. That person probably has developed a high level of literacy, a respect for time schedules, competitive skills, an ability to act independently of other people, certain interpersonal skills, skill in the use of standard English, and so forth. The kind of person who fits well in American society today has come to represent our image of what is normal. Psychological theories of normal development have been based on this standard and have helped us codify what normal development means in the form of various intelligence and personality tests.

The failure of some to develop "normally" can be explained in two different ways. Those who subscribe to the deficiency orientation see prevailing standards for "normal" development as universally correct and trace failures to achieve those standards to supposed deficiencies in one's home environment and culture and/or one's physiological and mental endowment. Those who subscribe to the difference orientation see prevailing standards as relative to the demands of a particular culture and hold that different cultural contexts produce equally healthy but different patterns of normal development.

However, those who subscribe to either orientation, and who see multicultural education as Teaching the Exceptional and the Culturally Different, share a common goal: helping those who deviate from a standard of "normal" to become as "normal" as possible through education so they can invest themselves in work that will bring them society's rewards. The approach assumes that ultimately this process has the best chance for eradicating poverty, unemployment, racism, sexism, and general social tensions because it helps everybody develop sufficiently to play a productive role in society and to share a common culture.

DEFICIENCY ORIENTATION

Those who subscribe to the deficiency orientation focus primarily on either presumed cultural deficiencies or physiological and mental deficiencies.

Cultural "Deficiency"

In our education classes, we have heard students refer to poor children as "disadvantaged," "socially deprived," "low socioeconomic," "culturally different," "culturally deprived," and "culturally deficient." Although different labels highlight different images—*socioeconomically* disadvantaged versus *educationally* disadvantaged—they all trace problems back to the child's living environment.

If you examine the education literature, especially what was written during the 1960s, you will not have difficulty locating a descriptive explanation of why the student was thought to be deficient. Goldberg's description is a good example:

> Beginning with the family, the early pre-school years present the child from a disadvantaged home with few of the experiences which produce readiness for academic learning either intellectually or attitudinally. The child's view of society is limited by his immediate family and neighborhood where he sees a struggle for survival which sanctions behavior viewed as immoral in the society at large. He has little preparation either for recognizing the importance of schooling in his own life or for being able to cope with the kinds of verbal and abstract behavior which the school will demand of him. Although he generally comes to first grade neat and clean and with his mother's admonition to be a "good boy," he lacks the ability to carry out those tasks which would make him appear "good" in the eyes of his teacher.
>
> Early difficulty in mastering the basic intellectual skills which the schools and thus the broader society demands leads to defeat and failure, a developing negative self-image, rebellion against the increasingly defeating school experiences, a search for status outside the school together with active resentment against the society which the school represents. The child early finds status and protection in the street and the gang which requires none of the skills which are needed in school but makes heavy use of the kinds of survival skills which he learned in his early home and street experiences. (1963, p. 87)[1]

Some of you are probably saying, "Yes, right, I agree, that's what I've heard about those students." Some of you may be saying, "Goodness," "Wow," "I did not know they had all of those problems." And some may be saying, "I question this description; how was this composite put together?" While acknowledging the comments of the first two groups of students, we believe it is important to respond to the

---

[1]Reprinted by permission of the publisher from Passow, *Education in Depressed Areas.* (New York: Teachers College Press, © 1963 by Teachers College, Columbia University. All rights reserved), p. 87.

question of the third group. What thinking lies behind this composite of the "culturally deprived" student?

One line of thinking promoted by Arthur Jensen (1969) held that children in poverty families, who are disproportionately of color, have inherited an inferior genetic stock, and their failure in school and society simply reflects that. Most educators, ourselves included, do not accept this line of thought, so we will not review it here.

Many educators who disagreed with the heredity explanation for the failure of students of color (especially Black students) explained these failures in terms of general environmental conditions. The environmental "explanations tried to emphasize the pattern of environmental conditions as the cause which depresses the ability of these children to learn—economic and job discrimination, substandard housing, poor nutrition, parental apathy" (Clark, 1969, p. 108). A number of specific psychological deficiencies were believed caused by "substandard" environments.

One psychological deficiency was poor perceptual skills. Klaus and Gray (1968) and Deutsch (1963) argued that homes in the ghetto provided too little visual and tactile stimulation and too much disorganized aural stimulation for normal perceptual development. A bare apartment with the TV blaring constantly—the image many people have of inner-city homes—was thought to retard a child's learning to discriminate among shapes and objects and learning to listen carefully to environmental sounds. Ausubel (1966a) cataloged a list of perceptual problems supposedly brought about by low-income homes that lacked sensory stimulation and systematic ordering of stimuli: "poor perceptual discrimination skills; inability to use adults as sources of information, corrections and reality testing, and as instruments for satisfying curiosity; an impoverished language-symbolic system; and a paucity of information, concepts, and relational propositions" (p. 251). Some believed that these deficiencies would not only hinder a child's ability to acquire information, but would also ultimately retard the child's development through Piaget's stages of cognitive growth (Hunt, 1961).

Language was another area of deficiency popularly attributed to the "culturally deprived." Many theorists believed that the language that lower-class children learned was so concrete and disorganized that it prevented them from learning to think abstractly. For example, Bernstein (1964) described middle-class language as "elaborated" because of its complex vocabulary and structures enabling the communication of hypotheses, relationships, and abstractions. In contrast, he saw lower-class language as "restricted" because of its high use of concrete words and short, simple sentences. Lower-class children were even described as being unaware of the separate words making up sentences and as being deaf to many words and parts of speech; as a result, they were believed unable to arrange words to express new meanings or use prepositions and conjunctions like "or" and "not" (Bereiter & Engelmann, 1966).

Children whose native language was not English were also not exempt from concern. It was not uncommon for language-biased teachers and counselors in Texas to place Spanish-speaking Mexican children in classes for the mentally retarded, as they assumed that not speaking English created a mental deficiency (San Miguel, 1987). Furthermore, many educators believed that Mexican migrant children failed to develop enough competence in either English or Spanish to enable complex learning, which was why their IQ scores were lower than those of Anglo children. Compensatory education for Hispanic students focused on language as the primary determinant of underachievement rather than other factors (such as quality of teaching or relevance of concepts being taught). This meant that Hispanic students' achievement was rarely discussed without reference to bilingualism, Spanish dominance, or lack of English skills and that other factors related to achievement were often overlooked (Walker, 1987).

A third supposed deficiency related to mental stability and integrity. Many educators believed that poor children, especially Black males, lacked appropriate role models and that this damaged their development. For example, Woronoff (1966) wrote that "the lower-class Negro adult male is seldom regarded as a worthwhile masculine model for the boy to emulate" (p. 293). He hypothesized that Black boys who grew up in female-headed households, exposed to Black males who held low-status jobs and served as "ineffective" family leaders, developed "problems of handling aggression, making decisions, accepting responsibility, and executing leadership, in addition to syndromes of neurotic behavior" (p. 293).

It was further believed that the cumulative effects of inability to learn, a poor environment, and neurotic disorders produced a low self-concept, which in turn produced more failure, further reinforcing the child's low self-concept (Conte & Grimes, 1969).

The culture of poor and minority people was seen as the main culprit for these psychological deficiencies, but some researchers also investigated the effects of poor health and nutrition. Pasamanick, for example, investigated how later cognitive development is influenced by prenatal maternal nutrition and complications during pregnancy and delivery. His main conclusion was that lower-class children suffered more nutritional deficits and much more from prenatal, natal, and postnatal complications than did middle-class children, producing a high rate of "organically injured Negro children who must contend with further consequences of socio-cultural disorganization" (Pasamanick & Knobloch, 1966, p. 292).

Taken together, educators subscribing to the cultural deficiency orientation believed that affected children developed the following learning characteristics: physical and visual rather than aural orientation, content-centered rather than form-centered orientation, external rather than internal controls, concrete rather than abstract thinking, inductive rather than deductive thinking, slow and inflexible rather than quick and flexible work style, nonverbal orientation, deficits in auditory skills, short attention span, large gaps in knowledge, and lack of feelings of success (Conte & Grimes, 1969). Set within human capital theory, such people seemed totally lacking in the knowledge and skills society needs and therefore lacking in the capacity to develop their human capital to a very great extent. They were even seen as lacking in the ability to raise children that would be able to escape poverty and unemployment more successfully. Many educators adopting this viewpoint simply gave up; others developed strategies for teaching that are described later in this chapter.

Physiological and Mental Deficiency

Much of the work in special education historically has sought to understand and learn to remediate physiological and mental deficiencies. You can accurately catalog these deficiencies (or supposed deficiencies) simply by listing the special education categories: visual impairment, hearing impairment, physical and health impairments, mental deficiency (in fact, a leading special education journal and professional organization have "mental deficiency" in their titles), emotional or behavioral disorders, and learning disabilities. For the most part, these disorders are believed to have primarily an organic or psychological basis, although mental retardation and emotional disturbance have also been thought strongly linked to the cultural "deficiencies" described earlier (Dunn, 1963).

Many of the same deficits in psychological functioning ascribed to the so-called culturally deprived have been ascribed to those labeled mentally retarded, emotionally disturbed, learning disabled, hard of hearing, and visually impaired. Most of these students are described as deficient in language and reading. Children classified as mentally retarded, for example, have been described as having the vocabulary and language skills of an intellectually normal but younger child; as Lenneberg (1967) put it, they use language "in 'frozen' but normal primitive stages" (p. 326). Children with hearing impairments also have difficulty learning oral language, owing to hearing loss. Many (perhaps even half) of those classified as learning disabled have been described as deficient is language skills. Bryan and Bryan (1978) noted that this group is deficient in their ability to handle grammatical inflections, comprehend and create complex sentences, define words, classify objects into categories, produce sentences, and recognize their own language errors.

Students with language and reading problems are often viewed as deficient in knowledge normally acquired verbally. Not only do such students frequently lack much information that their "normal" agemates have, but they also often lack some of the underlying concepts. For example, according to Kneedler (1984), mentally retarded children "learn concepts slowly if at all [and] have difficulty remembering things" (p. 51). Hearing impaired children are often behind academically because of their "difficulty succeeding in a system that depends primarily on the spoken word and written language to transmit knowledge" (Hardman, Drew, & Egan, 1984, p. 227). When you realize that much of what is taught in school is explained verbally or read, this makes sense: If you can't read the book, you won't learn the material in it.

Another area of deficiency attributed to most special education children is thinking skills. Hardman et al. (1984) described the moderately retarded as having "difficulty focusing on relevant stimuli, inefficient rehearsal strategies that help commit information to long-term memory, inability to learn from incidental learning cues, and difficulty transferring knowledge from one task to another" (p. 117). Children classified as learning disabled sometimes display difficulty with specific thinking skills, such as visualizing imagery, organizing information, abstracting, or synthesizing (Adelman & Taylor, 1983).

Finally, most students in special education are described as being deficient in social skills. For example, children classified as emotionally disturbed are frequently disliked by their peers because of their behavior, which has been found to be a major reason for their referral to special education (Rubin, Simson, & Betwee, 1966). And children classified as learning disabled often display "antisocial behavior" or inappropriate social behavior, owing to less positive and more negative reinforcement than most children receive, an impulsive cognitive style, hyperactivity, or visual-perceptual deficits that interfere with the ability to learn to read social cues (Bryan & Bryan, 1978).

Educators and researchers have used a variety of theoretical frameworks to understand these "deficiencies." The medical model assumes that the problems are caused by an organic defect, such as brain damage, chemical imbalance, or chromosomal abnormality. (For some handicapping conditions such causes are clearly documented; for others they are not.) The behavioral model assumes that the child's problems are due to reinforcement for the wrong behaviors, or a failure to have correct behaviors modeled and reinforced. The psychodynamic model assumes that they arise from repressed emotions caused by inadequate early experiences. The ecological model assumes that the child's problems are caused by a failure of factors in the child's environment to support positive characteristics and actions of the child.

Although these models suggest different factors responsible for children's problems, they all see certain children as deficient in the various areas. The deficiency orientation suggests that these areas must be remediated to enable the students to function more successfully in the classroom and later on in society. For that reason, a substantial portion of the school day usually is spent on remediation.

DIFFERENCE ORIENTATION

Our picture of the deficiency orientation was not very positive. We presented cultural deficiency in the past tense and set off certain words with quotation marks and qualifiers because few scholars today embrace the notion of cultural deprivation. A rich body of research counters it. We have noticed, however, that many teachers and lay people still accept it, largely on the basis of ignorance about the culture in question. The notion of physiological and mental deficiency is dying a harder death, although a number of special educators are raising serious objections to it.

Advocates of the difference orientation to Teaching the Exceptional and the Culturally Different approach agree with advocates of the deficiency orientation that there is a standard body of knowledge and a set of values and skills that all American citizens need to acquire. However, they believe that there are different models of healthy psychological development fostered by different cultural contexts or constitutional endowments. Rather than focusing on deficiencies that need to be remediated, they focus on strengths to build on to help children assimilate into the American mainstream. As Table 2–1 shows, the school goal of this approach is to teach traditional school knowledge more effectively by building on knowledge and skills students bring with them.

Cultural Difference

You probably have heard educators debate the pros and cons of using Black English to help teach inner-city students or of providing bilingual education programs. You also may have heard educators refer to the importance of understanding the learning and communication styles of students, for example, recognizing that looking down instead of looking the teacher in the eye may be a sign of respect in the student's home culture.

Many educators, particularly those of color, reacted strongly against the deficiency orientation. This reaction has prompted researchers to begin establishing a research base documenting that cultural differences in language and learning style are not deficiencies and can be built on to facilitate learning. A central concept here is cultural compatibility. Anthropologists have documented that discontinuities between one set of cultural practices and another can be confusing to the individual who must make a rapid transition between the two different sets. Perhaps the best example is to think of how you feel when you are traveling in a foreign country and find yourself among people who are culturally different from yourself. You may feel confused, a bit frightened and unsure of yourself, and perhaps annoyed when you repeatedly find yourself doing or saying the wrong thing. After a period of time, you learn to function in the new culture, but initially the discontinuity jolts you.

The same thing happens with children whose home culture is different from the culture of the school. The discontinuity may be particularly aggravating for the child who is expected to function within the school's culture without being taught it and who must make the leap between cultures twice a day—once when arriving at school, and then again when going home.

The main idea behind the Teaching the Culturally Different approach, then, is to ensure as much cultural compatibility as possible. There is no one right model of psychological development, and one's cultural context strongly influences how one will develop. In assimilating into American society, children should not be condemned for the language or culture they learn at home and should be encouraged to retain these. However, advocates of the Teaching the Culturally Different approach believe that all children still need to learn mainstream cultural values and knowledge. The psychological development of culturally different children may at times interfere or conflict with demands of the regular classroom, especially if the teacher is unaware of how children are interpreting and perceiving its demands. However, all cultural groups foster cognitive strengths that can be built on to facilitate classroom learning. As Abrahams and Troike (1972) put it,

> If we expect to be able to teach students from such [culturally different] groups effectively, we must learn wherein their cultural differences lie and we must capitalize upon them as a resource, rather than

doing what we have always done and disregarding the differences or placing the students in the category of "noncommunicative," thereby denigrating both the differences and the students. (p. 5)

Learning and communication style can be a major area of cultural incompatibility. We will first describe the style of learning and communication that schools tend to prefer, and then we will consider the styles often brought to the classroom by children of color. According to Cohen (1969), the following characteristics typify the approach to learning preferred in most classrooms: task rather than person orientation; focus on the parts of a whole; focus on formal and nonpersonal attributes; focus on decontextualized information; linear thinking patterns; nonemotional behavior; sedentary behavior; long attention span, regardless of personal interest; use of standard English; ability to communicate without reference to context or nonverbal cues; and formal roles, schedules, preplanning, and structure. These traits characterize the learning style fostered in most White, middle-class homes, in addition to the classroom. Since children develop a learning style at home, this point becomes very important.

On the other hand, research has found that Black and Mexican-American children tend to be more person-oriented than task-oriented, which means that they tend to become more interested in content that has a human, social focus and in teaching strategies that involve them with other people. They also tend to focus on the whole rather than the parts and to view the attributes of an object in relationship to the object's use rather than to a set of formal rules, such as classifying a cup as a drinking utensil rather than as a cylinder (Hale, 1982; Ramirez & Castaneda, 1974). Shade (1982) has suggested that Blacks have developed a strong interest in "reading" social information out of necessity: In a racist society in which one regularly encounters hostility, it is a matter of survival to learn to interpret social cues correctly. Hale has suggested that people who cannot afford to buy their children quantities of things to play with encourage a person orientation by offering the baby a body part (e.g., a finger) to play with rather than a toy. In addition, Cohen (1969) has argued that poor communities require more cooperation and sharing among members than do wealthier communities, which further contributes to this learning style. Although the mode of cognition fostered in many Black and Mexican-American homes is functional in most contexts, it conflicts with the requirements of most school tasks, which is why, Cohen argues, lower-class and minority children tend to do poorly in school. A teacher using the Teaching the Culturally Different approach would teach content by building directly on the skills and orientations the children learned at home.

The communication style of the teacher sometimes conflicts with the style of the students. Philips (1983) studied communication patterns among Warm Springs Indians, documenting, for example, wait time between utterances, how a person gains attention, how a person acknowledges that a message has been understood, and how people take turns in a conversation. She found that the patterns children learned in the community conflicted with the patterns used and expected by the Anglo teachers in school. As a result, the teacher and the students constantly responded to each other inappropriately, which fostered antagonism and lack of respect. For example, the children did not respond to the teacher's attempts to conduct recitation lessons, causing the teacher to view the children as slow and uncooperative and the children to view the teacher as rude and confusing. Philips suggested that teachers of Indian children could be much more successful if they learned to use the communication patterns of the local community.

The issue of communication has sparked more debate and research when it has involved dialect and language differences. Proponents of the cultural deficit orientation viewed the speech of lower-class Black children as incorrect, poor, and "destitute" (Newton, 1966). Since the mid-1960s, however, considerable research has established it as a distinct dialect, governed by its own rules of phonemics, syntax, morphology, and word meaning and as linguistically sound as standard English (Labov, 1969). This being the case, educators have wondered whether the dialect interferes with school learning conducted in standard English; for example, would Black children learn to read more easily in Black English than in standard English? Harber and Bryen (1976) reviewed research evidence on this question and did not find evidence that dialect difference does interfere, but acknowledged that research was still too limited to make any firm conclusions.

Even if the dialect does not prevent children from understanding the teacher, it can prevent teachers unfamiliar with it from responding constructively to the children. Gay and Abrahams (1972) have pointed out that "the child soon learns that if he [or she] writes the way he [or she] thinks the teacher is going to consider it all wrong," and therefore recommend that "if a teacher is to communicate with her [or his] Black students, she [or he] needs to learn to understand their language" (p. 207). In addition, accented English spoken by students whose native language is not English may cause a teacher to question the students' academic competence. Teachers have been found to associate the accented English of some language-minority students with a lack of comprehension in reading (Thonis, 1970).

There is no question, however, that language difference interferes with instruction when teacher and student do not speak the same language. Historically, most U.S. schools actively maintained an English-only policy, often prohibiting the use of any language other than English for instruction. Children whose native language was not English tended to be viewed as deficient and their home language and culture as inferior. Early strategies for dealing with linguistically and culturally different students included submersion in the English-language curriculum or placement in special English as a Second Language (ESL) classes. Neither approach successfully integrated the language-minority student into mainstream society. By the 1960s, spurred on by increased immigration from Castro's Cuba and the growing civil rights movement, education policymakers were desperately seeking another more promising approach. At the same time, parents, concerned teachers, and community activists began calling for the use of children's native language in schools (Schneider, 1976).

From its inception with the passage of the Bilingual Education Act in 1968, bilingual education programs were pushed into a compensatory mold. Although there are bilingual programs that use all the approaches to multicultural education described in this book, the majority continue to use the Teaching the Culturally Different approach. Such programs use the child's native language as a medium of instruction in the content areas until the child has learned enough English to get by in the English-only program. Bilingual programs oriented toward the Teaching the Culturally Different approach assume that English-language, middle-class, Anglo-American culture and traditional school knowledge need to be acquired by all American citizens, and that these programs form a standard in which all should gain competence. This competence will provide citizens the necessary key to "fuller participation in a free society" (Cordasco, 1975, p. 186).

This belief is overly simplistic and not always true and has lead to a controversial dichotomy in bilingual education program models between transitional and maintenance programs. Heated debates between these two camps have raged for years. In general, most programs in the United States follow the transitional approach already described, where the child moves from native-language instruction to English-only instruction as soon as possible, the average length of stay in such programs being 3 to 4 years. The less-practiced maintenance model strives to develop complete bilinguality in its students and to maintain it throughout the students' 12 years in public school. However, in reality, there are great varieties of program types and designs. Researchers have developed 3- 5- 7- and 19-part typologies of bilingual programs (Trueba, 1979).

There are several underlying assumptions of bilingual education regardless of a particular program's structure or its long-term goals. All programs assume that the language and culture a child learns at home can promote normal and healthy psychological development and communication competence. Moreover, lack of adequate first-language development may contribute to poor school achievement in the second language (Cummins, 1981; Skutnabb-Kangas, 1981). The work of Cummins and Skutnabb-Kangas has greatly influenced research and practice in bilingual education, and the evidence indicates that children with well-developed first-language skills acquire their second language with greater ease and success than children who are still learning their first language. This is explained by Cummins' "common underlying proficiency" model of language acquisition, which has helped to destroy, or at least weaken, the myth of a bilingual handicap.

If the school denigrates a child's native language, it may not only damage the child's self-concept (Kobrick, 1974), but also cut off normal communication development between the child and his or her parents. Many immigrant students, when enculturated with the Anglo, middle-class culture of the school, respond with shame and even hostility toward their parents and home language and culture.

Whether talking about learning style, communication style, or language, research indicates that achievement can be enhanced when teachers attempt to make the culture of the school compatible with the child's culture. For example, Jordan (1985) has reported a program in Hawaii aimed at improving the achievement of native Hawaiian children on standard measures of achievement in basic skills. She and her colleagues found a few key practices that were interfering with children's learning. Hawaiian children spend considerable time working with peers outside school; if they are punished for interacting with peers in the classroom, and especially if punishment involves isolating them, they will put their energy into establishing illicit contact with peers. If a moderate level of peer interaction is allowed, they tend to stay on-task. As another example, DeLain, Pearson, and Anderson (1985) found that Black students who exhibit competence in oral games, such as sounding, understand the use of figurative language better than White students. They suggested that teachers who incorporate Black students' verbal skills in language arts instruction will have a definite strength on which to build their achievement. Teachers who view Black English as incorrect or inferior, on the other hand, not only subject their students to unfair stereotyping, but also miss an opportunity to interface the demands of school with strengths in the students' culture.

Mental Difference

Children whose school performance is far below average are often considered mentally deficient. A teacher who views students such as those in classes for the learning disabled or educable mentally retarded as different rather than deficient is more likely to use an approach discussed later in this book than the approach being discussed in this chapter. For example, imagine a ninth-grade teacher with some special education students who read on a fourth-grade level. The teacher who wishes to assimilate these students may not believe they are permanently deficient, but will view the task of assimilating them into the classroom as virtually impossible without their reading deficiency being corrected first. An alternative for the teacher is to rethink the idea that there is a standard body of knowledge all should gain and that this should be done through reading. Once a teacher does this, he or she is moving away from the Teaching the Exceptional and Culturally Different approach.

Children who excel in certain areas, on the other hand, and who may be classified as gifted and talented can be considered mentally different. Conceptions of what the word *gifted* means range widely, from narrow definitions that include only the top 1% to 5% in academic achievement (Terman et al., 1976) to broad definitions that view many people as having gifts or talents in a variety of areas (Taylor, 1974). Many people believe that regardless of how one defines giftedness, gifted children need educational experiences that are different from those of "normal" children and that these experiences should ultimately help them provide the leadership needed in our technological society. Whether giftedness is caused primarily by genetic or environmental factors is not a major issue of debate; what is at issue is what to do about those who seem to excel in certain areas of learning. Proponents of the Teaching the Exceptional approach for the gifted believe that failure to employ this approach often results in the failure of abilities to develop, frustration and sometimes psychological problems on the part of the gifted, and a waste of a social resource. They condemn the belief that gifted children will "make it" on their own. For example, Robinson, Roedell, and Jackson (1981) concluded on the basis of two research studies that "superior abilities that are not nurtured will not develop" (p. 130). Proponents of this approach point to underachievers, dropouts, and even suicide victims, who have become frustrated with schooling and sometimes with life in general because their abilities were not being challenged or valued (Robbins, 1984). They point to medical, scientific, artistic, and social accomplishments that have been achieved for society by gifted people whose abilities were cultivated (Gallagher, 1979). For these reasons, they argue, some sort of differential education needs to be provided for this different group of children, whether it be within the regular classroom, a pull-out program, an accelerated program, a special class, or some type of extra enrichment program.

Gender Differences

Why do boys tend to outperform girls in mathematics and science, and why do they tend to dominate leadership roles? Can girls be better assimilated into these areas through the use of any particular teaching approach? We cannot give final answers to these questions, but we can outline some of the conclusions and suggestions that have been offered. You may wonder why we have placed this discussion under the difference rather than the deficit orientation, since the average performance of girls in these areas could be considered deficient to that of boys. We have placed it here because the "deficiency" seems to result mainly from a sexist culture that allocates the sexes to different roles and fosters in them different strengths and dispositions. Girls do not bring less learning to school than boys, only somewhat different learning. Nor are girls genetically inferior to boys for the task of learning mathematics and science. Crockett and Petersen (1984) reviewed research on biological determinants of male superiority in mathematics and science and found little conclusive evidence for it.

According to Fennema (1984), there are several factors that seem to explain why boys outperform girls in mathematics. One is that girls tend to have less confidence in their mathematical ability than boys and tend to attribute successes to luck or external causes and attribute failure to lack of ability (the reverse of boys' attributions). Another factor is that girls tend to see mathematics as a male domain and as less useful to their futures than do boys. These perceptions are often reinforced in mathematics classes by sexist teacher behavior and by a lack of female role models. This suggests that what girls need, then, to achieve in mathematics is a boost in their self-confidence and a belief that mathematics achievement will be useful to them.

Male dominance in the use of computers is also becoming increasingly noticeable in schools. According to Campbell (1984), boys are encouraged much more than girls to work with computers from childhood on. For example, examine a few currently popular video games to determine to which sex they were made to appeal. As a result of differential socialization, the sexes bring to school different skill, interest, and confidence levels for mathematics, science, and computer science learning.

Leadership position is another domain that men are better socialized to occupy. Block (1984) argues that men dominate positions of leadership and intellectual creativity largely because of sex-differentiated early socialization that coeducational schooling tends to reinforce. Boys are encouraged to experiment and seek solutions to problems themselves, while girls tend to be encouraged to develop social relationships at the expense of assertiveness and flexible, cognitive problem solving. In mixed-sex contexts, boys learn to dominate leadership and cognitive problem solving, and girls learn to let them dominate so as to maintain positive relationships with them (thus giving boys more practice in these areas at the girls' expense).

Those who wish to assimilate girls into traditional male domains believe that girls may at certain points in their lives require different teaching strategies or educational arrangements to help them acquire skills and attitudes that boys acquired in their early socialization. No matter how similarly teachers may try to treat boys and girls in school, there needs to be some compensation for the differential socialization that the sexes experience outside school.

Interestingly, there is much less discussion about how to assimilate boys into traditional female domains. While there is interest in determining how to teach girls to enjoy and succeed in mathematics and science, few people are attempting to discover ways to prepare boys to become secretaries. We think that this says something about which sex has controlled the more interesting, prestigious, and well-paying work.

RECOMMENDED PRACTICES

No classroom is completely homogeneous. Teachers learn to expect differences among their students. Invariably, for any set of standards to which a class of students is expected to adhere, some students will adhere better than others. The problem the teacher faces is what to make of those differences, and the more students vary from the standards the teacher values, the greater this problem.

Teachers who see strong reasons for maintaining their conceptions of a standard set of knowledge, skills, and attitudes for any given grade level and who want to see all their students achieve these goals as well as possible will search for ways to teach their exceptional or culturally different students. Whatever methods or techniques the teacher uses, he or she usually expects them to be temporary adaptations until the students are able to "swim" on their own. The teacher also does not expect to slow the pace or change the instruction offered to "average," or "normal" students: Those who differ from the norm need to adapt, not vice versa.

In this section, we will describe how a teacher or a school develops a program to teach the culturally different or the exceptional in a way that will help such students fit into society better. We will describe the main recommended practices, which we have organized around content, instructional process, and program structure. Keep in mind that a teacher may have as few as one or two students fitting into this category or as many as the entire class (e.g., in an inner-city school). The teacher may attempt to accommodate them entirely within his or her classroom or may rely on support service programs for much help.

Curriculum Content

The Teaching the Exceptional and the Culturally Different approach assumes that there is a standard body of content to be learned; as Table 2–1 shows, any deviations from that content should be temporary and for the purpose of either filling in major gaps in the students' knowledge or making the curriculum more relevant and understandable to the students.

Children classified as culturally "disadvantaged" and as learning disabled have been described as having learning profiles with hills and valleys: These children are not necessarily deficient in all areas of school knowledge for their grade level, but do have very glaring gaps (Taba & Elkins, 1966). To determine where these gaps lie, it is recommended that these students be assessed in relationship to the curriculum normally mastered by their age-mates. The mentally retarded are described as deficient in all areas and as needing basic instruction in everything: the three Rs, health, social skills, emotional security, home and community participation skills, leisure activities, and vocational skills (Kirk & Gallagher, 1979). One obvious gap that many culturally different children have is language. Transitional bilingual education and ESL are both aimed toward filling in the language gap as quickly as possible so that children with limited English proficiency can learn what American-born White children are learning.

A problem in compensating for knowledge gaps is that culturally different and exceptional children need to catch up as quickly as possible to compete and progress with their peers. As Bereiter and Engelmann (1966) put it, "They must progress at a faster than normal rate if they are to catch up" (pp. 6–7). To do this, educators recommend that content be very carefully selected so that time and effort are expended mainly on areas that will most help the child catch up. To some, this means immersing these children in as much of the world of the White middle-class child as possible, while to others it means teaching primarily school skills, basic academic knowledge, and thinking skills (Taba & Elkins, 1966; Webster, 1966). Many educators recommend repetition and "overteaching" material in short drill sessions spaced over time because they believe that children who have not learned expected content at the expected rate are likely to forget it without frequent review (Kirk & Gallagher, 1979).

Similarly, to help female students catch up with male students in mathematics, science, and leadership skills, some remedial or compensatory work may be necessary. Some recommend that girls be taught separately for the duration of a workshop, a few class periods, or even their entire secondary and/or college schooling (Block, 1984) so that they can develop the skills, attitudes, and self-confidence necessary to succeed in male domains. For example, Fennema (1984) describes two different workshops to teach girls about opportunities in mathematics-related careers and the importance (and realism) of girls achieving in mathematics. Both seem to lead girls to take more mathematics courses and view themselves as more capable in that subject. Campbell (1984) suggests that girls be given extra encouragement and instruction in school on using computers to duplicate what boys seem to be getting outside school. Block (1984) recommends greater use of single-sex schools to free girls from competition against male students (which many girls find discouraging), allow more girls to assume leadership positions, lessen the conflict between achievement and peer acceptance, and provide greater exposure to female role models.

The preceding recommendations are designed to fill in gaps by compensating for lack of knowledge in an expected area. Another problem with content is that it may not seem very interesting or relevant. Educators recommend that if the curriculum seems alien to the child, the child's interests and experiences should be used as a bridge to the school curriculum, and the curriculum should be made as relevant as possible. Students sometimes do not try hard when they do not see what they are being taught as useful or personally interesting. In addition, students need concrete examples to help them acquire new concepts. This means that White, middle-class curricula are inadequate for teaching the culturally different and that culturally relevant bridges are needed. For example, an urban teacher wrote that her Black students' "interest in Selma, Alabama, has created an interest in studying the map of the United States. Their knowledge of what Negroes in the South are enduring to try to vote has enabled me to motivate them into learning about the structure and function of government" (Levy, 1966, p. 432). In addition, educators have recommended that teachers teach children *why* a body of knowledge (or education in general) is useful to them. For example, Webster (1966) suggests that social studies will seem more worthwhile to disadvantaged students if the teacher starts with the "here-and-now" rather than the "there-and-then" and shows how what is taught can help students understand their own world now.

At the same time, advocates of the Teaching the Culturally Different approach argue that relevant material should not replace more conventional school knowledge. It should either supplement it or serve as a bridge to it. For example, Riessman (1966) stresses that "Negro history probably would interest Negro children, and might serve as a good *opener* for the development of further interest in history and social studies in general" (p. 59, emphasis his). He did not suggest that Negro history should replace the study of history "in general" or that students who were not Black should study it. Children's knowledge needs to be extended in the direction of mainstream culture, and although it is desirable to start where children are, a teacher should not stay there. Standard curriculum content becomes the compass a teacher uses for charting the direction in which to take his or her students. The same is true of curriculum for gifted students; Gallagher (1979) has cautioned against "fun and games" enrichment curricula that appeal to student interest at the expense of helping the student delve into advanced study in established disciplines. Established disciplines are useful for future professional opportunities; fun and games are not.

Instruction

More attention has gone into modifying instruction than into modifying curriculum content for the Teaching the Exceptional and the Culturally Different approach. The classroom teacher usually feels fairly confident about what students should be learning, but may be perplexed about how to help them learn it. It is generally recommended that teachers be familiar with a repertoire of instructional strategies and pick and choose those that seem most fruitful for individual students.

One strategy is to use a child's learning style as a vehicle for teaching new content. For example, Riessman (1976) recommends that "the method of teaching formal communication to inner-city children take advantage of their communication style by employing teaching techniques that stress the visual, the physical, and the active as much as possible" (p. 87). Kleinfeld (1973) recommends that teachers of Eskimo children use plenty of visual aids to capitalize on Eskimo children's well-developed visual skills. Some special educators recommend that students with visual deficits and auditory strengths be taught new content orally and that those with auditory deficits and visual strengths be taught new content visually (Bateman, 1965; Boder, 1971). Fennema and Peterson (1987) have found that girls learn mathematics better through cooperative learning than through competitive learning.

A second strategy, advocated particularly by those representing the deficiency orientation, is to individualize instruction, sequencing and pacing the program correctly for each individual child. For example, Taba and Elkins (1966) state that instruction for disadvantaged students needs to be broken down into "bite-size" learning tasks and carefully sequenced so that "each learning step must match the powers of the students" (p. 73). Ausubel (1966b) recommends that instruction be "geared to the learner's existing state of readiness," provide for "mastery and consolidation of all ongoing learning tasks before new tasks are introduced," and be "optimally organized to facilitate efficient sequential learning" (p. 468). A favorite procedure that many educators use to do this is direct instruction, especially for remediation. Direct instruction requires that specific learning objectives be set (preferably in behavioral terms) and that techniques of behavior modification be used to achieve them (Bereiter and Engelmann, 1966; Lovitt, 1977; Repp, 1983; Stephens, 1976). Direct instruction often uses task analysis, in which the teacher plans what to teach by stating the specific educational tasks to be learned, determining a sequence of steps for learning these tasks, and determining the specific behaviors needed to perform each task (Bateman, 1974).

The recommendation that strengths be built upon also has implications for language. Bilingual educators point out that it makes no sense to teach new knowledge and skills in a language a child does not understand and that achievement is higher when instruction makes use of a child's native language. For example, Garcia (1982) points out that "studies indicated that the bilinguals, who were initially taught in the vernacular, read with greater comprehension than those initially taught in the [language] of the school" (p. 138).

Whether or not one believes that the language-different child should develop competence in his or her native language, advocates of the Teaching the Culturally Different approach recommend that the teacher accept and not denigrate the child's language. For example, although Newton (1966) terms the speech of inner-city children "verbal destitution," she still recognizes that "rejection of the student because of his [or her] language inadequacy will inevitably lead to his [or her] alienation, and eventually to his [or her] disaffection for all things educational" (p. 336).

Students deemed exceptional and culturally different are often described as unmotivated or hard to motivate, and educators have suggested how to deal with this. One recommendation is to make sure these students experience immediate success by assigning tasks within their capability and rewarding them for successful performance. For example, special education students usually have a history of school failure, and teachers are told that those "who have faced failure may have developed low frustration tolerance, negative attitudes toward schoolwork, and possibly some compensatory behavior problems that make them socially unpopular." Teachers are told to "organize a day-to-day program presenting the child with short-range as well as long-range tasks in which to succeed" (Kirk & Gallagher, 1979, p. 163). Teachers are advised to use as motivators students' interests or prior experiences. For example, Taba and Elkins (1966) observe that "aspirations as a topic has no meaning or interest, but a study of ads for jobs—a good beginning—hits a lively concern" (p. 75). Lovitt (1977) suggests that the teacher deliberately bring into the classroom a variety of things to find out what actually turns kids on, and then deliberately use their interests as motivators and reinforcers. The point is that students who have done poorly in or been turned off by school will need some sort of "carrot on the end of a stick" to lead them willingly into more traditional content and instruction.

Program Structure

Programs are structured to teach the exceptional or culturally different in four different ways, distinguished by the degree to which they take the child out of "normal" education. One way of structuring a program is to keep the child entirely within the normal program but make sure that adaptations are offered that will enable the child to succeed. For example, low-vision students may be given large-print books and audio aids, or students from a different cultural background may be given culturally relevant materials and instruction based on their learning styles. Another example is team-taught bilingual programs, in which both languages are used. This is not just business as usual provided the teacher is actively attempting to develop students in the direction schools consider normal and is using many of the recommended practices to do this. The teacher tries to keep the curriculum and instruction as normal as possible, but at the same time offers whatever bridges are needed for students to learn successfully.

A second way of structuring a program is to keep the student in a full-day normal instructional program, but to provide help at the preschool level or before or after school. Probably the best example of this is Head Start, which attempts to provide school readiness skills for low-income students before their entry into school. After-school enrichment programs for gifted students also follow this arrangement.

A third kind of structure is a pull-out program, in which the child is in a normal classroom for much of the day, but in a special program for part of the day. This use of support services, as Table 2–1 notes, is a common structural arrangement for compensatory education pro-grams such as Chapter I, bilingual education, and special education.

A fourth kind of structure offers an entirely different education program for the different or exceptional child. Severely retarded and multiple-handicapped students are frequently educated most of the day in a separate, self-contained class. Moreover, children who do not speak English may be in a separate program all day until they learn enough English to be mainstreamed.

To illustrate the implementation of Teaching the Exceptional and the Culturally Different, we offer two vignettes.

Ms. Vanderbilt

Ms. Vanderbilt has been teaching a Head Start class on Chicago's Southwest side for 3 years. This was her first teaching assignment after acquiring her teaching certificate from a large university in the Midwest. The class this semester is typical of those she has taught since she began. Her students are Black and Hispanic res-idents of a poor socioeconomic community. The community mem-bers, including the parents of Ms. Vanderbilt's students, respect the school and look on it as the main institution that will improve life chances for their children.

There are 28 students in Ms. Vanderbilt's class. There are 16 girls—10 Black and 6 Hispanic. Two of the Hispanic girls are Span-ish-speaking. Of the 12 boys, 8 are Black; of the 4 Hispanic boys, 1 is bilingual. On entering Ms. Vanderbilt's classroom, you are struck by the richness and warmth of the environment. Colorful bulletin boards, colorful posters (mostly of nature), bushy plants in deco-rative pots, two aquariums, and two hamsters (in cages) capture your attention. Three learning centers, a library corner with Great Books for children, a rocking chair, and a large yellow carrel that students can climb up into are also prominent features of the room.

As you bring your eyes back from the room's artifacts to the teacher and students, you learn that the class is preparing for a field trip to the Art Institute, with a picnic lunch in nearby Grant Park. The class is discussing the lunch arrangements, and several of the students are calling out what they are planning to bring to eat. Ms. Vanderbilt calls their attention to the "basic four" food poster on the side wall and reminds them of the nutrition unit that concluded last week. She tells them that she expects their lunch to consist of the food categories that are pictured in the poster. She also tells them to review the worksheet on the three French painters—Monet, Manet, and Renoir—whose work they will see on the field trip. The recess bell rings, interrupting the discussion; Ms. Vanderbilt quickly gets the students ready for one of their favorite school activities and leads them out to the playground. She tells you as she leaves to meet her in the teachers' lounge for coffee.

When the two of you meet, she tells you that this is really a super class, and this is their fourth field trip downtown to take in a cultural event. She adds that next week they are going to attend the youth symphony. She says that, given time and an active enrichment program, most of the students will have a good opportunity for academic success in school. Her curriculum is geared to exposing the students to a way of life they have not been privileged to know. She points out that the information on the bulletin boards and posters is designed to help students learn about life on the other side of the tracks and that in her classroom every boy and girl will learn the same thing students in the suburbs learn.

Mrs. Stephens

Mrs. Stephens is a high school learning disabilities teacher. She has been teaching for 5 years in a suburban high school. During the course of a day, she sees about 30 students, most of whom are boys. Her classroom is small; it is furnished with two round tables, several chairs, several carrels, three well-stocked bookshelves, and a teacher's desk. Student work is displayed prominently around the room.

Mrs. Stephens tells you that her main job is to teach the students whatever she can to help them "make it" in the regular classroom and survive in the outside world. She has informally divided her students into two categories: those who can probably be remediated well enough to handle regular classes and maybe even college, and those who are too far behind to catch up for regular classwork and mainly need "real-world" survival skills, such as vocational training, skill in handling a checkbook, skill in filling out job applications, and so forth. The class you are about to observe consists of 10 students who are preparing themselves for a more academic course of study.

As the bell rings, the students enter class, laughing and shoving each other on their way to their seats. Mrs. Stephens jokes with them in a friendly manner. The second bell rings and the students quiet down.

Mrs. Stephens says, "Today we will continue with grammar. We will learn about the preposition." One boy jokes to a girl, "I'm gonna preposition you!"

Mrs. Stephens says, "I'm gonna preposition you, too. Brian, come up here." She gives him a poster with the word *to* written on it. She says, "You are a preposition. Hold this."

Mrs. Stephens calls up other students and gives them posters with words on them. She has the students arrange themselves in

various combinations to form various sentences, having them identify the subject and verb of each sentence. For each sentence, she
has students explain what words go with *to* and why.

Then she says, "You can all sit down. You are really getting
the idea."

Dave raises his hand. "My friend Marc, in the regular English
class, said they studied this stuff last month."

Mrs. Stephens nods her head. "Right. So far they have studied
a lot more parts of speech than you have, but by the end of the
semester, you should have pretty well caught up."

Joe asks, "Does that mean we won't need to be in here any-
more?"

Mrs. Stephens replies, "Not yet. You still don't have the vocabulary and reading skills the English teachers require, although
by next year some of you may be ready to handle Mr. Ross's class.
Now, let's get back to these prepositions."

Mrs. Stephens gives the students a list of prepositions on a
handout. She then writes several sentences on the board, and asks
the students to identify the parts of speech and explain which word
is the preposition. The last 10 minutes are spent playing a game
with prepositions.

After class, you ask how many of her students actually learn
to "make it" in school on their own. She replies, "Not that many. A
lot of this stuff I teach does stick, for a while at least, but they are
so far behind, it's like running after a moving train. Most of them
won't completely graduate from LD, but they will become more successful in their other classes, and some will need LD less and less.
Reading-oriented work just isn't their thing, so every day it's a
struggle."

You ask if the regular teachers assume any responsibility for
teaching them. She replies, "Oh, sure, a number of them do. They
give me new vocabulary words to review with the students, study
guides to help them with. Some let me give tests orally. Some make
allowances on their written work, have them do stuff orally, have
them work with a buddy. They don't change their whole approach to
teaching, of course. But a lot of them make modifications here and
there so my students can at least get something out of the class and
experience some success. A lot of high school teaching is heavy reading and lecture. Sometimes I wonder if it has to be that way, but
that's the way it is. I've got kids who would drop out before they'd
endure another day of heavy reading and lecture in a regular class. I
mean, I've got eleventh and twelfth graders who read on a fourth-
grade level. Without LD or something like it, they'd be on the streets,
and most regular teachers aren't at all equipped to deal with them.
But they are very cooperative about trying to modify things for the
students who are reading on maybe a junior high level."

CRITIQUE

Ms. Vanderbilt and Mrs. Stephens are both very concerned and caring teachers, and they give their best effort to implementing the approach described in this chapter. If they care about their students and do their jobs as well as they can, what arguments might one have for or against what they, or others adopting this approach, are doing?

Let us first synthesize the main criticisms of the cultural deficiency orientation, which were very cogently stated in 1970 by Baratz and Baratz. The notion of cultural deficiency was promoted by educators and social scientists who lacked an anthropological background and who took middle-class Anglo culture as their reference point for judging others. This culture was assumed to be the model against which to judge others, but no scientific evidence was ever put forth in support of that assumption. Those whose behavior, language, and cognition differed from this narrow standard were judged as "sick, pathological, deviant, and underdeveloped," with blame placed on their genes and/ or their environment (Baratz & Baratz, 1970, p. 31). There is abundant anthropological and linguistic data, however, that amply demonstrate that lower-class people and people of color have very well developed cultures that are simply different in some ways from that of middle-class Whites. Thus, the cultural deficiency position has been an ideological position that ignored a wealth of data from scientific research.

The notion of mental deficiency is similarly flawed, especially with respect to the categories of educable mental retardation, emotional disturbance, and learning disabilities. Very likely, you view these categories as "real" deficiencies that educators have discovered and are learning how to treat. Most non-special educators believe that special educators agree, for example, on what mental retardation is, how to identify a retarded child, and what to do about it. Actually, this is not the case, particularly with the largest special education category— learning disabilities. Ysseldyke and Algozzine (1982) have distinguished between objective categories—blindness and deafness—which have an objective, sensory basis, and subjective categories—learning disabilities, emotional disturbance, and mental retardation—which are "completely subjectively derived" (p. 43). Objective categories are fairly clearly caused by a physiological defect, and you don't need to be a professional to recognize members of these categories. For example, blindness is caused by damage to the eye or optic nerve, and you don't usually need to give a series of complicated tests to determine whether someone is blind, although you may need to do this to determine the visual limitations of a partially sighted person.

Subjective categories are different. How, for example, do you determine who is learning disabled and what causes learning disabilities? Although the learning disabled historically have been thought to be neurologically impaired, evidence that they actually are is questionable (Kavale & Forness, 1985), and professionals disagree among themselves on how the category should be defined and exactly which children should be in it. As another example, although most severely retarded children have identifiable organic impairments, about 90% of those classified as mildly retarded do not (Kneedler, 1984). A child may be classified as EMR in one school, but not in another. Some professionals may see a certain child as emotionally disturbed while others do not.

In a discussion of special education categories, Ysseldyke and Algozzine (1982) have argued that "the definition is the basis for the *existence* of the condition" (p. 48, emphasis theirs). In other words, people are mildly retarded, for example, because educators have chosen to regard certain behaviors that can be tested as defective. In fact, educators have tended to regard the same behaviors as symptoms of mental or emotional defect as they have regarded as symptoms of cultural deficiencies. For example, Mercer (1973) found that Black and Hispanic children in California were being disproportionately classified as retarded because institutions, and especially schools, had race-and class-biased notions of what constitutes intelligence and how one measures it. By defining differences as mental deficiencies, educators ignore the strengths and capabilities that children have and do so more on the basis of ideology than on the basis of science. Ysseldyke and Algozzine (1982) have warned that

> an elaborate, psychometrically inadequate system of identifying
> and explaining the extent of presumed important differences among
> individuals has evolved. . . . Educators are searching an empty field
> and expect to find solutions to problems they have created without
> recognizing the error of their omission. (p. 253)

The deficiency orientation is based on an additional fallacy. Imagine that you are forming a neighborhood basketball team and you decide that the main characteristic people should have is height. You round up your neighbors and discover you have more than enough for a team. You line them up by height, and because you can afford to, you define the shortest 5% of the neighborhood as deficient. The neighborhood could treat shortness as a serious problem and expend considerable energy looking for a remedy. Perhaps some of the shortest neighbors could even be cured of their defect by eating well. Soon there is a concerted effort among the neighbors to see that their children are fed well enough to grow tall. A year passes and heights sprout up. The next season, you line everybody up again, choose the tallest for your team, most of the rest for the bench, and again define the shortest 5% as deficient. Crazy? This is exactly what we do in using norm-referenced tests to determine who is mentally deficient. Norm-referenced tests are specifically constructed to rank-order people, to line them up by height, so to speak, except instead of height, we line them up according to reading level, skill in certain thinking processes, or general knowledge. We then decide where to draw the line between "normal" and "deficient." As long as we have enough workers for available jobs, we can afford to classify those on the lower end of our rank order as deficient.

To some extent, Mrs. Stephens in the vignette recognizes these problems. She realizes that the content and skills taught in the regular classroom form a yardstick for judging the extent to which her students are judged normal. Some of what she teaches has functional value outside school, and some has value mainly in helping her students cope with the demands of the regular classroom. Hence, she spends considerable time teaching concepts such as prepositions, while she wonders if time might be better spent helping her students develop their talents and interests more. She has sufficient sustained contact with her students that she gets to know most of them as interesting people with a variety of abilities, and she sometimes wonders if it is accurate or fair to call them "handicapped." But she also knows that our society has little tolerance for people who lack functional literacy skills, and so she builds her instruction around attempting to remediate these.

If mild mental "deficiencies" are socially constructed notions, what of physiological deficiencies, such as blindness and paralysis? We would be foolish to argue that a blind person is not impaired physiologically. Impairments to one's body do not usually prevent learning, although they may necessitate the development of skills and strategies that most people do not need. For example, manual communication lends itself better to a deaf person than does oral communication; but there is no evidence that deafness itself (or other physiological impairments, except clearly identifiable brain damage), or manual communication, or strategies that deaf people use to compensate for hearing loss retard their learning ability. Thus, although there may be differences in how some physiologically impaired people learn, these are not learning deficiencies.

The difference orientation corrects many flaws in the deficiency orientation. It focuses on strengths, recognizes the legitimacy of various cultural experiences and routes to becoming a mature person, and does not advocate that a child be ashamed of or give up anything he or she is. But the difference orientation also has its critics, although they are fewer in number. Valentine (1971) has charged the cultural difference orientation with a tendency to stereotype and oversimplify and to take an either-or position where none is needed. (These same arguments can be applied to the sex difference orientation.) It tends to stereotype by implying that all members of a given group share the same cultural and behavioral patterns. Although researchers who have developed the theory may recognize differences among individuals within a group, educators who use it often do not. (Witness the teacher who comments, "Mary is probably not doing well in science because girls see science as masculine." To what extent has the teacher looked into the reasons for *Mary's* poor achievement?) Furthermore, it assumes "that different cultures are necessarily competitive alternatives," that a person is competent in one but not in two or more cultural systems (p. 141). In addition, the orientation tends to assume that minority group people lack competence in the dominant culture. Valentine points out that much of this is erroneous. He notes that "members of all subgroups are thoroughly enculturated in dominant culture patterns by mainstream institutions, including most of the content of the mass media, most products and advertising for mass marketing," and so forth (p. 143). Most speakers of Black English, for example, comprehend standard English very well, and a teacher who assumes they do not is underestimating people's ability to become bicultural. Indeed, the teacher may be less bicultural than the students! Failing to recognize errors in these assumptions, many educators make needless adaptations—and excuses—for their culturally different students.

One outcome of the difference approach in dealing with language-minority students is that it has focused almost exclusively on the "language problem." One indication of the mistaken orientation of this approach can be seen in the continued high rates of school failure among groups of language-minority youth at the same time that bilingual education programs were expanding. This phenomenon is partially due to the compensatory model mandated and followed in many bilingual programs as well as to the finding that what has passed for bilingual education has lacked such essential elements as qualified teachers and native-language instruction (Orfield, 1986). Cummins (1986) argues that bilingual education and compensatory education have been unsuccessful because they have not significantly altered the relationships between educators and minority students and between schools and minority communities. This condition has prompted one researcher on Hispanic education to state, "Programs that attempt to address the educational outcomes of Hispanic students without a consideration of the school-based variables which give rise to those problems will only scratch at the surface," (Arias, 1986, p. 55).

Now let us look more broadly at the entire approach that has been presented in this chapter. Some of you probably agree with the foregoing criticisms, but still see the approach as sound. After all, many of the recommended practices seem like sensible, effective strategies that good teachers use. And there is both research evidence as well as experiential evidence of teachers that confirm their usefulness. For example, most teachers know that students become more interested in a concept that the teacher has tried to make relevant. And who would argue with the recommendation that the level of instruction be matched to the student's readiness level? What criticisms, then, have been directed toward this approach?

One of the main criticisms is that it is assimilationist, and as such, it seeks to eliminate minority cultures and make everyone like White middle-class people. Banks (1981) summarizes several problems that "Third World writers and researchers" have had with this (p. 66). One problem is that people of color have viewed assimilation as a "weapon of the oppressor that was designed to destroy the cultures of ethnic groups and to make their members personally ineffective and politically powerless" (p. 66). Another problem is that the melting pot idea never worked for people of color, even when they wanted to melt. No matter how hard some have tried to melt, White society is not color-blind and still devalues people of color. Finally, the assimilationist ideology is a "racist ideology that justified damaging school and societal practices that victimized minority group children" (p. 66), such as the use of culturally biased tests to classify minority children as mentally retarded. As Banks points out, "The assumption that all children can learn equally well from teaching materials that only reflect the cultural experiences of the majority group is also questionable and possibly detrimental to those minority group children who have strong ethnic identities and attachments" (p. 68).

By seeing minority group, female, and lower-class cultures as problems, the approach deflects attention away from the majority group and its culture. So long as majority group children are not seen as needing to learn another culture, implicitly they are being taught to accept "cultural elitism, meaning that minority groups are treated like second-class citizens, either in terms of a refusal to take their traditions and beliefs seriously or with a patronizing acceptance aimed at seducing or manipulating them" (Pratte, 1983, p. 23). Racism within White culture, sexism within male institutions, and the competitive individualism and Horatio Alger myth that upholds classism all remain unexamined. As Mukherjee (1983) puts it, this approach allows Whites to "externaliz[e] the issue" of race rather than "owning up to that racism" (p. 279).

For example, Ms. Vanderbilt sees her main task as teaching White, middle-class culture to Black and Hispanic children. She does not teach about things such as Black or Hispanic artists or racism encountered by artists of color who attempt to succeed in the mainstream of American society. She does not particularly think about these things: She believes that the children will learn a smattering of them at home and knows that this knowledge is not required for later school success. But implicitly she is also teaching that Whites are the main group to have accomplished worthwhile things and that discrimination would disappear if children of color did a better job of learning White culture.

This approach also allows males to externalize problems related to sexism. As long as sex equity is seen only as helping women to compete in male-dominated domains, women are the only ones seen as needing to change. This deflects attention away from the need for men to learn, for example, nurturing skills and attitudes that women normally learn in the process of their socialization. It also deflects attention away from examining the competitiveness, impersonality, and violence that often characterize the male-dominated world. It is worth pointing out that most female educators and researchers who study sexism, including most of those cited earlier in this chapter, do not subscribe wholly to the Teaching the Culturally Different approach for female students because of these limitations.

Finally, the approach completely ignores structural and institutional bases of oppression. It assumes that people do not succeed in life because they have not learned a certain repertoire of skills and knowledge that is the key to success. This implies that success is open to as many people as will avail themselves of the time and energy necessary for earning the key. It ignores the fact that our economy sustains a certain level of unemployment and a stratum of low-paying jobs, regardless of people's qualifications. (Witness the last recession and ask yourself whether the unemployment and suffering that people faced was caused by a sudden lapse in the cultural competence of the recession's victims.) It also ignores the fact that people develop culture around their life conditions and that cultural patterns tend not to change until the conditions supporting them change. Liebow (1967) illustrates the problem as follows:

> Many similiarities between the lower-class Negro father and son
> (or mother and daughter) do not result from "cultural transmission"

but from the fact that the son goes out and independently experiences the same failures, in the same areas, and for much the same reasons as his father. What appears as a dynamic, self-sustaining cultural process is, in part at least, a relatively simple piece of social machinery which turns out, in rather mechanical fashion, independently produced look-alikes. The problem is how to change the conditions which, by guaranteeing failure, cause the son to be made in the image of the father. (p. 223)

Most educators who study multicultural education, as well as most members of oppressed groups, do not subscribe to the Teaching the Exceptional and the Culturally Different approach for their own group. During the civil rights era in the United States, the approach gained some popularity and is still used by many. However, most of its acceptance has been on the part of White, middle-class teachers who take their own background and culture for granted and are searching for a way to incorporate or deal with those they view as different. It also tends to be accepted by those who see American society as the land of opportunity and as a good technological society that is constantly improving itself. People who do not share this view of American society tend to subscribe to one of the approaches discussed later in this book.

Let us hasten to add that most of these educators would not wish to throw the baby out with the bathwater. The approach does contain elements that are very useful in other approaches. Critics of this approach do not believe, for example, that all children should master one standard body of knowledge—which happens to be based primarily on the experience of White, middle-class males—but many do believe that there are some things, such as reading skills, that all citizens do need. The difference is, How much of the existing curriculum should be retained and taught to everyone? Many critics also warm to the idea of making the curriculum relevant, but take issue with the idea that relevance should be a temporary bridge. This approach offers some useful concepts of instruction, such as building instruction around student learning styles. But critics become concerned when teachers are searching desperately for instructional techniques that will help them fit round pegs into square holes. If a body of information is not being accepted well or making sense to a class of inner-city students, for example, perhaps the solution is not so much hitting upon the right teaching strategy as it is examining possible biases or lack of relevance in the information itself. Students' problems in schools may reflect problems *with* schools, rather than merely technical problems revolving around selecting the best instructional strategy.

TABLE 2–1 *Teaching the Exceptional and the Culturally Different*

Societal goals:	Help fit people into the existing social structure and culture
School goals:	Teach dominant traditional educational aims more effectively by building bridges between the student and the demands of the school
Target students:	Lower-class, minority, special education, limited English proficiency, or female students who are behind in achievement in main school subjects
Practices:	
Curriculum	Make relevant to students' experiential background; fill in gaps in basic skills and knowledge
Instruction	Build on students' learning styles; adapt to students' skill levels; teach as effectively and efficiently as possible to enable students to catch up
Other aspects of classroom	Use decorations showing group members integrated into mainstream of society
Support services	Use transitional bilingual education, ESL, remedial classes, special education as temporary and intensive aids to fill gaps in knowledge
Other school-wide concerns	Involve lower-class and minority parents in supporting work of the school

REFERENCES

Abrahams, R. D., & Troike, R. C. (Eds.) (1972). *Language and cultural diversity in American education.* Englewood Cliffs, NJ: Prentice-Hall.

Adelman, H., & Taylor, L. (1983). *Learning disabilities in perspective.* Glenview, IL: Scott, Foresman.

Arias, M. B. (1986). The context of education for Hispanic students: An overview. *American Journal of Education, 95,* 26–57.

Ausubel, D. P. (1966a). Effects of cultural deprivation on learning patterns. In S. W. Webster (Ed.), *The disadvantaged learner: Knowing, understanding, educating* (pp. 251–257). San Francisco: Chandler.

Ausubel, D. P. (1966b). A teaching strategy for culturally deprived pupils: Cognitive and motivational considerations. In S. W. Webster (Ed.), *The disadvantaged learner: Knowing, understanding, educating* (pp. 467–475). San Francisco: Chandler.

Banks, J. A. (1981). *Multiethnic education: Theory and practice.* Boston: Allyn and Bacon.

Baratz, S. S., & Baratz, J. C. (1970). Early childhood intervention: The social science base of institutional racism. *Harvard Educational Review, 40,* 29–50.

Bateman, B. (1965). An educator's view of a diagnostic approach to learning disorders. In J. Hellmuth (Ed.), *Learning disorders* (Vol. 1, pp. 219–239). Seattle: Special Child Publications.

Bateman, B. (1974). Educational implications of minimal brain dysfunction. *Reading Teacher, 27,* 662–668.

Bereiter, C., & Engelmann, S. (1966). *Teaching disadvantaged children in the preschool.* Englewood Cliffs, NJ: Prentice-Hall.

Bernstein, B. (1964). Elaborated and restricted codes: Their social origins and some consequences. *American Anthropologist, 66,* 55–69.

Block, J. H. (1984). *Sex role identity and ego development.* San Francisco: Jossey-Bass.

Boder, E. (1971). Developmental dyslexia: Prevailing diagnostic concepts and a new diagnostic approach. In H. Myklebust (Ed.), *Progress in learning disabilities* (Vol. 2, pp. 293–321). New York: Grune & Stratton.

Bryan, T. H., & Bryan, J. H. (1978). *Understanding learning disabilities* (2nd ed.). Sherman Oaks, CA: Alfred.

Campbell, P. B. (1984). The computer revolution: Guess who's left out? *Interracial Books for Children, Bulletin 15,* 3–6.

Clark, K. B. (1969). The cult of "cultural deprivation." In A. C. Ornstein & P. D. Vairo (Eds.), *How to teach disadvantaged youth* (pp. 108–121). New York: McKay.

Cohen, R. A. (1969). Conceptual styles, cultural conflict, and non-verbal tests of intelligence. *American Anthropologist, 71,* 828–856.

Conte, J. M., & Grimes, G. H. (1969). *Media and the culturally different learner.* Washington, DC: National Education Association.

Cordasco, F. (1975). The challenge of the non-English-speaking child in American schools. In E. J. Ogletree & D. Garcia (Eds.), *Education of the Spanish-speaking urban child: A book of readings* (pp. 179–187). Springfield, IL: Charles C. Thomas.

Crockett, L. J., & Petersen, A. C. (1984). Biology: Its role in gender-related educational experiences. In E. Fennema & M. J. Ayer (Eds.), *Women and education* (pp. 89–116). Berkeley, CA: McCutchan.

Cummins, J. (1981). The role of primary language development in promoting educational success for language minority students. In *Schooling and language minority students: A theoretical framework* (pp. 3–49). Los Angeles: California State University Evaluation, Dissemination and Assessment Center.

Cummins, J. (1986). Empowering minority students: A framework for intervention. *Harvard Educational Review, 56*, 18–36.

DeLain, M. T., Pearson, T. D., & Anderson, R. C. (1985). Reading comprehension and creativity in black language use: You stand to gain by playing the sounding game! *American Journal of Educational Research, 22*, 155–174.

Deutsch, M. (1963). The disadvantaged child and the learning process. In A. H. Passow (Ed.), *Education in depressed areas* (pp. 163–180). New York: Teachers College Press.

Dunn, L. M. (1963). *Exceptional children in the schools.* New York: Holt, Rinehart and Winston.

Fennema, E. (1984). Girls, women, and mathematics. In E. Fennema & M. J. Ayer (Eds.), *Women and education* (pp. 137–164). Berkeley: McCutchan.

Fennema, E., & Peterson, P. L. (1987). Effective teaching for girls or boys: The same or different? In D. C. Berliner & B. V. Rosenshine (Eds.), *Talks to teachers* (pp. 111–125). New York: Random House.

Gallagher, J. J. (1979). Issues in education for the gifted. In A. H. Passow (Ed.), *The gifted and the talented: Their education and development* (pp. 28–44). The 78th yearbook of the National Society for the Study of Education. Chicago: University of Chicago Press.

Garcia, R. L. (1982). *Teaching in a pluralistic society: Concepts, models, strategies.* New York: Harper & Row.

Gay, G., & Abrahams, R. D. (1972). Talking black in the classroom. In R. D. Abrahams & R. C. Troike (Eds.), *Language and cultural diversity in American education* (pp. 200–208). Englewood Cliffs, NJ: Prentice-Hall.

Goldberg, M. L. (1963). Factors affecting educational attainment in depressed urban areas. In A. H. Passow (Ed.), *Education in depressed areas* (pp. 68–100). New York: Teachers College Press.

Hale, J. E. (1982). *Black children: Their roots, culture, and learning style.* Provo, UT: Brigham Young University Press.

Harber, J. R., & Bryen, D. N. (1976). Black English and the task of reading. *Review of Educational Research, 46*, 387–405.

Hardman, M. L., Drew, C. J., & Egan, M. W. (1984). *Human exceptionality: Society, school, and family.* Boston: Allyn and Bacon.

Hunt, J. M. (1961). *Intelligence and experience.* New York: The Ronald Press.

Jensen, A. S. (1969). How much can we boost IQ and scholastic achievement? *Harvard Educational Review, 39*, 1–123.

Jordan, C. (1985). Translating culture: From ethnographic information to educational program. *Anthropology & Education Quarterly, 16*, 105–123.

Kavale, K. A., & Forness, S. R. (1985). *The science of learning disabilities.* San Diego: College Hill Press.

Kirk, S. A., & Gallagher, J. J. (1979). *Educating exceptional children*. Boston: Houghton Mifflin.

Klaus, R., & Gray, S. (1968). The early training project for disadvantaged children: A report after five years. *Monographs of the Society for Research in Child Development, 33* (4).

Kleinfeld, J. S. (1973). Intellectual strengths in culturally different groups: An Eskimo illustration. *Review of Educational Research, 43,* 341–360.

Kneedler, R. D. (1984). *Special education for today*. Englewood Cliffs, NJ: Prentice-Hall.

Kobrick, J. W. (1974). The compelling case for bilingual education. In F. Pialorsi (Ed.), *Teaching the bilingual* (pp. 169–178). Tucson: University of Arizona Press.

Labov, W. (1969). The logic of non-standard English. *Monograph Series on Languages and Linguistics,* No. 22.

Lenneberg, E. H. (1967). *Biological foundations of a language*. New York: Wiley.

Levy, B. (1966). An urban teacher speaks out. In S. W. Webster (Ed.), *The disadvantaged learner: Knowing, understanding, educating* (pp. 430–436). San Francisco: Chandler.

Liebow, E. (1967). *Tally's corner: A study of Negro street-corner men*. Boston: Little, Brown.

Lovitt, T. C. (1977). *In spite of my resistance. . .I've learned from children*. Columbus, OH: Merrill.

Mercer, J. R. (1973). *Labeling the mentally retarded*. Berkeley: University of California Press.

Mukherjee, T. (1983). Multicultural education: A black perspective. *Early Childhood Development and Care, 10,* 275–282.

Newton, E. S. (1966). Verbal destitution: The pivotal barrier to learning. In S. W. Webster (Ed.), *The disadvantaged learner: Knowing, understanding, educating* (pp. 333–337). San Francisco: Chandler.

Orfield, G. (1986). Hispanic education: Challenges, research, and policies. *American Journal of Education, 95,* 1–25.

Pasamanick, B., & Knobloch, H. (1966). The contribution of some organic factors to school retardation in Negro children. In S. W. Webster (Ed.), *The disadvantaged learner: Knowing, understanding, educating* (pp. 286–292). San Francisco: Chandler.

Philips, S. U. (1983). *The invisible culture*. New York: Longman.

Pratte, R. (1983). Multicultural education: Four normative arguments. *Educational Theory, 33,* 21–32.

Ramirez, M., & Castaneda, A. (1974). *Cultural democracy, bicognitive development, and education*. New York: Academic Press.

Repp, A. C. (1983). *Teaching the mentally retarded.* Englewood Cliffs, NJ: Prentice-Hall.

Riessman, F. (1966). The culture of the underprivileged: A new look. In S. W. Webster (Ed.), *The disadvantaged learner: Knowing, understanding, educating* (pp. 53–61). San Francisco: Chandler.

Riessman, F. (1976). *The inner-city child.* New York: Harper & Row.

Robbins, W. (1984). Student's suicide stirs new interest in gifted. In C. A. Grant (Ed.), *Preparing for reflective teaching* (pp. 281–283). Boston: Allyn and Bacon.

Robinson, H. B., Roedell, W. C., & Jackson, N. E. (1981). Early identification and intervention. In W. B. Barbe & J. S. Renzulli (Eds.), *Psychology and education of the gifted* (3rd ed. pp. 128–141). New York: Irvington.

Rubin, D., Simson, C., & Betwee, M. C. (1966). *Emotionally disturbed children and the elementary school.* Detroit: Wayne State University Press.

San Miguel, G., Jr. (1987). *"Let all of them take heed": Mexican Americans and the campaign for educational equality in Texas, 1910–1981.* Austin: University of Texas Press.

Schneider, S. G. (1976). *Revolution, reaction or reform: The 1974 Bilingual Education Act.* New York: Las Americas.

Schultz, T. W. (1977). Investment in human capital. In J. Karabel & A. H. Halsy (Eds.), *Power and ideology in education* (pp. 313–324). New York: Oxford University Press.

Shade, B. (1982). Afro-American cognitive style: A variable in school success? *Review of Educational Research, 52,* 219–244.

Skutnabb-Kangas, T. (1981). *Bilingualism or not? The education of minorities.* Clevedon, Avon, England: Multilingual Matters.

Stephens, T. M. (1976). *Directive teaching of children with learning and behavioral handicaps* (2nd ed.). Columbus, OH: Merrill.

Taba, H., & Elkins, D. (1966). *Teaching strategies for the culturally disadvantaged.* Chicago: Rand McNally & Co.

Taylor, C. W. (1974). Multiple talent teaching. *Today's Education, 63,* 71–74.

Terman, L. M., Baldwin, B. T., Bronson, E., DeVoss, J. C., Fuller, F., Goodenough, F. L., Kelley, T. L., Lima, M., Marshall, H., Moore, A. H., Raubenheimer, A. S., Ruch, G. M., Willoughby, R. L., Wyman, J. B., & Yates, D. H. (1976). *Genetic studies of genius: Mental and physical traits of a thousand gifted children.* Stanford: Stanford University Press.

Thonis, E. (1970). *Teaching reading to non-English speakers.* New York: Collier Macmillan International.

Trueba, H. (1979). Bilingual education models: Types and designs. In H. Trueba & C. Barnett-Mizrahi (Eds.), *Bilingual multicultural education and the professional: From theory to practice* (pp. 54–73). Rowley, MA: Newbury House.

Valentine, C. A. (1971). Deficit, difference, and bicultural models of Afro-American behavior. *Harvard Educational Review, 41,* 137–157.

Walker, C. L. (1987). Hispanic achievement: Old views and new perspectives. In H. Trueba (Ed.), *Success or failure? Learning and the language minority student* (pp. 15–32). Cambridge, MA: Newbury House.

Webster, S. W. (1966). Social studies for disadvantaged students. In S. W. Webster (Ed.), *The disadvantaged learner: Knowing, understanding, educating* (pp. 586–594). San Francisco: Chandler.

Woronoff, I. (1966). Negro male identification problems and the education process. In S. W. Webster (Ed.), *The disadvantaged learner: Knowing, understanding, educating* (pp. 293–295). San Francisco: Chandler.

Ysseldyke, J. E., & Algozzine, B. (1982). *Critical issues in special and remedial education.* Boston: Houghton Mifflin.

CHAPTER 3

Human
Relations

What comes to mind when you hear the term *human relations?* "Getting along," "tolerance," "interactions between individuals and groups," and "learning how to resolve differences between individuals and groups" were some of the responses our students gave to this question. Our students also said that human relations means trying to reduce prejudice and stereotypes between the races, helping men and women to eliminate their gender hang-ups, and helping all people to feel positive about themselves. Central to most definitions was the development of positive interactions between individuals or groups.

GOALS

Our students' statements were consistent with goal statements by educators who advocate a Human Relations approach. As we note in Table 3–1, the goals of this approach are to promote positive feelings among students and reduce stereotyping, thus promoting unity and tolerance in a society composed of different people (see p. 100). For example, in a pamphlet entitled *Improving Human Relations*, the National Council for the Social Studies (Cummings, 1949) listed the following among its six major aims of human relations or intergroup education: "to foster desirable human relationships in students' daily living" and "to help all, majority and minority group members, to participate fully in American life" (p. 4). According to Taba, Brady, Robinson, and Dolton (1950), "Intergroup education [which they used synonymously with human relations] is concerned with children's present relationships. It is also concerned with preparing children for wider, more diverse intergroup relationships in the future" (p. 1). Grambs (1960) listed three components of human relations: looking at social groups of which one is a member, and at how society views them; looking at friendship groups, the meaning of group membership, and group skills; and developing attitudes of acceptance and friendship between groups (p. 19). In this chapter we will examine how advocates of human relations education suggest developing positive relationships among individuals or groups that differ from one another.

Some proponents of the Human Relations approach (often called intergroup education) directly relate it to the study of prejudice and intergroup hostility. Proponents claim that because so many complex factors, such as home background, social situations, health, income, intelligence, and aspirations, affect human interaction and human relationships, intergroup education must take into account one's total personality. Examine Grambs's (1960) comment:

> Research workers now claim that intergroup relations cannot
> properly be understood in a narrow sense at all but must be consid-
> ered in terms of the total personality, the interaction of persons in
> groups, the sources of group tension and conflict, and the cultural
> context within which people grow and learn. In fact, the field is now
> often defined as "human relations" rather than as intergroup relations.
> (p. 5)

The importance of this concept, argue Colangelo, Foxley, and Dustin (1979), is that it "encompasses a recognition of the humanness of people" (p. 1), which Wesley (1949) claims is "more important in a democratic society than land, sea or sky" (p. 30). Wesley believes this is because human relations will reduce prejudice and develop attitudes of racial tolerance:

> The teaching of facts about race will not solve race problems but
> it will develop attitudes of tolerance where hitherto there were emo-
> tional reactions in disintegrated personalities based upon lack of
> knowledge. Is there anything more tragic in human relations than to
> see the college graduate refuse association with another college gradu-
> ate who happens to be of different religious faith or a different na-
> tional origin or color? There is something wrong with an education
> which leads to such results. (p. 30)

We would synthesize these various goal statements by saying that the Human Relations approach is directed toward helping students communicate with, accept, and get along with people who are different from themselves; reducing or eliminating stereotypes that students have about people; and helping students feel good about themselves and about groups of which they are members without putting others down in the process. This approach is aimed mainly at the affective level: at attitudes and feelings people have about self and others. It attempts to replace tension and hostility with acceptance and care. Human relations, or intergroup education, is an idea that needs to be fostered in everyone to make our democracy work—equality and justice for all. Taba, Brady, and Robinson (1952) believe that every school has difficulty educating for human understanding—schools in the rich suburbs as well as schools in the inner-city ghettos.

Systematic attention to intergroup–human relations education began during World War II and grew rapidly right after the war owing to a number of different factors (Taba, et al., 1952). Prior to the war, organizations such as the Anti-Defamation League of B'nai B'rith, the Urban League, the National Association for the Advancement of Colored People, and the National Conference of Christians and Jews had over the years fought to eliminate discrimination and prejudice and were encouraging legislation that would help to do this. World War II brought about some specific changes that fueled the efforts of these organizations to draw serious attention to this area. World War II created jobs, and people often had to move to other regions to take advantage of them. This brought together people who were not used to being together and sometimes caused intergroup conflicts, for example, when Blacks and Whites from the South moved to the North and West and had to interact under different rules. As poor people and people of color became integrated, they also began to experience a more fulfilling and enriched life and began to demand a larger slice of the American apple pie. War veterans, especially those of color, believed that they and their people deserved fair treatment because they had fought and died for democracy—democracy not just for some citizens, but for all citizens. Intergroup and human relations education was seen as a way to bring about harmony among these different groups.

During the war, the United States was especially concerned with maintaining and improving its relations with its neighboring countries, Canada and Mexico. Roosevelt's Good Neighbor policy had implications for educators in Texas. Pressure from the Mexican government was brought to bear that exposed the poor treatment of Mexican-American students in schools. To respond to this, the Inter-American Education movement developed, which held conferences, developed curricula, and conducted studies aimed at improving relations between Anglos and Mexicans in the schools.

Another factor supporting attention to intergroup education was the belief that America's concern about human interactions was being ignored while we invested the country's financial and human resources in the technological race. There was more interest in the atom than in relationships among people. Many believed that our role as free-world leader and as champion of the democratic way of life throughout the world was inconsistent with the way of life experienced by many U.S. citizens.

To advocate justice and fair play abroad, we had to put these into practice at home. Minority and majority group relations had to be improved. Finally, the war itself had produced some devastating consequences that pointed strongly to a need to promote better intergroup relations. The Holocaust demonstrated how inhumanely one group can treat another group, and the bombing of Hiroshima and Nagasaki revealed to the world a more terrible and destructive kind of weapon than had ever been used before in human history.

These events and circumstances gave human relations and intergroup education a big push, and interest in this concept grew rapidly within a few years. Many books, pamphlets, articles, and lectures and discussions at professional association meetings were produced in a short period of time to provide the momentum for this growing concept. Another big push for human relations came a decade later with the school desegregation and civil rights movements. School desegregation meant that in many cases, people of color and White people would have to share the same facility (school). Human relations and intergroup education programs were often put into place (and many still exist) to help promote harmony between racial groups.

During the late 1970s and 1980s, following the passage of PL 94-142, human relations was seen as important in mainstreaming special education students. As students who previously had been segregated from the regular classroom and school were increasingly placed into them, educators became concerned about negative attitudes on the part of both regular students and teachers, particularly since one reason for the mainstreaming movement was to develop acceptance of the handicapped. By the early 1980s, books and articles began to appear with some frequency on how to modify attitudes toward the handicapped and increase their social integration.

THEORIES BEHIND HUMAN RELATIONS

The theoretical underpinnings for the Human Relations approach have come mainly from general psychology and social psychology. Human relations is a field that examines relationships among people, regardless of whether race, social class, gender, or handicap is involved. For example, there is a body of literature on human relations in formal organizations and a cadre of people who conduct human relations workshops for businesses. For this chapter, we will draw only on that which develops human relations as an approach to multicultural education; it is a subset of this larger body of thought and rests on much the same theoretical foundations.

Some theorists have emphasized the development of prejudice and stereotyping within individuals; others have emphasized the development of prejudice and hostility between groups; still others pay more attention to individual self-concept. These ideas are not mutually exclusive; in fact, as Allport (1979) notes, no one theoretical formulation by itself can account for prejudice, although different people see different theories as being the most persuasive.

Development of Prejudice Within Individuals

Gordon Allport (1979) was probably the main theorist who wrote about the development of prejudice in individuals. He focused on individuals for two reasons: Not everybody in any given society is prejudiced, which leads one to wonder why some people are much more prejudiced than others; and prejudice and discrimination are acted out by individuals. Allport drew mainly on cognitive development theory and psychoanalytic theory. We will explain these theories, incorporating examples (some used by Allport, some not) to show how they apply to race, gender, social class, and handicap. We will also provide elaborations of these ideas offered by other theorists.

According to cognitive development theory, the mind has a need to relate, organize, and simplify phenomena in order for experiences to make sense. Thus, on the basis of concrete experience, people create categories to organize similar phenomena. As they mature and acquire an increasingly broad range of experience, they attempt to assimilate as much of their new experiences as possible into existing categories. Occasionally, people have to restructure (accommodate) categories to fit experience. How does this apply to prejudice?

By age 3 or 4, children are aware of visible differences among people, including skin color (Goodman, 1952), physical impairment (Weinberg, 1978), and gender (Kohlberg, 1966). Initially, these differences do not suggest stereotypes or evaluations, although Allport suggests that children often associate dark skin with dirt. At the same time, children are also learning language, and with it, labels for categories and the emotional overtones of those labels. In fact, children sometimes acquire a label and its emotional overtone (e.g., "homosexual") before they have constructed a category to which the label applies, or before they have connected the label with a category. Allport cites an example:

One little boy was agreeing with his mother, who was warning him never to play with niggers. He said, "No, Mother, I never play with niggers. I only play with white and black children." This child was developing an aversion to the term "nigger" without having the slightest idea what the term meant. (p. 305)

By late childhood, children tend to overcategorize and stereotype many things. Their categories have acquired many descriptive attributes that they apply to whomever or whatever seems to fit the category. Thus, all dogs are large and brown, or all people in wheelchairs are friendly (or quiet, or stupid, or whatever the child has experienced with one or two members of that category). Finding their system of organizing experience useful, they overuse it, often without recognizing its limitations. Pogrebin (1981) gives an example of a girl who insisted that women could not be doctors, even when her own mother was a physician. Her experience with doctors told her that women were not doctors, and she dealt with exceptions by refusing to accept them as true.

As children mature, their categories modify to varying degrees to fit reality better. Allport describes people in general as operating under the "principle of least effort," which means that the mind will avoid restructuring its categories unless it has to. As one encounters people who do not fit a designated category, one tends to view them as exceptions to the rule. For example, upon meeting a man who is acting as homemaker, a person who sees homemakers as women would see the man as an exception, rather than restructuring the category to make it genderless. Most people learn to allow for numerous exceptions and qualifications and do not see the boundaries of their categories as fixed and rigid. Thus, one can say, "Some of my best friends are Jews," allowing one to retain a stereotypical image of "Jew," while admitting many exceptions (Allport, 1979, p. 309).

Allport notes the important role that perception plays in this process. When the mind perceives, "it selects, accentuates, and interprets sensory data" (p. 166). To view a diverse group of people (such as "the poor") as a category, we need to pay special attention to the attributes that members of the category are believed to have in common. In the process of doing this, we tend to accentuate those attributes unconsciously. For example, we look for skin color so we can identify a person's race, and in the process, we exaggerate the importance of skin color and diminish our attention to attributes that people have in common. Or, the adult viewing a young child searches for clues to the child's gender, and overemphasizes these unconsciously in the process.

Thinking in terms of categories and stereotypes is natural and does not necessarily, by itself, lead to prejudice and hostility. Why do some people hate groups unlike themselves, while other people are simply curious and accepting of others? For an answer to that, Allport (and others) turned to psychodynamic theory. Essentially, psychodynamic theory holds that the mind has built-in urges and capacities that manifest themselves in feelings and needs. Only a portion of these reach the conscious level in any individual; a large portion remain at the unconscious level, where they nevertheless direct our thoughts and behaviors, but in ways we are unaware of. Allport describes several needs or capacities that are built into the human mind: aggression, affiliation with others, fear of strangers, need for status, and need for a positive self-image. Early in life, children attempt to form relationships with others, build positive self-images, and acquire status, some with more success than others. Lack of success leads to frustration. Many people learn to channel frustration productively (e.g., it becomes a motivation to try harder until success is achieved), while others allow it to smolder inside. People who do not learn to handle frustration develop a free-floating hatred that can be directed against any convenient group or individual, and that hatred can turn into active aggression against that target.

Projection is the main process by which frustration becomes directed against a group. Allport defines projection as "the tendency to attribute falsely to other people motives or traits that are our own, or that in some way explain or justify our own" (p. 382). Projection is based on feelings of guilt, fear, or anxiety about traits or urges within ourselves or factors in our own lives. For example, many people develop feelings of guilt about their own homosexual thoughts, and because they are unable to deal with these feelings at a conscious level, they project fear of their own urges onto others who are openly homosexual. This group becomes a target for hate. People who fear losing their jobs, either because of their own inadequacies or because of economic conditions, often project this fear onto a group, often a minority group, that they can blame for "stealing" jobs from people who deserve them. Such groups become scapegoats.

It is here that the content of stereotypes becomes important but hard to change. The categories in which we place people contain beliefs and attitudes about members of those categories. For example, take the category of "fat person": What do you believe most fat people are like? How do you feel about fat people? Feelings cannot be tested to determine how true they are. Beliefs can, but feelings strongly influence one's willingness to test the truth of one's beliefs. If one believes that fat people are greedy, for example, one could check the accuracy of that belief by observing a number of fat people. If one's attitudes about the group were not passionately negative, one would revise the belief upon observing fat people who are not greedy. If, however, one hated fat people because one was unable to deal constructively with one's own appetite, one may well resist altering the stereotype or may substitute another negative stereotype. ("Well, they may not be greedy, but they are certainly sloppy!") As Allport puts it, "We cannot help but strive to put flesh and clothes upon the skeleton of an attitude" (p. 317). In so doing, we construct and hang on to a stereotype that justifies a hostile attitude, regardless of its accuracy.

You may be thinking that although this makes some sense, many people do *not* externalize their problems and blame others. Why are some people prone to hate much more than others? Psychodynamically oriented research by Adorno, Frenkel-Brunswik, Levinson, and Sanford (1950) and by Harris, Gough, and Martin (1950) strongly suggests that certain child-rearing styles develop personality types that are prone to be either prejudiced or open. People who scored high on prejudice scales tended to come from homes that were authoritarian, where parents expected rules to be obeyed without question, where all rules were handed down by parents, and where parents punished broken rules or behavior they saw as immoral. People who scored low on prejudice scales tended to come from homes in which love was given uncondi-tionally and where matters of daily living were dealt with flexibly (but not chaotically). The authors suggest that children from authoritarian homes develop feelings of guilt about things such as sex or develop resentments toward their parents, and these smolder at the uncon-scious level until later directed against others. In addition, such chil-dren fail to develop self-confidence and self-reliance, since they have been continually directed by someone else, and they adopt their parents' view of things as being black or white and rigid. Children from dem-ocratic homes, on the other hand, develop self-confidence because they are allowed to make some decisions and express themselves; they learn to accept others in spite of their perceived shortcomings because their parents allowed them to recognize shortcomings in family members without withdrawing love or approval. Allport argues that the tendency for prejudice becomes a core personality trait and is due in large part to family upbringing. A person with a prejudiced personality will direct hostility against virtually any available target group.

Psychodynamic theory suggests another process that can foster prejudice: identification. As Allport points out, most children identify with their parents. When identifying with one's parents, a child accepts their beliefs and actions as desirable. Children who identify with prej-udiced parents thus tend to acquire their prejudices, often without being aware of it. Children also tend to rely on their parents to tell them which social groups they belong to and how they should behave toward others. Answers are usually accepted by young children without question and form the basis for attitudes and behavior patterns that will condition further learning about a group.

Social learning theory, as developed by Bandura and Walters (1963), expands on these ideas. Bandura and Walters explain that much social behavior is learned through imitation and reinforcement. Children learn behaviors and responses by watching others; they develop tendencies to copy what they see by having their actions reinforced by others. Parents provide particularly powerful models as well as reinforcers.

With respect to prejudice, parents model for children "whom they should hate and for what reasons, and how they should express their aggression toward the hated objects" (Bandura & Walters, 1963, p. 19). To reduce a child's prejudice, it is insufficient simply to teach the child that prejudice is unfounded or irrational, so long as the child is receiving positive reinforcement from loved ones for prejudicial behavior. Instead, positive behavioral patterns need to be modeled and their use reinforced by some means that the child finds genuinely rewarding. For example, children who beat up on weaker and unattractive peers would need to learn not only why this is inappropriate, but what behaviors would be preferable and what positive consequences will follow using these behaviors.

Dissonance theory provides additional insight. According to Watts (1984),

> Dissonance occurs whenever an individual simultaneously holds two cognitions (ideas, beliefs, opinions) which are psychologically inconsistent. Because dissonance is an unpleasant motivational state, people strive to reduce it through a cognitive reorganization that may involve adding consonant cognitions or changing one set of opinions. (p. 44)

An example Watts provides is a person who believes that cigarette smoking is dangerous to the health, but smokes nonetheless. To reduce dissonance, the person could belittle research on lung cancer or could decide to quit smoking. An example related to prejudice is the child who thinks retarded people are distasteful, but then begins to play with a retarded neighbor. The child could reduce dissonance between his or her attitude and behavior either by clinging to the attitude and ceasing to play with the retarded child or by adopting a more positive attitude that would support their play relationship.

Development of Prejudice and Hostility Between Groups

Many social psychologists see the preceding theories as inadequate for understanding prejudice and discrimination. For example, can we say that the Germans constructed death camps for the Jews in the 1930s because, for some reason, most Germans experienced levels of frustration they could not handle and so projected their individual guilts and failings on the same target group? While to some extent this may have happened, it does not account very well for groups mobilizing against groups. To understand intergroup relations, we turn to reference group theory developed by Sherif and Sherif (1966).

The Sherifs conducted numerous observations and some experiments with small groups to understand how groups form interactions with other groups. One notable set of experiments took place in a number of boys' summer camps, in which situations were constructed to encourage groups to form, and these groups were then studied in isolation from, as well as in contact with, one another. Those of you who have attended camp yourself may well remember the sense of "we-ness" that can develop among tent-mates or cabin-mates and the friendly rivalry that often develops between cabins.

According to reference group theory, people derive much of their identity from association with others. All people belong to a set of in-groups, beginning with one's family during early childhood. As one matures, the number of groups to which one belongs expands. People identify with some groups more than others; in fact, one can identify with a group to which one does not even belong. For example, an aspiring basketball star might initially identify with the neighborhood basketball team with whom he or she plays, but shift identification to the Lakers as his or her perception of his or her own potential as a great basketball player shifts. A reference group is any group with which one identifies. We all have reference groups, and they are a central regulator of our identities.

We all willingly conform to groups with which we identify, and we may deliberately behave in ways that distinguish us from other groups. For example, the Sherifs found that the boys in camp adopted colors for their group; having done so, they avoided wearing the colors of other groups. During the late 1970s, many girls adopted the "preppie" look, which identified them with conservative, upper- or upper-middle-class White girls. One visible badge of group membership was a string of real pearls; particularly if the rest of one's garb on a given day was ordinary, the pearls would indicate that one had the money to sport expensive jewelry, even with jeans.

In and of itself, group formation does not necessarily cause prejudice and discrimination. However, the Sherifs noted that when groups come in contact, they begin to make a concerted effort to define and maintain group boundaries. To encourage group members to stay within the group and loyal to the group, they begin to picture themselves as superior to out-groups and try to convince one another that this is so. Hostility develops as soon as groups perceive themselves to be in competition with one another. Sherif and Sherif noted that groups need not even *really* be competing; as long as they *believe* another group is competing for something they want, hostility and rejection of the out-group result.

This theory can easily be applied to ethnic group, gender group, social class group, and handicap group relationships, as well as to relationships among other kinds of groups. In so doing, one can combine it with psychological theories described earlier. For example, take gender. According to cognitive development theory, children learn early that sex is an important way to categorize people. They also learn early to which category they belong. Once they know, most children actively strive to conform to that category as part of constructing a self-identity. If a little girl believes that girls wear only dresses, she will not wear anything but dresses. In early childhood, there is some sex segregation and rejection between the sexes as each group seeks to maintain its boundaries and to conform to its image of its own sex. "Sissies" and "tomboys" are regarded disdainfully because they threaten the integrity of group boundaries, group norms, and personal understanding of what "male" and "female" mean. As the children grow up, the opposite sex becomes a target group for individuals with psychological problems described by psychoanalytic theory; hence, rape and wife beating take place. When people perceive the sexes to be competing over things such as jobs, stereotyping and hostility develop: males are seen as "chauvinist pigs" and females as aggressive "libbers" who are failing to provide a secure home for their children.

When victimized, according to Allport, most individuals and groups react, and some reactions further intensify the problem. Reactions that intensify the problem include becoming obsessively concerned with prejudice (e.g., reading anti-Semitism into remarks that were not intended that way); withdrawing or becoming passive (which reinforces stereotypes such as that the handicapped are unassertive); covering up hurt by clowning; strengthening in-group ties (which can make outsiders see the group as too clannish or too different); rejecting one's own group; striving extra hard to succeed in spite of discrimination (which reaffirms stereotypes that the group is cunning or works too hard); militancy (which reaffirms the idea that the group is hostile); and allowing the prophecy to be self-fulfilling. Such reactions can unwittingly intensify prejudice and stereotyping.

Self-Concept Theory

Human relations deals with self-concept as well as intergroup relationships. Intergroup and interpersonal relationships can be thought of as attitudes toward other people, self-concept as attitudes toward oneself. For this discussion, the main concern is self-concept as one sees one's own membership in a particular group. We will not discuss self-concept theory in general, but only that which directly relates to group membership.

Purkey and Novak (1984) have defined self-concept as "our view of who we are and how we fit into the world" (p. 25). Advocates of the Human Relations approach are particularly concerned about how members of oppressed groups view themselves and see their place in the world. Banks (1981) has developed a typology for conceptualizing how people view themselves in relation to their membership in an ethnic group; it can also be applied to other kinds of groups, such as sex groups. This typology has six stages of ethnicity; research by Banks and others has demonstrated that people can be located in these stages and can advance from lower to higher stages. The lowest two stages have particular relevance for the Human Relations approach. The lowest stage Banks calls *ethnic psychological captivity*. This stage is experienced mainly by members of oppressed social groups who internalize society's negative perceptions of them. According to Banks, an individual experiences ethnic psychological captivity when he or she "inculcates the negative ideologies and beliefs about his/her ethnic group that are institutionalized within the society. Consequently, he/she exemplifies ethnic self-rejection and low self-esteem" (p. 130). There is research evidence that members of oppressed groups often internalize society's negative images of themselves and that the same psychological processes involved in learning stereotypes about other groups apply. For example, Clark (1963) found that young children become aware of their own skin color at the same time that they become aware of the skin color of others, and they learn attributes that others ascribe to their own as well as other people's skin color. This forms the basis for their ethnic self-concept. He put it this way: "The individual child develops an awareness of his [or her] own personality through recognizing his [or her] own physical characteristics and learning what value others in the society place on those characteristics. This becomes an important part of what he [or she] thinks about himself [or herself]" (p. 42).

Clark performed certain experiments, the results of which strongly suggested that Black children had internalized negative perceptions of their own skin color. In one experiment, children were shown an assortment of brown and white dolls made from the same mold. They were asked to select the doll they preferred and the doll they thought was most like themselves. The majority preferred the white doll, and many of the lighter-skinned Black children said that the white doll was most like themselves. The researchers also administered a coloring test in which White and Black children were given an assortment of pictures to color and a box of 24 crayons. The children were told that one of the pictures was to represent themselves. All the light-skinned Black children used the white or yellow crayon, as did 15% of those with dark skins. Clark concluded that many of the children associated whiteness with desirable characteristics and rejected their own blackness; he saw these children's behavior as the beginning of self-hatred.

Clark's work has been criticized, and there is evidence that children of color have strong self-concepts. For example, Stone (1981) has argued that Black children are provided considerable love and validation of self-worth in their homes and neighborhoods and that it is a mistake to assume that they have internalized White society's low esteem for people of color. Still, when children enter school, school can damage students' self-concepts by treating them and their communities as failures that have little or nothing of value to contribute.

Banks believes that people at Stage 1—ethnic psychological captivity—can move to a higher stage. Because schools historically have taught mainly or solely the culture of the White middle class, he recommends that schools develop the self-concept of members of oppressed groups, or at least counteract the tendency of White institutions to devalue people of color, by teaching them about the history and contributions of their own group. This will enable these children to recognize that neither they nor their families nor their ethnic groups are to blame for problems such as poverty, but rather that such groups have been victimized; it will also enable the children to appreciate contributions that group members have made.

Banks' second stage of ethnicity is called *ethnic encapsulation.* It is similar to the first stage in that the individual holds a stereotypical image about his or her ethnic group, but it is the opposite of stage 1 in that the image is unrealistically positive. A person in this stage, in fact, sees his or her group as superior to others and has an inflated sense of self. Banks sees members of the dominant social group as tending to cluster at this stage, as well as members of oppressed groups who have previously been at Stage 1 but have undergone consciousness-raising. For people in Stage 2, Banks advocates a Human Relations approach to help them reexamine their stereotypes about themselves as well as about others and reduce their sense of superiority over others.

Some Thoughts on Theory

We believe that reference group theory and cognitive development theory provide the strongest explanations for the development of prejudice and discrimination, primarily because they both deal with groups of people. Cognitive development theory helps us understand how individuals learn to categorize people into groups and apply stereotypical descriptions to those groups. In a society that is already somewhat segregated and stratified on the basis of race, sex, family background, and handicap, cognitive development theory explains how individuals construct sense out of the social world they encounter. Reference group theory helps explain why racial, gender, social class, and handicap prejudice are group phenomena rather than isolated individual problems. This theory helps us understand why people tend to hold tenaciously to certain values and perceptions and reject people they see as nonmembers of their group and why tension can exist between groups even when individuals have no personal reason to dislike those who belong to the out-group.

Psychodynamic theory and social learning theory help explain why some people are more prone to reject out-group members than others, but their focus on the individual does not help explain intergroup relations on a large scale. In fact, as Clark (1963) has pointed out, viewing prejudice and discrimination as emotional disturbances overlooks advantages that social stratification confers on the dominant group. By acting in ways that help maintain racism, Whites preserve certain economic and political benefits for themselves. By maintaining sexism, males preserve benefits for themselves. Acting on the basis of self-interest may at times be morally questionable, but is not necessarily the product of emotional instability.

For example, take the wealthy White neighborhood in which families hire women of color as "cleaning ladies." The White employers may harbor positive attitudes toward their employees, have learned positive behaviors for interacting with them, and manifest great emotional stability in their own lives and in their acceptance of people. Yet at the same time, they may accept it as natural that women do housework and that women of color do other people's housework for minimum wage. They may accept stereotypes about this category of person and see the category as an out-group, yet a group that has a useful function. This is not to say that individual members of the neighborhood may not harbor negative feelings about women of color; some may dislike them intensely. But others may feel they treat their cleaning ladies well and like them personally. At the same time, they can still see them as different and as conforming to stereotypes about women of color, and they accept their lower status.

The strategies that follow are based mainly on reference group, cognitive development, social learning, dissonance, and self-concept theories.

STRATEGIES

Human Relations strategies for classrooms are based on the theories we just discussed with the major exception of psychoanalytic theory. Allport (1979) and Cook and Cook (1954) have recommended individual counseling and therapy to help people who have unusually hostile attitudes toward others. Counselors and therapists have at their disposal psychotherapeutic techniques for helping people resolve their inner frustrations and conflicts and develop more positive attitudes toward others. This is not normally done in classrooms, nor is it recommended for classrooms.

Advocates of the Human Relations approach have developed several strategies for classroom use; these strategies are summarized in Table 3–1. These advocates have also developed five underlying principles that teachers should consider before selecting specific strategies. We will present these principles first.

General Principles

First, the Human Relations program should be comprehensive (Stendler & Martin, 1953; Taba et al., 1952). This means that it should be infused into several subject areas and it should be school-wide to avoid giving children mixed messages. For example, a school attempting to promote social acceptance of mentally retarded students is working at cross-purposes if lessons in social studies are aimed at prejudice reduction, but language arts and mathematics classes are ability grouped, with the retarded composing the lowest group, and school clubs are dominated by the most academically successful students.

Second, diverse strategies should be used (Stendler & Martin, 1953; Taba et al., 1952). Different strategies accomplish different things, and no single strategy has been found to be *the* strategy for promoting positive human relations.

Third, strategies actively involving children tend to be most effective (Watts, 1984). Although there is value in presenting information or demonstrating, strategies that place children in a passive role have less impact than those placing them in an active role.

Fourth, the program should start with the children's real-life experiences (Stendler & Martin, 1953; Taba et al., 1952). Educators recommend, for example, starting with interpersonal relationships in the classroom or intergroup hostilities in the school. This enables the children to see the point of developing human relations involving more distant and abstract groups.

Finally, each child should be able to experience success in the classroom, and the success of some should not be contingent on the failure of others (Stendler & Martin, 1953; Turnbull & Schulz, 1979). Often in classrooms, children compete for grades or rewards. This teaches them to devalue the feelings and accomplishments of others, because others must do poorly for oneself to look good. Those who consistently come out on or near the bottom tend to suffer some rejection by others and may develop feelings of personal inadequacy. These feelings run counter to the goals of the Human Relations approach.

These principles govern the use of a number of strategies, including providing accurate information, using group process, using vicarious experience and role playing, involving students in community action projects, and teaching social skills.

Providing Accurate Cognitive Information

In multicultural education programs, providing accurate cognitive information means providing accurate information about various ethnic, handicap, gender, or social class groups. At the very least, it means making sure that classroom materials do not contain overt stereotypes and biases (Clark, 1963; Cook & Cook, 1954). Most educators advocate going beyond the removal of stereotypical materials, and presenting accurate and comprehensive information. This is important because, as noted earlier, people learn stereotypes, and they focus attention on attributes of categories of people (such as skin color) that exaggerate traits, oversimplify, and in many cases misrepresent people. The strategy of providing accurate cognitive information seeks to replace stereotypes and misconceptions that the children may already have.

Human Relations educators agree that this information should stress "the *commonality* of people as well as their *individuality*" (Colangelo et al. 1979, p. 1, emphasis theirs). For example, Taba et al., (1952) recommended that teachers teach children about cultural differences by stressing ways in which culture is a reasonable response people make to their particular life conditions in an effort to resolve common human problems. They give an example regarding teaching about the Chinese diet. Anglo children may view the preponderance of rice in the Chinese diet as peculiar until they are made aware of the preponderance of wheat in the Anglo diet and until they learn why all people need a grain product. Similarly, Turnbull and Schulz (1979) recommend that teachers with handicapped students stress similarities among all students so that differences are placed in perspective rather than assuming exaggerated importance.

Grambs (1968) recommends that representatives of minority groups be invited to school as classroom speakers because "using the 'real thing'—the live representation of the thing we wish to demonstrate—speaks far louder than the words we say" (p. 34). Donaldson and Martinson (1977) have made a similar recommendation regarding the handicapped: Speakers who are themselves members of handicap groups have more impact on students than information out of a book.

Educators see limitations to presenting information as a primary teaching strategy: It does not necessarily change behavior or attitudes. For example, Watts (1984) reviewed research studies on the impact of persuasive information on attitudes. He found that information is most likely to change attitudes when the person is not already committed to the target attitudes or when the attitudes are not directly connected to core beliefs. Attitudes that help anchor a person's core beliefs are resistant to change, and the information may simply be ignored.

However, presenting children with positive information about their *own* group can be very helpful if it counters negative perceptions. Generally, people want to feel good about themselves and look for information that will validate their self-worth. School curricula tend not to include much positive, substantive information about many groups, such as women of color, contemporary American Indians, or handicapped people. This sends a message to members of these groups that they are relatively unimportant, which can be detrimental to their self-concepts. For example, when an Indian child is taught about his or her tribe's accomplishments, this information is embraced with more enthusiasm than information that suggests that Indians in the 1980s are an artifact of U.S. history.

Group Process

Group process can be defined as the "use of the group to educate its members" (Cook & Cook, 1954, p. 243). Human Relations educators usually advocate the use of heterogeneous groups (i.e., racially mixed, sex mixed, or containing both special education and regular students). Group process strategies relate to two of the theories discussed earlier. One is cognitive development theory. As a result of direct contact with members of another group during carefully structured situations, students should be able to gain accurate information about that group that will challenge stereotypes. For example, if a student believes that hearing-impaired people are unsociable, but then works on a class project with one who is gregarious, that stereotype might weaken or be eliminated. The other theory the strategy builds on is reference group theory. By building groups of heterogeneous students, teachers attempt to construct in-groups out of those who had previously regarded each other as out-group members. For example, in a sex-segregated classroom, cross-sex team members would begin to identify with teammates of both sexes, in addition to identifying with members of the same sex who are on other teams. In addition, the peer group within the entire class would develop a norm against sex discrimination (or race or handicap discrimination) as students on each team saw value in interacting with teammates of the opposite sex.

Depending on how a teacher structures group-work, it can be either very successful or disastrous. Some teachers mistakenly believe that contact by itself among members of different groups is beneficial. Actually, contact by itself can aggravate stereotyping, prejudice, and social rejection. For example, imagine a teacher in a desegregated school who has White, middle-class students who have attended suburban schools with good teaching and Black, lower-class students who have previously attended schools that had inferior teaching. Suppose that this teacher makes racially mixed groups that are assigned to complete a library research project on the Industrial Revolution. It is quite possible that the Black students' prior schooling would not have prepared them as well for this task as the White students' schooling. Consequently, if the White students believe that Blacks are inferior, the contact experience might reaffirm that belief. And if the Black students believe that Whites are arrogant, this too might be reaffirmed.

Allport (1979) has specified conditions under which cross-group contact can be beneficial:

> Prejudice (unless deeply rooted in the character structure of the individual) may be reduced by *equal status* contact between majority and minority groups in the pursuit of *common goals*. The effect is greatly enhanced if this contact is sanctioned by institutional supports . . . and provided it is of the sort that leads to the perception of common interests and common humanity between members of the two groups. (p. 281, emphasis ours)

David Johnson and Roger Johnson, as well as Robert Slavin, have done considerable work developing this into teaching strategies and researching their effects. Considerable evidence points to cooperative learning in classrooms as a successful strategy for reducing stereotyping and social rejection across handicap, race, and gender lines (Johnson & Johnson, 1984; Johnson, Johnson, & Maruyama, 1983; Sharan, 1980; Slavin & Madden, 1979). Briefly, the strategy involves organizing heterogeneous groups to accomplish a common project (such as creating and putting on a play or competing in a tournament) and structuring the project so that each member can successfully contribute something of approximately equal value.

Various cooperative learning models are available. For example, in using the group investigation models, the teacher in the desegregated school mentioned earlier would make sure that resource materials were available on a range of reading levels and topics so that all students would be able to contribute. The teacher would encourage the final product to be one that depends on a variety of skills rather than a written report. Creating a newspaper, for example, requires articles that have diverse writing styles, drawings, and attention to layout design. In using the jigsaw model, the teacher would use two groupings to complete an assignment. In the first grouping, each group would study a different but related piece of a topic, and group members would work together to make sure each became an "expert." The students would be regrouped so that each new group had one or two "experts" on each piece. A task would then be given requiring students to pool their expertise. In the team games model, students would be divided into heterogeneous groups. All the students would be expected to master a body of skills or knowledge, but they would compete as a team against other teams in some form of tournament; the main way for teams to succeed is for group members to tutor each other. (See Johnson & Johnson, 1975, or Slavin, 1983, for guides to using these strategies.) Although evidence is still sparse concerning the duration or carryover of effects of these strategies, they do build positive intergroup relationships and reduce stereotyping and prejudice within the classroom.

Vicarious Experience and Role Playing

Cook and Cook (1954) have described vicarious experience as "an experience *in*, a contact *with*, rather than reading *about*" (p. 291, emphasis theirs). Group dynamics, described earlier, fosters direct face-to-face contact; vicarious experiences promote contact with symbols of reality. Vicarious experiences include experience through role playing, sociodrama, literature, and film, in which the student takes the perspective of a member of another group.

Vicarious experiences are rooted in different theories, depending on how the experiences are structured. They may be structured primarily to reduce stereotyping. For example, if some students who believe all Asians are quiet view a film depicting a realistic story involving Asians who do not conform to that stereotype, the stereotype may be weakened (depending on the believability of the film).

Vicarious experiences can also reduce social distance and develop feelings of empathy. For example, a boy who plays the role of a woman trying to raise a family single-handedly on a secretary's salary may reevaluate his stereotypes about working women, as well as discover the problems such women face and feel more concern for their situation. According to dissonance theory, the boy would experience a discrepancy between his previous negative attitude and his feelings while playing the role. The experience could lead to a change in attitude, provided the role playing was realistic. Simulations of handicapping conditions are currently popular for preparing regular education students for mainstreamed special education students. According to Kitano, Stiehl, and Cole (1978), research has found role playing and simulation to be a helpful approach to improving attitudes toward the handicapped.

Community Action Projects

Community action projects, another form of direct contact experience, move the students out of the classroom and place them in contact with members of a target group in the community to do some sort of service project. Cook and Cook (1954) explain that

> the idea is to provide learners with direct, perceptual experience
> in area life, issues, and affairs. This is seldom easy and it is never
> safe, yet it is hard to find any better way by which abstractions can
> take on meaning and be acted on. (p. 249)

Like group dynamics, this strategy provides contact in an effort to reduce stereotyping. For the strategy to be most effective, students performing community service must behave in a constructive and positive manner. Like role playing, this can create dissonance between behavior and prejudiced attitudes.

Watts (1984) has discussed projects such as this, using the term *counterattitudinal behavior*. He argues that research supports their effectiveness in changing negative attitudes and reducing prejudice when several interrelated conditions are present: The student must commit himself or herself to the task voluntarily; the student must feel personally responsible for negative consequences of any negative behavior he or she displays; and the student must not justify acting in a negative manner in the situation. For example, suppose that a student is assigned to do volunteer work in a welfare office as a way of dealing with prejudice against the poor. The student should not be coerced to perform the service, as this in itself could engender increased hostility.

The work situation should be structured so that the student feels personally responsible for his or her own actions; if the student talks to a client in a condescending manner and the client becomes angry, the student should realize that his or her behavior triggered the anger by observing that other clients do not become angry when being helped. Furthermore, there should be a supervisor who can help the student realize that the condescending behavior was inappropriate. If the student behaves in a positive and helpful manner over a period of time, he or she will probably develop positive relationships with some clients, as well as see firsthand the sorts of problems they face, which may lead to a change in attitude.

Social Skills Training

Teaching social skills to someone who does not interact positively with a member of another group can facilitate cross group relationships and positive attitudes. This strategy has two rather different kinds of applications. One application is primarily for members of dominant groups who may behave toward others in a manner that breeds hostility or simply indifference. Johnson (1972) provides examples of the sorts of skills one could teach: self-disclosure, developing and maintaining trust, listening, responding, sending clear messages, expressing feelings both verbally and nonverbally, and confronting others constructively. Some educators have trained teachers and students to use these skills in interracial situations to facilitate positive and constructive communication (Banks & Benavidez, 1981).

A second application has been for handicapped students or socially unpopular students; such students are taught skills to facilitate their social relationships with regular education students. For example, Oden and Asher (1977) studied the effects of teaching the following skills to socially unpopular children:

> participation (e.g., getting started, paying attention); cooperation (e.g., taking turns, sharing materials); communication (e.g., talking with the other person, listening); and validation support, referred to as being friendly, fun, and nice (e.g., looking at the other person, giving a smile, offering help or encouragement). (p. 499)

In a control group design study, the researchers found that children who were taught these skills rose in popularity, with results persisting in a one-year follow-up study.

Social skills are usually taught using a variety of techniques, including modeling, coaching, and role playing. Positive reinforcement is given consistently, immediately following a child's use of the desired positive social behavior. Students should be helped with skills development until they are able to use the skills appropriately in real-life situations.

How does a Human Relations approach get into a school? What kinds of considerations and problems make it seem useful? The following vignette describes one morning in a typical junior high school, where problems with human relationships suddenly assume great importance.

A Blue Monday Morning

Mr. Mack, a junior high social studies teacher, was not feeling the greatest this morning as he sped along the expressway to Hemingway school, located in the suburbs. He was annoyed with himself for arguing with his wife about where to spend spring vacation. She wanted to go to San Francisco to see their new niece and then rent a car and drive along the California coast for a second honeymoon. He wanted to go to Boston to see a few Celtics games and spend some time in the Harvard library doing research on his thesis. Not only was he annoyed for having lost the argument that had occupied most of their attention over the weekend, but he had spent too much time this morning making a final plea for his position (last day for supersaver fares) and was really late for school. And the nonverbal communication conveyed by his principal, Mrs. Wilson, literally hung staff members by their thumbs when they arrived late. His feelings were further compounded by having been late Thursday of last week.

When he pulled his car into the first open space in the school parking lot, a glance at his Timex informed him that he had 1½ minutes before being late. He figured that if he walked fast across the playground, he could make it and not have to endure the scowls of Mrs. Wilson. He was halfway across the playground and beginning to feel like he just might get in under the wire when he suddenly saw three boys from his class—Ernest, Ken, and Harold—yelling and chasing Victor Cheng, the new boy in school. He wondered if he had correctly heard what they were shouting. He called the boys over to him. As they arrived—28 seconds left before the scowl—he told Ernest, Ken, and Harold to meet him in his classroom. He then took Victor gently by the arm and continued his trek to the office. On the way, he asked Victor why the boys were chasing him and what they were calling him.

He scribbled his name and time of arrival on the time sheet— just as the bell sounded, alerting all faculty that the workday had officially begun (and telling any teacher who hadn't yet signed in that he or she was late). Victor told him that the boys had said that they didn't like wormy Chinese food or people who try to act smart in class. He said that they had told him that if he didn't bring some fortune cookies to school they would "do him in," and he hadn't brought the cookies to school.

Mrs. Wilson overheard this conversation from her vantage point near the sign-in sheets, and she moved closer to listen. After Victor finished his story, she asked Mr. Mack to have Victor wait in the library while they had a talk.

Mrs. Wilson told Mr. Mack that this was the ninth name-calling and fighting incident that had come to her attention in the last few days. She said, "We have had basically a peaceful integration of students of color into the school, but the name calling, fighting, and writing of graffiti—words like Nigger and Chink—on the boys' bathroom wall suggest that the students need to have some human relations orientation." She suggested that Mr. Mack organize a committee of three other teachers to recommend some school-wide and classroom human relations activities that could help reduce the prejudice, stereotyping, and name calling. She suggested that they consider bulletin boards that point up the similarity of people and the importance of brotherhood and sisterhood.

Mr. Mack said, "Okay, I'll get back to you this afternoon with the names of the other committee members."

As he left Mrs. Wilson and headed to pick up Cheng, he thought, "Human relations are important on the job *and* off!"

CRITIQUE

One can criticize the Human Relations approach, not for what it aims to do, but for what it does *not* aim to do. Few can quarrel with the desirability of reducing prejudice and stereotyping and reducing tension and hostility between groups. In fact, one is hard-pressed to find criticisms of this approach because these are goals that most people support, and the approach itself does not threaten or attack any group.

However, it is rejected by many for a variety of reasons. Advocates of the Teaching the Exceptional and Culturally Different approach see it as too "soft." It does not directly address how to teach the existing curriculum better, which that first approach did. For example, in the vignette, the teachers were probably ignoring Victor Cheng's ethnic background, as well as that of other students, until a social problem erupted. They were probably teaching students as if they were all alike, and if the school was predominantly White, as if all the students were

White. Student diversity became an object of concern only when it threatened harmony within the school. Actually, these first two approaches can be used simultaneously, but teachers who try to do so usually emphasize one or the other—teaching the existing curriculum or improving feelings in the classroom.

The Human Relations approach is usually not the approach adopted by enthusiastic advocates of multicultural education because by itself it is too limited. It reduces social problems to the inability of people to get along. Imagine two children fighting at school, one being lower-class Black and the other middle-class White. One can teach them to play together rather than fight, and one can teach that Blacks are not necessarily violent (contrary to the White child's stereotype) or that Whites are not necessarily arrogant (contrary to the Black child's stereotype). But these teachings do almost nothing to change the fact that the Black child, like many Black children, is living in poverty, that middle-class Whites tend to accept other people's poverty and see it as the other person's fault, and that the White child will have doors of opportunity open to him or her that will be closed to the lower-class Black child and in many cases the middle-class Black child. Perhaps this particular White child will deal more humanely with people of color as a result of human relations teaching, but kind treatment on the part of individuals does not by itself eliminate poverty, powerlessness, social stratification, or institutional discrimination. As in the vignette, the other students may learn to interact pleasantly with Victor and to enjoy Chinese food, but this is no guarantee that they will learn about issues such as the poverty of Chinatown or the psychological devastation many Asian immigrants face when they realize they must surrender much of their identity to assimilate into American society.

Human relations curricula do not address these issues in much depth, if at all. For example, we reviewed *Rainbow Activities* (Ethnic Cultural Heritage Program, 1977), which contains 50 human relations lessons for grades K–8. The lessons are in four categories: cultural pluralism, self-image, values, and feelings. Written objectives inform the user that the lessons aim to teach children that diversity is beautiful, people of different colors have contributed to America and this "makes America beautiful and unique" (p. 13), there is diversity within ethnic groups, individual uniqueness should be cherished, no cultural group is better or worse than any other, and everyone has feelings. These are worthwhile purposes, and the lessons are creatively and skillfully written to accomplish them. However, the lessons do not teach about injustices that have happened, either in the past or currently. They do not teach that groups in real life compete for wealth and power, that power positions in America are dominated by White males of wealth, or that unemployment is high in central cities partly because businesses do not find it profitable to locate there, and many businesses are set up to value personal profit more than sharing with others. Such lessons do not teach that many women who head households and need jobs often lack child care facilities for their children and are forced to choose between holding a job and leaving their children unsupervised or staying home with their children but having to live on welfare.

These are problems that are not resolved by teaching individuals to get along better and value diversity. In fact, it is possible to interpret valuing diversity to mean believing, for example, that Mexican-Americans *should* eat beans rather than steak because beans are "more Mexican." Beans are also cheaper, and such thinking can glorify the way people have adapted to poverty and powerlessness without facing the fact that many people who eat beans do so because they cannot afford steak.

In a very real sense, the Human Relations approach can be assimilationist. Educators who adopt a Human Relations approach often do not address issues of assimilation versus pluralism; often, cultural differences are addressed as much as needed to improve feelings toward self and others. Other Human Relations educators do address cultural diversity, stressing mainly the acceptance of differences without necessarily examining critically which differences are of most value and which are artifacts of historic or present injustices. In addition, by failing to focus adequately on social problems and structural inequalities, the approach implicitly accepts the status quo. It asks people to get along within the status quo rather than educating them to change the status quo.

Because of what the approach does not address, it has not been adopted by most educators interested in fighting sexism or classism, and many people of color who adopted the approach at one time have since shifted to one of the later approaches in this book. The Human Relations approach can be incorporated into other approaches, so one need not give up a fight against prejudice and stereotyping to adopt another approach. We would suggest that this approach currently has popularity with those who work with the handicapped because most people who write about and teach the handicapped are not themselves handicapped. A recent book on exceptional children (Hardman, Drew, & Egan, 1984) concludes with a chapter on handicapped adults, and the main message of the chapter is that little is known about them. Educators see problems of human relations in schools, but tend not to view handicapped people as socially oppressed because they become almost invisible as a group outside school and have few visible spokespeople setting an agenda of needed social action. Thus, educators often define the problems of the handicapped more as human relations problems than as problems of institutionalized poverty and discrimination.

TABLE 3-1 *Human Relations*

Societal goals:	Promote feelings of unity, tolerance, and acceptance within existing social structure
School goals:	Promote positive feelings among students, reduce stereotyping, promote students' self-concepts
Target students:	Everyone
Practices:	
Curriculum	Teach lessons about stereotyping, name-calling; teach lessons about individual differences and similarities; include in lessons contributions of groups of which students are members
Instruction	Use cooperative learning; use real or vicarious experiences with others
Other aspects of classroom	Decorate classroom to reflect uniqueness and accomplishments of students; decorate with "I'm OK, You're OK" themes
Other school-wide concerns	Make sure activities and school policies and practices do not put down or leave out some groups of students; promote school-wide activities, such as donating food for the poor, aimed at peace and unity

REFERENCES

Adorno, T. W., Frenkel-Brunswik, E., Levinson, D. J., & Sanford, R. N. (1950). *The authoritarian personality.* New York: Harper & Row.

Allport, G. W. (1979). *The nature of prejudice* (25th anniversary ed.). Reading, MA: Addison-Wesley.

Bandura, A., & Walters, R. H. (1963). *Social learning and personality development.* New York: Holt, Rinehart, & Winston.

Banks, G. P., & Benavidez, P. L. (1981). Interpersonal skills training in multicultural education. In H. P. Baptiste, Jr., M. L. Baptiste, & D. M. Gollnick (Eds.), *Multicultural teacher education: Preparing educators to provide educational equity* (pp. 177–201). Washington, DC.: Association of Colleges & Teacher Education.

Banks, J. A. (1981). *Multiethnic education: Theory and practice.* Boston: Allyn and Bacon.

Clark, K. B. (1963). *Prejudice and your child* (2nd ed.). Boston: Beacon Press.

Colangelo, N., Foxley, C. H., & Dustin, D. (1979). *Multicultural nonsexist education: A human relations approach.* Dubuque, IA: Kendall/Hunt.

Cook, L. A., & Cook, E. (1954). *Intergroup education.* New York: McGraw-Hill.

Cummings, H. H. (Ed.). (1949). *Improving human relations.* Washington, DC: National Council for the Social Studies.

Donaldson, J., & Martinson, M. (1977). Modifying attitudes toward physically disabled persons. *Exceptional Children, 43,* 337–341.

Ethnic Cultural Heritage Program. (1977). *Rainbow activities.* South El Monte, CA: Creative Teaching Press.

Goodman, M. E. (1952). *Race awareness in young children.* Cambridge, MA: Addison-Wesley.

Grambs, J. D. (1960). *Understanding intergroup relations.* Washington, DC: National Education Association.

Grambs, J. D. (1968). *Intergroup education: Methods and materials.* Englewood Cliffs, NJ: Prentice-Hall.

Grambs, J. D. (n.d.). *Group processes in intergroup education.* New York: National Conference of Christians and Jews.

Hardman, M. L., Drew, C. J., & Egan, M. W. (1984). *Human exceptionality.* Boston: Allyn and Bacon.

Harris, D. B., Gough, H. B., & Martin, W. E. (1950). Children's ethnic attitudes: II, Relationship to parental beliefs concerning child training. *Child Development, 21,* 169–181.

Johnson, D. W. (1972). *Reaching out: Interpersonal effectiveness and self-actualization.* Englewood Cliffs, NJ: Prentice-Hall.

Johnson, D. W., & Johnson, R. (1975). *Learning together and alone.* Englewood Cliffs, NJ: Prentice-Hall.

Johnson, D. W., & Johnson, R. (1984). Classroom learning structure and attitudes toward handicapped students in mainstream settings: A theoretical model and research evidence. In R. L. Jones (Ed.), *Attitudes and attitude change in special education: Theory and practice* (pp. 118–142). Reston, VA: Council for Exceptional Children.

Johnson, D. W., Johnson, R., & Maruyama, G. (1983). Interdependence and interpersonal attraction among heterogeneous and homogeneous individuals: A theoretical formulation and meta-analysis of the research. *Review of Educational Research, 53*, 5–54.

Kitano, M., Stiehl, J., & Cole, J. (1978). Role-taking: Implications for special education. *Journal of Special Education, 12*, 59–74.

Kohlberg, L. (1966). A cognitive-developmental analysis of children's sex-role concepts and attitudes. In E. E. Maccoby (Ed.), *The development of sex differences* (pp. 82–173). Stanford, CA: Stanford University Press.

Oden, S., & Asher, S. R. (1977). Coaching children in social skills for friendship making. *Child Development, 48*, 495–506.

Pogrebin, L. C. (1981). *Growing up free.* New York: Bantam.

Purkey, W. W., & Novak, J. M., (1984). *Inviting school success* (2nd ed.). Belmont, CA: Wadsworth.

Sharan, S. (1980). Cooperative learning in small groups: Recent methods and effects on achievements, attitudes, and ethnic relations. *Review of Educational Research, 50*, 241–271.

Sherif, M., & Sherif, C. W. (1966). *Groups in harmony and tension.* New York: Octagon Books.

Slavin, R. E. (1983). *Cooperative learning.* New York: Longman.

Slavin, R. E., & Madden, N. A. (1979). School practices that improve race relations. *American Educational Research Journal, 16*, 169–180.

Stendler, C. B., & Martin, W. E. (1953). *Intergroup education in kindergarten–primary grades.* New York: Macmillan.

Stone, M. (1981). *The education of the black child in Britain.* London: Fontana.

Taba, H., Brady, E. H., & Robinson, J. T. (1952). *Intergroup education in public schools.* Washington, DC: American Council on Education.

Taba, H., Brady, E. H., Robinson, J. T., & Dolton, F. (1950). *Elementary curriculum in intergroup education.* Washington, DC: American Council on Education.

Turnbull, A. P., & Schulz, J. B. (1979). *Mainstreaming handicapped students: A guide for the classroom teacher.* Boston: Allyn and Bacon.

Watts, W. A. (1984). Attitude change: Theories and methods. In R. L. Jones (Ed.), *Attitudes and attitude change in special education: Theory and practice* (pp. 41–69). Reston, VA: Council for Exceptional Children.

Weinberg, N. (1978). Examination of pre-school attitudes toward the physically handicapped. *Rehabilitation Counseling Bulletin, 22*, 183–188.

Wesley, C. H. (1949). Education and democracy. In H. H. Cummings (Ed.), *Improving human relations* (pp. 27–31). Washington, DC: National Council for the Social Studies.

CHAPTER 4

Single-Group Studies

Y ou probably have not heard the term *Single-Group Studies* before. You are correct in assuming that we made it up. It refers to an approach to multicultural education that is characterized by attention to a *single* group, for example, women, Asians, Blacks, Hispanics, Native Americans, or the working class. To refer to this approach as ethnic studies, women's studies, or Black studies would mislead and confuse and would not correctly identify the various populations that can be addressed.

GOALS

Most advocates of the Single-Group Studies approach to multicultural education hope to reduce social stratification and raise the status of the group with which they are concerned. Table 4–1 states their main goal as promoting social equality for and recognition of the group being studied (see p. 131). They hope to broaden what counts as mainstream culture (e.g., education) so that it includes wider cultural diversity (i.e., the group in which they are interested). Essentially, the Single-Group Studies approach attempts to change attitudes and provide a basis for social action by providing information (in this case through schooling) about the group and about the effects of discrimination on the group. In the school, this approach is often implemented by way of a unit (e.g., Hispanic holidays) or a course of study (e.g., women in the 19th century).

This approach became popular during the civil rights struggle of the late 1960s, particularly on college campuses. Advocates of the approach have usually instituted it as a way of counterbalancing the study of White, middle-class males, which is what the traditional curriculum emphasizes. A common argument for the study of racial groups is that the United States is a racially pluralistic country. Advocates of studying Mexicans, Asians, Blacks, and Native Americans argue that there is no one model American. The portrayal of a dominant national cultural group completely controlling daily institutional and cultural processes is inconsistent with reality. This statement by Hazard and Stent (1973) explains: "The melting-pot ideology has failed. . .cultural pluralism is both a fact and a concept which has not been given due recognition. The fact that the United States includes citizens of diverse cultures cannot be challenged" (p. 13). Guerra (1973), discussing the need for bilingual education, argues as follows:

> Monolingual and monocultural education in America has traditionally ignored the cultural pluralism of American society. We acknowledge ethnic and racial differences, religious variances, and a cultural heterogeneity of our cities, but the criteria of our value judgments, our value system, and our social consciousness remain predominantly White Anglo-Saxon Protestant—that is, representative of the monolingual, monocultural predominant society. The dichotomy between this cultural pluralism of America on the one hand, and the imposing conformity of the monolingual and monocultural predominant society on the other, is something that has never been reconciled. (pp. 27–28)

Various goals are stated by racial groups for the study of their own group. One goal is to present a more accurate version of American history by including groups that were left out and to meet economic, political and cultural demands by people of color from both within and without local communities (Giles, 1974). Garcia (1982) has pointed out that every ethnic group has a unique history set within a definable geographic region and should therefore be studied in an ongoing, in-depth fashion, rather than piecemeal, with bits and pieces of its history tacked onto Anglo studies. Another goal is to provide the teacher with an understanding of the background, reality, and problems the students are facing (Giles, 1974). For students of color, the Single-Group Studies approach should inspire higher student achievement (Giles, 1974), provide the intellectual offensive for the social and political struggle for liberation and cultural integrity (Cortada, 1974), and provide leadership for the group in escaping from physical and psychological bondage (Pentony, 1971, p. 62). It should also give students of color a sense of their history and identity in American society, increase their awareness and self-confidence, and provide a greater sense of direction and purpose in their lives (Suzuki, 1980). Single-Group Studies should support intellectual inquiries into the political, economic, and historical forces affecting the group (Nakanishi & Leong, 1978). Finally, it should help eliminate or reduce White racism (Nakanishi & Leong, 1978).

The preceding goals apply to Native Americans as well, but the historical circumstances differ somewhat from that of other racial groups. As Dupris (1981) explains, the U.S. government declared Indians its "wards"; having done so, "the value of the American Indians' culture was designated as 'dysfunctional' and was, therefore, to be eliminated" (p. 70). This was done by turning the task of education over to the White-controlled Bureau of Indian Affairs, in which policies were overtly assimilationist. The results were disastrous. According to Dupris, Cherokees had had literacy rates of 90% 100 years ago; 70 years of White-controlled schooling has resulted in a Cherokee dropout rate of 75% and a literacy rate of only 60%. The rationale for Indian education controlled by Indians is to restore a language and culture that have been partially lost as well as to strengthen identity and improve achievement of Indian children.

The woman's story—her history, contributions, successes, and failures—has been mostly absent from mainstream accounts of society. Women's studies correct this imbalance, teaching about the oppression that women face and providing women with a true knowledge, purpose, and understanding of themselves. "To change the sexist world" is the way Westkott (1983) describes it. Rutenberg (1983) says that women's studies "rose as a critique to the traditional disciplines" (p. 75). Boneparth (1978) argues that "the justification for women's studies is based upon the need to provide meaningful educational experiences for female students to search out their own identities. Knowledge for women is as important as knowledge of women" (p. 22). Also, women's studies are needed to provide women and men with the knowledge and skill to confront gender issues and promote equality of the sexes. Schramm (1978) summarizes many of the goals of women's studies this way:

> (1) increasing the visibility of women's accomplishments; (2) dispersing information and resources on women which ordinarily are by-

passed; (3) defining feminism for the community; (4) contributing to the legitimacy of a movement which aims for nothing less than human liberation; (5) facilitating consciousness-expansion in others; and (6) increasing the levels of consciousness of Women's Studiers themselves. (p. 4)

Labor studies have a long history, dating back to the turn of the century. Dwyer (1977) has documented how the rationale and main focus of labor studies shifted as the political and economic context changed. During the 1920s, workers' education existed primarily as a political movement concerned with reconstructing the social order; it was allied with the Socialist political agenda as much as it was with trade unionism. After the Depression and passage of the National Labor Relations Act, labor education was much more pragmatic: Its primary purpose was to train labor union members in the day to day aspects of collective bargaining (Douty, 1950). In the last 2 decades, labor studies have developed goals similar to those of women's studies and ethnic studies: to provide "working men and women students with a theoretical background of their life experiences as well as equipping them with an understanding of the practical tools utilized by workers and trade unions to improve working conditions" (Dwyer, 1977, p. 202). Rooted within the social sciences, labor studies programs offer a study of the nature of work; a study of the political, economic, and social problems workers face; and a study of the processes by which modern organizations respond to these problems.

You may have noticed that the various purposes of these Single-Group Studies can make it difficult to determine whom the programs should be aimed at. For example, are Black studies for Blacks or for everyone? Are women's studies for women or for both sexes? We can find goals directed mainly toward the target group, as well as goals directed toward students who are not necessarily members of that group. Both kinds of goals usually go into the establishment of a Single-Group Studies program, and this, as we will see later, can create something of a problem.

Elementary, secondary, and university administrators (who are not necessarily true advocates of Single-Group Studies) have their own reasons for instituting these programs. Often the reason is to keep peace. In a review of Black studies programs in public schools, Giles (1974) comments that "black studies programs seem to have been implemented in response to demands from the local community and political pressures outside the community to which school administrators feel compelled to respond" (p. 11).

PHILOSOPHICAL FRAMEWORK

The Single-Group Studies approach has its roots in educational philosophical orientations that argue that education is not a neutral process, but is used by government and significant others (e.g., labor and business) for social and political purposes. Because of the social and political nature of education, Single-Group Studies advocates argue that study of their group be included in schooling. This approach also has roots in the philosophical arguments that schooling should encourage individuals to become critical thinkers able to reflect on and guide their own behavior and that schooling should teach and encourage cultural analysis, evaluation, and a critical consciousness.

Whether one examines writings about Black studies, women's studies, or Asian studies, for example, one will find similar philosophical tenets considering issues such as the nature of knowledge, the nature of society, and the purposes of schooling. We invite you to consider the issues raised by Single Group-Studies advocates.

Myth of the Neutrality of Education

One question that needs consideration regards the nature of knowledge. Is knowledge neutral? Are the processes by which it is taught neutral? Although most of us can point to particular biases held by particular teachers, when the entire experience is taken in its totality, is it ideologically neutral?

Many see education as essentially a neutral process. In other words, many see education as *not* promoting a particular ideology or point of view. For example, we asked an undergraduate class of 36 beginning education students if education (schooling) was neutral, or if their schooling—kindergarten through high school—had a particular message. About half of these college juniors said that education was neutral and that their schooling did not argue a particular point of view or present one group's point of view over another. Several students who believed this pointed out that they could remember their teachers making a point of being neutral. But many others were quick to argue that their peers were naive. They offered examples of how education is not neutral, but serves as a socialization process to help the young (from 8 to 80) buy into and fit into a particular conception of the American way of life. For example, some pointed out that until very recently, women were for the most part omitted from textbooks, causing the young to accept male domination of society.

By the time this 2-hour discussion was over, the majority of the class had concluded that schooling was not neutral. Schooling, they argued, must be regarded as a social process: It is related to the country's political structure (often its present political scene), to its political and social history, and to its beliefs and ideals.

The two previous approaches to multicultural education—the Human Relations approach and the Teaching the Exceptional and the Culturally Different approach—view schooling as politically neutral. The Human Relations approach concerns itself with what schools teach only insofar as the schools help alleviate sterotyping by providing more information about groups that people frequently stereotype and more positive portrayals of groups to which all students belong. The Teaching the Culturally Different approach advocates modifying what schools teach only as needed to make it more relevant to students who might have trouble catching on. But both approaches see most of the content and processes of schools as essentially fair and desirable and as politically neutral—not biased in favor of any particular group.

Single-Group Studies advocates argue that education is not neutral. Norman (1975), in an article entitled "The Neutral Teacher?", concludes that "questions about what to teach and how to teach it can be answered only in the context of some political perspective or other" (p. 187). Newton (1939) tells us that any form of neutrality, paradoxical though it may seem, becomes a form of positive social action. To allow for and encourage diverse viewpoints is to encourage the value of diversity and open debate. Schooling is purposive, meaning that schooling in the United States has an explicit purpose: to promote democracy or "the American way." In discussing schooling and democracy, Newton states:

> If democracy is to be conserved and fully realized, the American people must understand the meaning of democracy, both in its historical development and in its social bearings and implications for the world of today . . . *The first responsibility of organized education is, then, to enable children, youth, and adults to acquire this understanding of democracy and its problems. Every part of the educational system and every area of education is involved, the university no less than the high school, the arts and the sciences as well as the social studies.* (p. 94, emphasis ours)

Schooling that teaches about democracy is not neutral, but offers a particular point of view. Although this view may be related to freedom, justice, and equality, it is nevertheless a point of view. You may be thinking that *this* viewpoint—the teaching of democracy—is the viewpoint that encourages discussion of issues from a neutral position. (As one student commented, her "teacher was neutral.") It is true that democracy enables different viewpoints to be discussed, but it does represent teaching from a particular point of view. For example, schools in a republic using democratic principles teach a different viewpoint and offer a different curriculum than do schools in a totalitarian country. However, promoting democracy has not meant fully representing the viewpoints of all Americans. The predominance of a particular point of view in our schools can be traced back through U.S. history. For example, Tyack (1966) points out that to some degree Thomas Jefferson, Noah Webster, and Benjamin Rush all saw the function of public school as teaching a balance between order and liberty. Tyack writes:

> Not content with unconscious and haphazard socialization provided by family, political meeting, press, and informal associations, not trusting in the "giveness" of political beliefs and institutions, these men sought to instruct Americans deliberately in schools. Having fought a war to free the United States from one centralized authority, they attempted to create a new unity, a common citizenship and culture, and an appeal to a common future. In this quest for a balance between order and liberty, for the proper transaction between the individual and society, Jefferson, Rush, and Webster encountered a conflict still inherent in the education of the citizen and expressed still in the injunction to teachers to train students to think critically but to be patriotic above all. (p. 31)[1]

This same idea is also seen in comments by Ellwood Patterson Cubberley (1909), a recognized educational leader in the early 1900s:

> Everywhere these people [immigrants] tend to settle in groups or settlements, and to set up here their national manners, customs, and observances. Our task is to break up these groups or settlements, to assimilate and amalgamate these people as part of our American race, and to implant in their children, as far as can be done, the Anglo-Saxon conception of righteousness, law and order, and popular government, and to awaken in them a reverence for our democratic institutions and for those things in our national life which we as a people hold to be of abiding worth. (pp. 15–16)

In other words, historically, schools have taught not only skills for democratic participation, but also allegiance to a culture defined primarily by Anglo-Saxon men of at least moderate wealth. And this is the concern of advocates of Single-Group Studies: Whereas democracy *should* be fostered in schools, democracy is a sham if it incorporates only the concerns and perspectives of those who already dominate politically and economically. For there to be true democracy, the points

---

[1]Tyack, David, "Forming the National Character," *Harvard Educational Review*, 36, 29–41. Copyright © 1966 by the President and Fellows of Harvard College. All rights reserved.

of view of oppressed people must also be given full expression. Note the statement given to undergraduates at the University of Wisconsin–Madison from the Afro-American Studies Department (1970):

> Although the Afro-American community has had a unique histor-ical experience, has evolved a distinct culture, and faces a special set of problems in American Society, scholars have tended either to greatly distort or to completely dismiss the black experience as an unpleasant footnote to the larger American experience. (p. 1)

Consider also the observation by Spender (1981) as she addresses male dominance in theoretical frameworks for educational research:

> From a feminist perspective one of the dominant theoretical frameworks of education is that of male dominance, but it is a frame-work which goes unquestioned and which has not been made the sub-stance of educational enquiry. Unless and until education begins to examine male dominance as a fundamental issue in the entire educa-tional process, the impact of feminism will be minimal. (p. 157)

Even the teacher who refuses to take a position when presenting an issue makes numerous decisions throughout the school day about what and how to teach—decisions that could suggest a particular point of view. For example, a teacher who decides to teach the American novel could be teaching points of view that have race, gender, and class implications. If the teacher decides to use *The Adventures of Huckle-berry Finn* (Mark Twain), *The Catcher in the Rye* (J. D. Salinger), *Deliverance* (James Dickey), and *The Grapes of Wrath* (John Stein-beck), then this teacher has in essence decided to omit (at least so far) *Manchild in the Promised Land* (Claud Brown), *To Kill a Mockingbird* (Harper Lee), *Forever* (Judy Blume), and *The Color Purple* (Alice Walker). The points of view given to the students in the two sets of novels could be very different, since the second set includes novels by two women and two persons of color. If used over an extended period of time, neither set of materials is politically neutral. The question is, What political implications are there for any given set of decisions that teachers make about what to teach, whether those decisions are conscious or uncon-scious?

Social Purpose of Schooling

Schools are society's agencies (or institutions) of socialization. Newton (1939) argues:

> Education is a form of socialization. The purpose of education is to modify behavior, to make the individual a different person from

what he would otherwise be. It is for this reason that educational policy is always social policy and that, in the modern world, the school is
employed, deliberately, for the achievement of definite social purposes,
becomes, in fact, a crucial element in national policy. (p. 203)

Schools have a daily impact on students and serve to prepare them for
the roles they will have as adults. Besides being used to teach about
democracy, schooling is used as a form of social control by influencing
attitudes and modifying behavior. For example, historically, schools
were charged with teaching self-discipline and the literary skills required for reading the Bible. In the 20th century, schools increasingly
prepared a mass citizenry for an industrial labor market. Spring (1973),
describing the school as an instrument of social control, observes:

By the beginning of the twentieth century, industrialization and
urbanization had severely eroded the influence of family, church, and
community on individual behavior. As the power of these institutions
waned, the school became increasingly important as a primary instrument for social control. It became the agency charged with the responsibility of maintaining social order and cohesion and of instilling
individuals with codes of conduct and social values that would insure
the stability of existing social relationships. Although a preserving institution, the school was viewed as a form of internal control—and
therefore more in the "democratic" tradition than such external forms
as law, government, and police. (p. 30)

Advocates of Single-Group Studies would explicitly describe the "codes
of conduct" and "social values" that Spring discusses as having been
prescribed mainly by White, middle-class males. For example, proper
conduct for middle-class women included deferring to men, serving
men, and running an orderly home; schooling reinforced this. Children
of color were taught to value and respect the culture and language of
Whites and to devalue that of their families.

  The school carries out its control through a process referred to
as socialization. Socialization is a lifelong process, basic to human
activity and occurring in the classroom, as well as in the family and
religious institutions. Schools contribute to the process of socialization
by helping the student to fit into an established cultural or social tradition and by aiding in the student's development of personality or
individual identity. Through participation in various social experiences
in the school, the student becomes familiar with or learns knowledge,
attitudes, behavior, and values. Schools are considered by many as
society's instrument for inculcating the "right" values and social attitudes into the young. For example, some educators claim that in school,
habits such as obedience, industriousness, neatness, and punctuality

are taught as important social values that will help students grow to adulthood and become useful and productive members of society.

As already noted, the social control that schools orchestrate in this democratic society is not neutral or unbiased. According to Bowles and Gintis (1976) it is biased along race, social class, and gender lines:

> Schools foster legitimate inequality through the ostensibly meritocratic manner by which they reward and promote students, and allocate them to distinct positions in the occupational hierarchy. They create and reinforce patterns of social class, racial and sexual identification among students which allow them to relate "properly" to their eventual standing in the hierarchy of authority and status in the production process. Schools foster types of personal development compatible with the relationships of dominance and subordinance in the economic sphere. (p. 11)

For example, lower-class students tend to be sorted into lower-ability and remedial classes, while upper-class students tend to be sorted into college-bound classes. On the surface, this process appears fair because it uses objective testing and professional guidance. Once sorted, students learn to view their own status as acceptable and learn to relate to each other in a leader-follower fashion. The status quo is reproduced, but in a manner that appears natural.

What does this mean specifically for children who are members of different social groups in society? Banks's (1981) stages of ethnicity help us understand the way schools shape student self-concept and aid in maintaining social control. As noted in chapter 3, members of ethnic minority groups, females, the poor, and the handicapped are often socialized, in schools as well as in other social institutions, to occupy a state of "Ethnic (or Gender, or Class) Psychological Captivity." Taught that members of their group rarely make notable achievements, contributions, or political decisions, children of oppressed groups often see themselves and their group as powerless and worthless. This may be aggravated when they are simultaneously taught that we live in a free democracy in which everyone can do as he or she chooses and people get what they work for. If the Black female child sees few Black women who seem to have contributed anything of social value, implicitly she is being taught that Black females—herself included—must not have much to contribute. This is a message of powerlessness and hopelessness.

White, middle-class male students tend to find themselves in a stage of "Ethnic (or Gender, or Class) Encapsulation." They are taught that people like themselves have run this country since its earliest history and have contributed its greatest achievements in literature, art, music, and science. This is a message of arrogance. It is also a message that teaches those in control that they have rightfully earned that control and that they have little need to understand oppression or the experiences of the oppressed. It is because of the school's role in the socialization process that advocates of Single-Group Studies want to become more involved in the schooling process.

If advocates of Single-Group Studies criticize the social purpose to which schools are normally put, what social purpose do they advocate? The purpose they advocate is based not only on a critical view of the nature of society, but also on an optimistic view of human nature. Is human nature essentially active or passive? Do children by nature want to learn, or do they need to be coaxed? Is learning essentially a process of meaning-making or a process of imprinting a body of information on blank minds?

The Single-Group Studies approach sees the student as willing and eager to learn, capable of making decisions, and committed to reflection about his or her learning. Education is consistent with Newton's (1939) observations:

> Education must aim, first of all, at the building of minds that are sensitive to the social realities of the world in which they live, that are free, that have acquired the capacity for thinking for themselves, because they have had opportunity to think for themselves. (p. 213)

From the perspective of Single-Group Studies, this means that schools should develop in students what Freire (1970) calls a "critical consciousness." When students learn about their heritage and contributions to society, they participate in a process of self-discovery and increasing social consciousness. This results in the realization that, contrary to the myth of their inferiority, their actions can be a transforming process in the United States and in the world. In other words, as they learn about their group, they grow in pride and knowledge about themselves; and as others learn about their group, they, too, will change in relationship to their new knowledge. Dominant groups will learn that their dominance was usually seized rather than earned and that its use has been more often than not biased and unfair. The preamble of the Constitution of the National Women's Studies Association (1977) directly addresses the point of consciousness-raising when it states: "Women's studies is the educational strategy of a breakthrough in consciousness and knowledge" (p. 6).

Examples of students who have had to be coaxed into learning probably spring readily to your mind. But students only need to be coaxed to learn material that has no personal meaning. Schooling for many young people is alienating when it is not about themselves; it is highly motivating when it is.

In the summary, the Single-Group Studies approach is aimed toward social change. It attacks primarily the knowledge normally taught in schools, arguing that knowledge reinforces control by White wealthy men over everyone else. "Business as usual" attempts to socialize the young into accepting the status quo as "right," at the same time alienating children of color, children of the poor, and female children from social institutions. Schooling needs to offer an in-depth study of all major social groups for the purpose of empowering group members, developing in them a sense of pride and group consciousness, and helping members of dominant groups appreciate the experiences of others and recognize how their own groups have oppressed others.

RECOMMENDED PRACTICES

The main goal of Single-Group Studies programs is to promote willingness and knowledge among students to work toward social change that would benefit a specific group, as stated in Table 4–1.

Single-Group Studies programs have been developed the most comprehensively at the university level. During the 1960s and 1970s, many college and universities offered courses of study leading to majors and minors in Single-Group Studies areas at both the undergraduate and graduate levels. At the high school level, such courses were added to the curriculum, usually within departments, but sometimes across departments. At the elementary and middle school levels, one finds units or lessons about specific groups. Such units are usually more simplistic and superficial than the more in-depth courses of study. Regardless of level of schooling, however, and regardless of which group one is concerned with, advocates recommend fairly similar practices.

Content (Curriculum)

There are many ways to prepare curriculum for a Single-Group Studies course, program, unit, or lesson. However, most Single-Group Studies curricula have a good deal in common; the main commonalities are summarized in Table 4–1. The curriculum often contains a history of the group, starting with the country the group originates from or, in the case of women, the history of women. For racial groups, the history may explain reasons for immigration (e.g., of Asian-Americans) or enslavement (in the case of Black Americans). The history might also provide information on early relationships with White settlers (e.g., in the cases of Native Americans and Mexican-Americans) or, in the case of Native Americans, the history of legal settlements and conflicts with Whites.

The group's great heroes and heroines, both past and present, are very often discussed in great detail, as well as the group's contributions to the United States and the world in the fields of arts, letters, and sciences. For example, the background, struggles, and achievements of noted authors, musicians, scientists, and civic workers are provided. In addition, many of the Single-Group Studies programs include selections of art, music, and other cultural expressions. Traditional and contemporary perspectives are offered to provide insight into the group's culture. For example, Mexican-Americans are known to have very strong extended family ties and certain views related to male and female behavior. One can see these concepts reflected in the art and literature of Mexican-Americans.

Experiences that the group has had are often included, such as the internment of Japanese-Americans during World War II, the Trail of Tears that Native Americans experienced during their forced immigration, the work of Rosie the Riveter in the defense plants during World War II, and the role of labor unions in collective bargaining. Many courses or programs contain information addressing diversity within the group; for example, women's studies may address the problems and strengths arising from the fact that the group is made up of both women of color and White women. Puerto Rican studies may discuss the relationship of skin color to job opportunities. Discussions of stereotyping, myths, and cultural and institutional bias also occur.

Finally, contemporary issues of concern to the group are usually studied. For example, women's studies usually address economic inequalities between the sexes, the status of gays and lesbians, and women's health care. Chicano studies may address the status of agricultural workers in the Southwest, as well as the illegal alien issue.

You may be wondering, How is all this content normally packaged? To illustrate the similarities as well as differences across courses, we will now present a few outlines of Single-Group Studies courses. The first, a syllabus from a Black studies course, Black History I, taught in a Detroit high school, gives the titles of chapter units and provides an example of the content:

I. Introduction to Black History

II. African Past

III. Slave Trade

IV. Slavery Develops in English America, 1619-1790

V. The Constitution

VI. Black Protest Against Slavery

VII. Emancipation Proclamation

VIII. Reconstruction and Aftermath

IX. New Black Leadership

X. Blacks Who Contributed

XI. Blacks Organize—Why?

XII. What Now? Integration? Nationalism?

XIII. Political Power Now (Black Officeholders) (Giles, 1974)

In Madison, Wisconsin, there are two courses (Black Studies 1 and 2) offered in one of the high schools. The description for the courses reads as follows:

Black Studies 1: Examines Black History from the great African Kingdoms to 1877. Deals with such topics as "the slave revolts," "Abraham Lincoln—Racist," and "Reconstruction failure."

Black Studies 2: Covers Black History from 1877 to the present. Deals with such topics as "Jimcrowism," the "Harlem Renaissance," "Booker T. Washington and Frederick Douglass," "segregation and racism in America," and "Where does Black America go from here?"

The 1973–1974 syllabus from Dwight Morrow High School in Englewood, New Jersey, illustrates the content of a women's studies course titled "American Studies: Women in American History."

I. Overview
   A. What is history? How can it be understood? Why study history?
   B. Major events, movements in U.S. history

II. The Role of Women
   A. Examination of the student's own attitudes and stereotypes
   B. Women as presented in traditional history texts
   C. Institutional support of women in certain roles: family, church, government, economy

III. Women in Early America
   A. Status and role of women in different regions: New England, Middle Atlantic states, the South
   B. Role played by women in different social classes, races, ethnic groups

    IV. Major Social Changes Bring Change in Role of Women During
        Late 1800's
        A. Feminist movement grows from abolitionist movement
        B. Effects of the Civil War in increasing roles of women
        C. Industrial Revolution increases role of women outside the
           home
        D. Effects of the great migrations: westward movement,
           immigration, urbanization
        E. Educational expansion
     V. Twentieth-Century Technology Affects Women
        A. Changing household technology
        B. Mass media influences life styles, values and expectations
           through radio, movies, women's magazines, advertising,
           television
        C. The automobile and the move to suburbia
    VI. Biography: in-depth study of one woman's life by each student
    VII. Today's Women's Movement: examination of change and
        resistance to change in current history   (Ahlum & Fralley,
        1976)

Students can complete an undergraduate major in American Indian studies from the University of Wisconsin–Eau Claire. Students are required to take at least 15 semester credits from the following core courses:

    Introduction to Cultural Anthropology

    North American Indians

    Contemporary American Indian Issues

    American Indian Art

    Introduction to Literature of the American Indian

    Major Works in American Indian Literature

    The History of Native Americans, 1492–1900

Students may also choose from the following elective courses:

    Folk Religion

    Racial Minorities and Schools

    History of Westward Expansion

    The Minority Press in America

    Race and Ethnic Relations

As you can see, Single-Group Studies programs may be put together somewhat differently. But they all have important components of history, group culture, and contemporary issues.

Implementation

The day-to-day teaching strategies for Single-Group Studies programs are no different than for traditional classroom teaching, although as noted in Table 4–1, many teachers try to adapt instruction to the learning styles of students, especially students who are members of the group being studied. It is the content and the interest in social action that distinguishes Single-Group Studies. However, in planning a program and designing a curriculum, a teacher must make certain decisions about its relationship to the rest of the school program, and these decisions have implications for planning and teaching.

One decision is whether Single-Group Studies will be separate from the regular curriculum or integrated with it in an attempt to provide a more balanced curriculum. Most advocates—especially those doing elementary and secondary teaching—recommend integrating their study into the content of the mainstream curriculum. This approach would encourage including information about the group's historical and cultural experience in present courses of social studies, government, history, literature, art, and music. Not to do so, they argue, would make the Single-Group Studies curriculum separate and supplementary to the main curriculum. Banks (1979) argues, "If ethnic content is merely added to the traditional curriculum, which in many ways is ineffective, efforts to modify the curriculum with ethnic content are likely to lead to a dead end" (p. 83). Banks's argument is consistent with data reported in an *Education U.S.A.* survey (cited by Giles, 1974), which reports that most educators believe that the best way to handle material on racial groups is to make it an integral part of the regular kindergarten-through-12th grade (K–12) curriculum.

There is a flip side to this approach, however. In a discussion of women's studies, Bowles and Klein (1983) argue that women's studies need to be researched and developed as an area in its own right. Perhaps after it has become as well developed as the more traditional "men's studies," then integration would make sense. But to push prematurely for integration would greatly overwork women's studies scholars by giving them two jobs rather than one (i.e., redesigning traditional knowledge for a traditional set of colleagues in addition to conducting research on women). It would also weaken the efforts of women to develop new conceptual frameworks for understanding, since research and curricula currently have very well entrenched frameworks that would resist displacement by fledgling ideas. The same can be said of ethnic studies. Another argument for separatism is that educators believe that they need to offer older students separate courses to make up for all the years that this area was excluded from their education (National Schools Public Relations Association, 1970).

Currently, when Single-Group Studies are implemented, the integrative approach is not usually used. A day to celebrate a particular heroine or hero, a unit during a special time (e.g., Black History Week), a festival or ethnic cookout is more typically the manner in which attention is given to Single Group-Studies. We have observed that the major implementation strategy for Single-Group Studies in the public schools is the four Fs: fairs, festivals, food, and folktales. Usually, when it is done in this manner, there is no well thought-out reason for having it separate. There is also no in-depth study of the group itself. Perhaps it seems easier to add on special activities and lessons to the existing instructional plan. However, such add-ons are usually devoid of any strategy to change the existing program substantially, even though substantive change of school curricula is a primary goal of serious Single-Group Studies practitioners, whether they advocate integration or separatism.

A second decision that must be made is how many disciplines will be involved and in what relationship to each other. The teacher has essentially three choices: using a single discipline, using a multidisciplinary approach, and using an interdisciplinary approach. The least complex, and probably the most common approach in high schools, is the single-discipline approach. This means, for example, that a history teacher would develop units or an entire history course in Black history, or a literature teacher would develop units or a course on Asian-American literature.

The multidisciplinary approach involves teachers or professors in several disciplines, each contributing a unit or a course to a Single-Group Studies program. For example, an Indian studies program may have courses in anthropology, art, history, and religion. A women's studies program could offer courses in biology, literature, history, and psychology. Boneparth (1978) offers an argument in favor of this approach, saying that it would facilitate moving from a separate to an integrated program:

> The rationale for the multidisciplinary approach is clear: the traditional disciplines have universally ignored women and have failed to integrate the study of women into their course offerings. Therefore, outside efforts to push the discipline into a concern with women are necessary and well spent. (p. 23)

The interdisciplinary approach is the most complex. It requires integrating two or more disciplines in the study of issues of concern to them. For example, in a Black studies program using the interdisciplinary approach, teachers of history, literature, and art could develop a study of artistic expression by Black people through history, examining the impact of historical events on works of art and literature.

Using the interdisciplinary conceptual approach, Banks (1973) argues, is important because it helps students make reflective decisions so that they can institute social change. He believes that the social science disciplines (e.g., sociology and anthropology) must be brought together and that analytical concepts within these disciplines (e.g., values and norms) must be used to help make decisions about complex societal problems such as racism or sexism. He states:

> A social studies curriculum which focuses on decision-making
> and the Black experience must be *interdisciplinary;* it should incorpo-
> rate *key* (or organizing) concepts from all of the social sciences. Knowl-
> edge from any one discipline is insufficient to help us make decisions
> on complex issues such as poverty, institutionalized racism and
> oppression. To take effective social action on a social issue such as
> poverty, students must view it from the perspectives of geography, his-
> tory, sociology, economics, political science, psychology, and anthro-
> pology. (p. 156, emphasis ours)

How one teaches Single-Group Studies often depends on the availability of materials and the preparation of the teachers (Giles, 1974). This is especially true at the elementary and high school levels, where the instructors may or may not have had the opportunity to develop the area of specialization.

Teachers must also be aware that students may be sensitive to materials and embarrassed to ask questions about their culture or about racial or sexual dynamics. Therefore, the teacher, says Butler (1981), "should always be approachable and should frequently encourage students to take advantage of his/her office appointment hours to discuss topic papers, clarify classroom discussion" (p. 117). Finally, the most important ingredient for teaching Single-Group Studies, we have found, is the awareness, commitment, and dedication of the teacher to the kind of job he or she thinks needs to be done.

Single-Group Studies and Bilingual-Bicultural Education

In an earlier chapter, we noted that most bilingual education programs could be subsumed under the Teaching the Culturally Different approach. One can also find a few bilingual-bicultural education programs that have more in common with Single-Group Studies than with any other approach. Essentially, such programs include a strong component about the culture of the group with which the language is associated, and they do so for the purpose of enhancing students' competence in that culture, rather than for the purpose of enabling non-Anglo children to learn traditional school subject material more competently.

Trueba (1976) distinguishes between bilingual education and bilingual-bicultural education. The main purpose of bilingual education is usually to teach English to children whose home language is not English: "The main purpose of this curricular model is to equip ethnic children with native-like skills in the second language in order that they may 'perform' almost as native English speakers in an all-English curricular module" (p. 11). This is essentially assimilationist. Bilingual-bicultural education, on the other hand, seeks to teach children as much about the Hispanic, or Chinese, or Indian culture, for example, as about the dominant Anglo culture.

When bilingual-bicultural programs are open to children of diverse backgrounds and seek to promote what Ramirez and Castaneda (1976) have called "cultural democracy"—equal status of two cultures and of the people who represent those cultures—the program is a variant of Single-Group Studies. Kjolseth (1976) has described some essential characteristics of this type of program. He argues that it involves the political mobilization of the ethnic community: They are as involved in the development and implementation of the program as is the dominant group. The program is "two-way with members of both the ethnic and nonethnic groups learning in their and the other's language" (p. 126); the cultures of both groups are stressed equally in all curricular areas; and the program "encourages a democratic forum for the resolution of conflicts and differing interests within and between the ethnic and nonethnic communities" (p. 127).[2]

How widespread is the use of the Single-Group Studies approach to bilingual education? It is relatively rare. Kjolseth analyzed files of reports on bilingual programs collected by the U.S. Office of Education, classifying programs as either pluralistic (described above) or assimilationist. He found that "the great majority of bilingual programs (well over 80 percent) closely approximate the extreme of the assimilationist model, while the remaining few are only moderately pluralistic" (p. 132). Gaardner (1976) made a similar point in his analyses of espoused versus real practices. He found all projects he examined to have a

[2]We disagree with Kjolseth's equation of the dominant group with a nonethnic group. To us, there is no such thing as a nonethnic group. White ethnics who have "melted" and who no longer have strong ties to European countries, which is probably the group Kjolseth refers to as nonethnic, can be considered ethnically Euro-American: Their ancestors came from Europe, and their culture has European roots that have developed a distinctive American character; Euro-Americans can be distinguished visually as well as culturally from, for example, Afro-Americans.

"profession of emphasis on the 'history and culture' of the child who has a mother tongue other than English" but few to give serious attention to culture (p. 152). Probably one of the best examples of this model has been found in Miami, particularly in Coral Way Elementary School (Mackey & Beebe, 1977). We would guess that the 1980s are seeing less attention to culture in bilingual education and increased use of the program for assimilation. Thus, the study of a group's culture may be advocated by some, but it appears to be practiced in only a few settings.

Señor Ricardo Gomez and Ms. Kathy Bennett

As Ricardo entered the school, he had mixed emotions. He was very pleased and proud that his college days were behind him and that he had his teaching certificate. He was sad and annoyed that in 1 week he would be 28 years old—28 years old and just getting his first real job. Sometimes he counted the 2 years he spent in Vietnam as a real job and other times he didn't. He felt he had really grown up in Nam. He lost his two best buddies—Juan and Pedro—and got banged up pretty badly himself. Badly enough to remain in the hospital for 6 months.

The three had joined the Marines the day they graduated from Lakeview High School. So many of his Hispanic brothers, he now thought, had lost their lives in Vietnam. Before Ricardo could allow that thought to go any further, a little kid hollered up to him, "Are you the new P.E. teacher?" Ricardo said, "No—I am the new social studies teacher."

Kennedy Junior High School was located in the suburban area of a large metropolitan area. The school was upper-middle-class with a student population of 88% White, 4% Black, 2% Asian, and 6% Hispanic. All the students of color were bused in from the inner city.

In a short time, Ricardo established himself as one of the "good" teachers at Kennedy. He was assigned three classes in American history and one in world geography. The students liked and respected him, and the other teachers saw him as friendly and professional, but also as a man in a hurry.

Ricardo had been a history buff for as long as he could remember. He was very interested in what the past teaches us about the present and future. In short order, his classroom took on an attractive and museumlike appearance, with pictures and historical artifacts everywhere.

George Glenn had been principal of Kennedy Junior High School for 6 years. One of his responsibilities was evaluating all his teachers, especially the new ones. According to district policy, he had to observe new teachers at least three times over the school year. When Mr. Glenn came to observe Ricardo, he was informed that he was to see a lesson on the Fall of the Alamo. What Mr. Glenn saw was not a lesson that featured Davy Crockett and his rifle Betsy along with some Texans as fallen heroes of the Alamo, but a lesson that featured the Mexican general Santa Anna and his army putting down a revolt against the Mexican government. Around the room were bulletin boards, posters, and other classroom artifacts that featured the Hispanic culture.

Later, during their conference, Ricardo explained to Mr. Glenn how important it was to provide his students with a broad perspective of history. He said that he believed it was his responsibility as a Hispanic American to include in his teaching not only the Anglo perspective of American history, but also the Hispanic perspective. He asked Mr. Glenn why more attention wasn't given to the Hispanic culture in the daily practices of the school. He said that the school curriculum and activities were exclusively Anglo in policy and practice. Mr. Glenn was taken aback by Ricardo's comments and had difficulty responding. Ricardo continued, saying that not only were the Hispanics in the school being cheated by not having their history taught, but so were the other students, especially the Anglos, many of whom displayed ethnocentric attitudes. Mr. Glenn nodded his head and concluded the conversation by saying that they should talk about this again soon and that he had another observation to make in 5 minutes.

Kathy Bennett had been vice principal of Kennedy for 12 years. In fact, she had been Mr. Glenn's mentor teacher when he started teaching. Kathy was becoming increasingly disenchanted with her job and the school system in general. She had been passed over for a principalship so often that she now believed that it could never happen. The "word" on her was that she was too aggressive and would not fit in with the other administrators—all of whom were male. Kathy and her friends never would have described her as aggressive, but more as a person who believed in being in charge of her own life and who knew what she wanted and where she wanted to go.

Kathy did have a personal and professional concern related to the career goals of the female students at the school. Too many of them, she believed, were too passive and too much into playing the helpless female. Their career goals were very traditional. It was as if they were living in the 1940s and early 1950s. Kathy had started an after-school club called "You Too Can Do." In the club meeting room were pictures and posters of women in both traditional and nontraditional jobs. There were books by female authors and stories of famous and not-so-famous women who had really taken charge of their lives without relying on the male species. "You Too Can Do" met twice monthly. During each meeting, there was usually a discussion of some work accomplished by a woman or a guest speaker who addressed some aspect of feminism.

Mr. Glenn was aware of Kathy's club and her special attention to the female population of the school; but he tried to ignore it because she was fair with the boys and it did not particularly interfere with her job. However, he was not personally assertive in helping her get a principalship, as he had been with Robert Wilson, his vice principal before Kathy.

As Mr. Glenn left Ricardo's room, he saw Kathy in the hall and asked her to come and chat with him. He said he was concerned about Ricardo's curriculum and teaching. He described what he had observed in Ricardo's room, and as he did, he became more upset. Kathy told him that although she had never seen Ricardo teach, she had heard that he was "different." However, she said, the students for the most part enjoyed it. She then added, "You know, I have similar feelings about the girls and feminist issues in the school." At that comment, Mr. Glenn looked at Kathy with a facial expression that turned from puzzlement to greater annoyance, and said, "I have an observation to do. I will see you later."

Ricardo and Kathy continued, each in his or her own way, to influence their students' education. Ricardo's lessons always contained both the Anglo and Hispanic perspectives, and Kathy's "You Too Can Do" club continued to meet and discuss feminist issues.

Mr. Glenn, meanwhile, tried to ignore the teaching behavior of these two staff members. However, he did on numerous occasions, in a friendly manner, suggest to Ricardo that he would probably prefer teaching in the urban barrio.

CRITIQUE

To critique Single-Group Studies is to realize that many positive statements can be made about this approach to multicultural education. The Single-Group Studies approach can be seen as a beginning. It is a beginning because people must first understand themselves before they can hope to understand others. Banks (1979) puts it this way: "Another important goal of ethnic studies is to help individuals clarify their ethnic identities and function effectively within their own ethnic community. This must occur before individuals can relate positively to others who belong to different racial and ethnic groups" (p. 21). Single-Group Studies can also be described as a beginning because the civil rights movement of the 1960s started with *one* group—Blacks—demanding their social, political, and economic rights, and from that beginning, other groups of color and women have also demanded their rights. Although the struggles of women and of labor were not new, their demands to be included in the curriculum as legitimate groups of study were articulated with renewed, and in many cases new, vigor. The Single-Group Studies approach has generated ethnic pride and a desire to discover one's roots. Congress was so swayed by this interest in ethnic heritage that in 1972 it passed legislation enacting the Ethnic Heritage Studies Program. Similarly, Title IX of the Elementary and Secondary Education Act (ESEA) and the Women's Educational Equity Act also came about because women demanded equality.

For the teacher who doesn't have a strong knowledge of feminist issues, class issues, or race diversity, the Single-Group Studies model serves as a starting place in which to focus. For the teacher working with a student population that is basically Asian or Hispanic for example, the Single-Group Studies approach provides a beginning point to help those students develop pride in who they are and understand how their group has been victimized. Ricardo Gomez's Hispanic students, for example, knew little about themselves as Hispanic people before enrolling in his class. They learned some Hispanic culture informally at home, but in school had never been taught their own history, literature, and so forth. In fact, constituting only 6% of the student body, they were ignored in the curriculum and treated as invisible by the school.

The Single-Group Studies approach does have certain limitations, however, and what one sees as its limitations depends on one's perspective. From the perspective of Teaching the Culturally Different, the Single-Group Studies approach spends too little time on the things that subordinate groups need most, and too much time on things that will not help them. This model has been criticized for keeping students of color and White female students out of the mainstream and for promoting cultural separatism. Critics fear that minority students, for example, will fail to acquire a sufficient grasp of mainstream culture if they spend too much time studying their own culture. A knowledge of Black history, for example, will not help much on the SATs or in a traditional American history class, and the system requires success in the traditional curriculum, not in the study of oppressed groups. One can argue that this vividly illustrates how the system oppresses some groups, but advocates of Teaching the Culturally Different reply that teachers must nevertheless prepare students to succeed within the system, since this is the most realistic course of action.

From the perspective of Human Relations, Single-Group Studies can be seen as counterproductive. Human Relations advocates support studying contributions of diverse groups, but fear that the study of oppression will only exacerbate tension and hostility. Furthermore, studying separate groups separately will not promote unity. Rather than examining painful issues in our past, Human Relations advocates would rather seek ways of drawing people together in the present. For example, Kathy Bennett's students will, at one time or another, experience anger toward men as they learn how women have been oppressed. Some of this anger will probably be directed toward male students, male teachers, brothers, and fathers. Similarly, Ricardo's Hispanic students will experience anger toward Whites and may display some hostility toward White students and teachers in the school. Human Relations advocates prefer that students learn to appreciate their similarities and their cultural differences and learn to interact as unique individuals, rather than exploring the pain and injustice of past oppression and victimization.

To those who accept and support the intent of Single-Group Studies, the main limitation is that it leaves the regular curriculum unreformed. This is not a fault of advocates and practitioners of the approach, for most are keenly aware of a need to reform the curriculum. It is this need that prompted the development of Single-Group Studies countercurricula. But as a separate program of its own, Single-Group Studies allows the rest of the education program to proceed as "business as usual." For example, Mr. Glenn has no intention of changing anything in his school and tries hard to ignore Kathy and Ricardo. As long as their activities can be compartmentalized into a separate course or an after-school activity, they are tolerable. Champions of the status quo can argue that students are being provided with ethnic, gender, or class-relevant experiences and that teachers such as Ricardo and Kathy are being allowed to "do their thing." Too often, such programs remain add-ons, supplemental to the main business of the school. And, in so remaining, they tend to draw as students only members of the group being studied. For example, Black studies programs ideally should be taken by members of all racial groups, and teachers within such programs see as much need for changing White attitudes toward Blacks as for educating Blacks about Blacks. But when Black studies programs are supplemental and elective, as they almost always are, they are attended mainly by Blacks. Although some students who are members of dominant groups find such courses enlightening and worthwhile, others feel threatened, particularly when they are in the minority as class members, and find it more comfortable to avoid such courses. Those students who may need reeducation the most can comfortably stay away, pursuing their education in the unchanged mainstream.

Another problem is that Single-Group Studies programs do not necessarily work together. The goal of most advocates of Single-Group

Studies is curriculum reform that would involve the inclusion of the various ethnic groups, the working class, and women into the curriculum. Ultimately, of course, this would mean rewriting the curriculum, since its main conceptual frameworks currently derive from upper-middle-class White male studies. This goal is often more rhetoric than demonstration. Most writings about Single-Group Studies suggest including other groups, but rarely in the example they provide do they accomplish this goal. Specifically, ethnic studies often focus on the males of a given ethnic group; labor studies often focus on White, working-class males; and women's studies often focus on White, middle-class women. Bowles and Klein (1983) acknowledge this point when they say that women's studies, as it presently exists, "has its own problems with heterosexism, classism and racism in its predominantly White programs—all inherited from patriarchal culture" (p. 5). Ricardo's study of Hispanics, for example, emphasized the male Hispanic experience; most likely he was not even aware of this. And Kathy's study of feminism centered around the concerns of White, middle-class females. While not intending to exclude others, each of these teachers prioritized the concerns of one group, and in so doing, implicitly accepted other existing biases.

Giles (1974) has identified several weaknesses of Single-Group Studies programs in the public schools. Referring to Black studies programs, he notes that they are taught only in schools that have a significant percentage of Black students. Moreover, guides developed by school districts were not being used because, the teachers complained, they were not useful in dealing with certain types of learned attitudes, nor did the guides stress or emphasize what the students or community defined as Black studies. In other words, topics or concepts for study identified by the students or community may not be included or may be only partially included.

Another weakness of Single-Group Studies is its limited scope. Unlike the next two approaches, Multicultural Education and Education that is Multicultural and Social Reconstructionist, it does not attempt to change the total school environment, but focuses more on curriculum revision. Although certain Single-Group Studies educators might extend their reform efforts beyond the curriculum to include the process of instruction, relationships with the community, and so forth, the main element of the school experience that is changed is the curriculum.

There is often confusion among teachers as to when they are really using a Single-Group Studies approach. We have observed teachers who believed they were using this approach when they taught a 2- or 3-week unit, for example, on Asian-Americans, this being their main substantive attempt to teach about a group other than Whites for the entire school year. Advocates of Single-Group Studies would tell such teachers that they are not doing Single-Group Studies, but what we described in the first chapter as "business as usual." Single-Group Studies is an in-depth, comprehensive study of a group. Superficial lessons about groups do not really meet the goals and objectives of Single-Group Studies and may only promote stereotyping. Furthermore, they leave the rest of the teacher's teaching still upper-middle-class White male studies, or "business as usual." However, if such teachers taught the unit on Asian-Americans and also taught similar units on other ethnic groups, class groups, or women, then advocates of the approach would probably argue that the teacher had Single-Group Studies as part of his or her curriculum, if for no other reason than that the teacher was at least reducing White male studies to one group that is receiving attention comparable to that given other groups. "Time on task," a phrase becoming very familiar to teachers, is an important aspect of teaching any of these approaches to multicultural education.

You probably have noticed that we have said nothing about the disabled during this entire chapter, and you may be wondering why. The reason is that the study of the disabled within a Single-Group Studies framework is virtually nonexistent. It *should* exist, but it does not. You may be feeling puzzled, perhaps recalling a unit of study on the blind or a university course on exceptional children. In all probability, however, these could not truly be called Single-Group Studies, primarily because they were not designed by disabled people. Most studies of the disabled are designed by people not considered disabled, and they tend to emphasize a deficit perspective. They focus on the group's problem or deficit area (such as blindness or physical disability), on the causes of the problem, and on how to remediate it.

A true Single-Group Studies approach to the handicapped would start with the perspective that the group is not deficient, although in some respects distinctive. Such a study would examine positive contributions and life experiences of group members, the history of how the group has been treated, and issues that the group presently faces in dealing with nongroup members. For example, a Single-Group Studies program on deaf and hearing-impaired people would include a study of Amslan and other language systems; deaf cultural forms, such as the theater; deaf scholars, scientists, and artists; how the hearing world historically has stereotyped, isolated, and oppressed deaf people; and issues of concern today for the deaf and hard of hearing. Such a program has, in fact, been recently advocated by Reagan (1985), who makes the following point:

Educators involved with bilingual education, minority students, and multicultural education . . . have generally tended to ignore the deaf, save in discussions about blacks, Latinos, and so forth, who happen also to be deaf. The notion that being deaf in and of itself might have important cultural and linguistic implications appears to have been overlooked. (p. 277)

One may find isolated bits and pieces of such study in schools and institutions of higher education populated by large numbers of disabled people, but these studies do not exist in a comprehensive form, as do women's studies or Asian-American studies, for example.

TABLE 4–1 *Single-Group Studies*

Societal goals:	Promote social structural equality for and immediate recognition of the identified group
School goals:	Promote willingness and knowledge among students to work toward social change that would benefit the identified group
Target students:	Everyone
Practices:	
Curriculum	Teach units or courses about the culture of a group, how the group has been victimized, current social issues facing the group—from the perspective of that group
Instruction	Build on students' learning style, especially the learning style of that group
Other aspects of classroom	Use decorations reflecting culture and classroom contributions of the group; have representatives of the group involved in class activities, (e.g., appearing as guest speakers)
Other school-wide concerns	Employ faculty who are members of group being studied

REFERENCES

Afro-American Studies Department Curriculum. (1970). Pamphlet. Madison, WI: University of Wisconsin–Madison, Dept. of Afro-American Studies.

Ahlum, C., & Fralley, J. (1976). *High school feminist studies.* Old Westbury, NY: Feminist Press.

Banks, J. A. (1973). Teaching black studies for social change. In J. A. Banks (Ed.), *Teaching ethnic studies* (pp. 149–179). Washington, DC: National Council for the Social Studies.

Banks, J. A. (1979). *Teaching strategies for ethnic studies* (2nd ed.). Boston: Allyn and Bacon.

Banks, J. A. (1981). *Multiethnic education: Theory and practice.* Boston: Allyn and Bacon.

Boneparth, E. (1978). Evaluating women's studies: Academic theory and practice. In K. O. Blumhagen & W. D. Johnson (Eds.), *Women's Studies* (pp. 21–30). Westport, CT: Greenwood Press.

Bowles, G., & Klein, R. D. (1983). Introduction: Theories of women's studies and the autonomy/integration debate. In G. Bowles & R. D. Klein (Eds.), *Theories of women's studies* (pp. 1–26). London: Routledge & Kegan Paul.

Bowles, S., & Gintis, H. (1976). *Schooling in capitalist America.* New York: Basic Books.

Butler, J. E. (1981). *Black studies: Pedagogy and revolution.* Lanham, MD: University Press of America.

Cortada, R. E. (1974). *Black studies.* Lexington, MA: Xerox College Publishing.

Cubberley, E. P. (1909). *Changing conceptions of education.* Boston: Houghton Mifflin.

Douty, A. (1950). *American workers' education in action.* Paris: Economic Cooperation Administration, Mimeographed paper. Cited in R. Dwyer (1977), Workers' education, labor education, labor studies: An historical delineation. *Review of Educational Research, 47,* 179–207.

Dupris, J. C. (1981). The national impact of multicultural education: A renaissance of Native American Indian culture through tribal self-determination and Indian control of Indian education. In *Proceedings of the Eighth Annual International Bilingual Bicultural Conference,* (pp. 69–78). Roslyn, VA: InterAmerica Research Associates.

Dwyer, R. (1977). Workers' education, labor education, labor studies: An historical delineation. *Review of Educational Research, 47,* 179–207.

Freire, P. (1970). *Pedagogy of the oppressed.* New York: The Seaburg Press.

Gaardner, A. B. (1976). Bilingual education: Central questions and concerns. In F. Cordasco (Ed.), *Bilingual schooling in the United States* (pp. 150–158). New York: McGraw-Hill.

Garcia, R. L. (1982). *Teaching in a pluralistic society.* New York: Harper & Row.

Giles, R. H., Jr. (1974). *Black studies programs in public schools.* New York: Praeger.

Guerra, M. H. (1973). Bilingual and bicultural education. In M. D. Stent, W. R. Hazard, & H. N. Rivlin (Eds.), *Cultural pluralism in education* (pp. 27–34). New York: Appleton-Century-Crofts.

Hazard, W. R., & Stent, M.D. (1973). Cultural pluralism and schooling: Some preliminary observations. In M. D. Stent, W. R. Hazard, & H. N. Rivlin (Eds.), *Cultural pluralism in education* (pp. 13–26). New York: Appleton-Century-Crofts.

Kjolseth, R. (1976). Bilingual education programs in the United States: For assimilation or pluralism? In F. Cordasco (Ed.), *Bilingual schooling in the United States* (pp. 122–140). New York: McGraw-Hill.

Mackey, W. F., & Beebe, V. N. (1977). *Bilingual schools for a bicultural community.* Rowley, MA: Newbury House Publishers.

Nakanishi, D. T., & Leong, R. (1978). Toward the second decade, a national survey of Asian American studies programs. *Amerasia Journal, 5,* 1–2.

National Schools Public Relations Association. (1970). *Black studies in schools.* Special report. Washington, DC: National Schools Public Relations Association.

Newton, J. H. (1939). *Education for democracy in our time.* New York: McGraw-Hill.

Norman, R. (1975). The neutral teacher? In S. C. Brown (Ed.), *Philosophers discuss education* (pp. 172–187). Totowa, NJ: Rowman & Littlefield.

Pentony, D.V.E. (1971). The case for black studies. In J. E. Blassingame (Ed.), *New perspectives on black studies* (pp. 60–72). Urbana: University of Illinois Press.

Ramirez, M., & Castaneda, A. (1976). *Cultural democracy, bicognitive development, and education.* New York: Academic Press.

Reagan, T. (1985). The deaf as a linguistic minority: Educational considerations. *Harvard Educational Review, 55,* 265–277.

Rutenberg, T. (1983). Learning women's studies. In G. Bowles & R. D. Klein (Eds.), *Theories of women's studies* (pp. 72–78). London: Routledge & Kegan Paul.

Schramm, S. S. (1978). Women's studies: Its focus, idea, power, and promise. In K. O. Blumhagen & W. D. Johnson (Eds.), *Women's studies* (pp. 3–12). Westport, CT: Greenwood Press.

Spender, D. (1981). Education: The patriarchal paradigm and the response to feminism. In D. Spender (Ed.), *Men's studies modified: The impact of feminism on the academic disciplines* (pp. 155–173). New York: Pergamon Press.

Spring, J. (1973). Education as a form of social control. In C. Karier, P. Violas, & J. Spring (Eds.), *Roots of Crisis: American education in the twentieth century.* Chicago: Rand McNally.

Suzuki, B. H. (1980). *An Asian-American perspective on multicultural education: Implications for practice and policy.* Paper presented at the Second Annual Conference of the National Association for Asian and Pacific American Education, Washington, DC.

Trueba, E. T. (1976). Issues and problems in bilingual bicultural education today. *Journal for the National Association of Bilingual Education, 1*, 11–19.

Tyack, D. (1966) Forming the national character. *Harvard Educational Review, 36*, 29–41.

Westkott, M. (1983). Women's studies as a strategy for change: Between criticism and vision. In G. Bowles & R. D. Klein (Eds.), *Theories of women's studies* (pp. 210–218). London: Routledge & Kegan Paul.

CHAPTER 5

Multicultural Education

How can we have a Multicultural Education approach to multicultural education? We realize that this may be a bit confusing, so allow us to explain. *Multicultural education* is the popular term educators increasingly use to describe education policies and practices that recognize, accept, and affirm human differences and similarities related to gender, race, handicap, and class. Because of the popularity of the term and what it advocates, many educators who use other approaches (e.g., Teaching the Exceptional and the Culturally Different) say that they are doing multicultural education. Thus, it is important to clarify what most advocates of multicultural education mean when they use the term.

GOALS

Based on a review of the literature on multicultural education, Gollnick (1980) has described it as having five goals:

1. Promoting the strength and value of cultural diversity
2. Promoting human rights and respect for those who are different from oneself
3. Promoting alternative life choices for people

4. Promoting social justice and equal opportunity for all people

5. Promoting equity in the distribution of power among groups

Although different educators emphasize and highlight one or two goals more than the others, most who advocate this approach embrace all five.

At present, many people who use this approach deal only with race (Banks, 1981, distinguishes in this regard between multicultural and multiethnic education) or only with gender (often termed *sex equity* or *nonsexist education*). Increasingly, those interested in mainstreaming are beginning to apply this approach to handicap; and those interested primarily in social class tend not to adopt this approach for reasons we will explain later. But even though different terms may be used when educators discuss different groups, they advocate similar goals for their group, draw on much the same theories for achieving those goals, and recommend similar or identical practices in schools. Recognizing this, some educators explicitly give equal attention to multiple groups (Gollnick & Chinn, 1986), and others who focus on one form of diversity at least acknowledge other forms (Stockard et al., 1980). This chapter will discuss race, gender, and disability, since these can be integrated and educators are increasingly doing so.

The Multicultural Education approach began in the late 1960s and grew energetically during the 1970s. As Gay (1983) has described, three forces converged during the mid-1960s and gave birth to this approach: The civil rights movement matured, school textbooks were critically analyzed, and assumptions underlying the deficiency orientation (described in chapter 2) were reassessed. The civil rights movement began as a passive, nonviolent way of changing laws that oppressed specific racial groups; by the late 1960s, it had become an energetic movement joining all Americans of color and directed toward self-determination and power. One institution that was severely criticized was the schools: As schools were desegregated, it became apparent that curricula were written solely or primarily about Whites. It also became apparent that many teachers knew little about minority students and treated cultural differences as deficiencies needing to be remediated. As Gay describes, "The student activists, abetted by the efforts of textbook analysts and by the new thinking about cultural differences, provided the stimulus for the first multiethnic education programs" (p. 561).

During the 1970s, these early ideas about school reform were tried and developed in many classrooms. Educators received encouragement and support from a variety of sources. Ethnic groups all around the United States developed expression of their heritage and identity. The women's movement got well under way. Court cases and federal legislation supported diversity, such as the *Lau* decision supporting bilingual education, the Ethnic Heritage Act funding multiethnic curriculum development, and the adoption by many states of goal statements supporting teaching for cultural pluralism. These kinds of supports have diminished in the 1980s, but the approach has continued to develop conceptually, and its popularity has continued to grow.

IDEOLOGY AND MULTICULTURAL EDUCATION

We distinguish in this chapter between theory and ideology because this approach, more than the others, has experienced a mixing of the two that can be confusing. Essentially, ideology prescribes what ought to be, whereas theory describes how social systems or human psychology actually works. Is equal opportunity a theory or an ideology? What about cultural pluralism? These are terms frequently employed by advocates of this approach. To understand and evaluate more clearly what advocates mean, we have divided our discussion into ideology first and then theory.

Newman (1973) describes an ideology as prescribing what "ought to be," and Mannheim (1956) says that ideologies are "those complexities of ideas which tend to generate activities toward changes in the prevailing order" (p. xxi). The large discrepancy between what "ought to be" and the current prevailing order in society encourages proponents of the Multicultural Education approach to argue for it in school policies and practices.

Some of the earlier writings in multicultural education were based on the belief and knowledge that there is no one model American (Hunter, 1974); that the United States is a pluralistic nation, and its racial and cultural diversity needs to be recognized and prized (Stent, Hazard, & Rivlin, 1973); that women's history and point of view have been systematically ignored and omitted from the schools (Spender, 1982); and that poor people and handicapped people have been rendered invisible. Advocates saw a need to correct the beliefs and ideas espoused by the prevailing order and to make school policies and practices affirm American diversity.

The vision of what ought to be was a major substance that fed the intellectual and emotional activities of the early advocates. The ideology of Multicultural Education is one of social change—not simply integrating those who have been left out into society, but changing the very fabric of that society. This ideology has two main components:

cultural pluralism and equal opportunity. These are noted as both societal goals and school goals in Table 5–1 (see p. 168) and are described below.

Cultural Pluralism

Advocates of Multicultural Education often compare U.S. society to a tossed salad or a patchwork quilt. Both metaphors depict an array of materials and objects of various sizes, shapes, and colors. Each is independent of the others, and each is unique, and they therefore form a collective total that is distinguished by its difference and diversity. There are a number of formal definitions of cultural pluralism in the education literature. Although they vary, all suggest that cultural pluralism includes maintenance of diversity, respect for differences, and the right to participate actively in all aspects of society without having to give up one's unique identity.

The National Coalition for Cultural Pluralism (1973) describes the concept as

> a state of equal co-existence in a mutually supportive relationship within the boundaries or framework of one nation of people of diverse cultures with significantly different patterns of beliefs, behavior, color, and in many cases with different languages. To achieve cultural pluralism, there must be unity with diversity. Each person must be aware of and secure in his [her] own identity, and be willing to extend to others the same respect and rights that he [she] expects to enjoy himself [herself]. (p. 14)

Explicit in these definitions of cultural pluralism is reference to race and ethnicity. Recently, advocates of the Multicultural Education approach have also begun arguing that since gender and class are also very important determinants of what happens, how it happens, and why it happens in society, these status attributes must also be considered in conceptualizing pluralism.

Applying cultural pluralism to gender, advocates desire a society where gender does not even hint at a particular sex role image and where females are evaluated not in comparison to males but to best practices. For example, many women who enter into the corporate structure emulate the performance style of the successful male, "making it in the man's world" instead of deciding what works in the "world of work" and basing their style on that. Advocates contend that both males and females should have equal opportunity for the occupation or profession of their choice and that society's socializing practices for the young should be nonsexist.

Androgyny provides one model of nonsexist choice making. As Ferguson (1977) explains:

> An androgynous person would combine some of each of the character-istic traits, skills, and interests that we now associate with stereotypes of masculinity and femininity. . . . He or she would have the desire and the ability to do socially meaningful productive activity (work), as well as the desire and ability to be autonomous and to relate lovingly to other human beings. (pp. 45–46)

This means opening up choices of roles and personality traits to *both* sexes. As Tavris and Wade (1984) observe:

> When people speak of liberating women and ending discrimination, they are generally thinking of how to get women out of the home and into the work force; they are generally not thinking of how to get men to do more at home. (p. 352)

Cultural pluralism related to gender means that males, as well as fe-males, should have a gender-free repertoire of roles and styles to choose from.

Many advocates of this approach agree on the need to live in a society where poverty, as well as racism, does not exist. Their vision of society would expunge the need for food stamps and the existence of substandard housing would ensure the provision of suitable clothing for every individual. However, descriptions of how to make this vision become a reality present a frontal attack on racism and only an indirect attack on class. It is as if advocates of this approach view race and class as overlapping factors that are mostly one and the same.

Equal Opportunity

Equal opportunity is the other main pillar of the ideology of multicul-tural education. Equal opportunity as a legal right in education was established in 1954 in *Brown v. Board of Education*. In that decision, Chief Justice Warren wrote:

> In these days it is doubtful that any child may reasonably be expected to succeed in life if he [or she] is denied the opportunity of an educa-tion. Such an opportunity, where the state has undertaken it, is a right which must be made available to all on equal terms.

Since that decision, exactly what school practices constitute equal op-portunity has been an issue of considerable debate, and as Gee and

Sperry (1978) put it, "equal educational opportunity may mean all things to all people" (p. E-9).

The "business as usual" position is that since it is illegal to deny students access to education on the basis of race, sex, or handicap, schools that comply with equal opportunity laws and court decisions such as Title IX, PL 94-142, and *Lau v. Nichols* are providing equal opportunity. According to O'Neill (1977):

> On this view, once the rules governing admissions to places of education, appointments to jobs and promotions are fair, a society is an equal-opportunity society. . . . If women are not barred from engineering school on account of their sex, then they have equal opportunity to become engineers—and the fact that very few do so cannot be attributed to any inequality of opportunity. (p. 179)

Advocates of the Multicultural Education approach do not see it as sufficient simply to remove legal barriers to access and participation in schooling. So long as groups do not gain equal outcomes from social institutions, those institutions are not providing equal opportunity. So long as White, middle-class children succeed and leave school with higher achievement scores than other children, so long as disproportionate numbers of boys enter mathematics and science fields and girls enter human service or domestic work after schooling, so long as children leave school seeing White male contributions as most important, schools have not provided equal opportunity. O'Neill (1977) argues that "an equal-opportunity society on the substantive view is one in which the success rates of all major social groups are the same" (pp. 181–182).

Plenty has been written from a Multicultural Education perspective about what equal educational opportunity should mean in schools as it relates to race, culture, language, gender, and handicap. We will summarize the main ideas.

Advocates of equal educational opportunity related to gender wish to promote for members of both sexes an equal opportunity to choose occupational roles and life-styles, to express feelings and interests, and to be rewarded for work. Gough (1976) voices these goals in raising questions about the extent to which an education program is nonsexist:

> Does it give girls the freedom to have "doctor" and "professor" in their matrix of career choices along with "truck driver," and "telephone lineperson," or whatever else suits their interests and talents? Does it make boys comfortable with expressing gentleness, grief, delight in small children, dislike of athletics? (p. 33)

In other words, the whole spectrum of roles, careers, emotions, and behavioral patterns should be equally available to male and female alike, without regard to gender.

Schools should not only encourage children to make choices free of sex role conditioning; schools should themselves reflect equal opportunity. In chapter 1, we described ways in which they often do not. As Stockard et al. (1980) point out;

> In the elementary school, the principal is probably a man and the first-grade teacher a woman. . . . Men often teach science, social studies, and math; women more often teach English and foreign languages. . . . Where allowed to take elective classes, girls and boys usually do not choose the same ones. . . . Principals are usually men, and superintendents and assistant superintendents are almost certainly men. . . . Among the nonprofessionals, virtually all members of the clerical and secretarial staff are women; men are usually employed as custodians. (pp. 3–5)

Advocates of equal educational opportunity related to handicap generally wish to see all handicapped children educated in the least restrictive environment, and they particularly wish to see the regular classroom accommodate differences better than it usually does. Sarason and Doris (1979) argue that "every effort should be made to allow a handicapped child to be an integral member of his [her] peer-age group, and only when such membership is not possible should one employ the least restrictive alternative" (p. 24). Many would argue that schools and classrooms that do not provide for differences in learning style, rate, interest, and so forth, *make* children handicapped by defining them as deviant. Ysseldyke, Thurlow, Graden, Wesson, and Algozzine (1983) have found that the main determinant of whether a child is classified as handicapped is whether a regular education teacher was bothered by the child enough to refer him or her for psychoeducational evaluation:

> From 3% to 6% of the school-age population is referred each year for psychoeducational evaluation. Of those referred, 92% are tested. Of those tested, 73% are declared eligible for special educational services. . . . When we investigated the specific determinants of referral, we found that teachers tend to refer students who bother them. (p. 80)

Thus, equal educational opportunity should mean that regular classrooms accommodate a wide enough spectrum of human diversity that only those children who would be seen as handicapped in virtually any social setting (e.g., children who are blind or severely retarded) would be seen as exceptional in school. Such classrooms would prevent large numbers of children from ever being labeled as handicapped and would welcome those who truly are handicapped for at least a portion of their school day.

Advocates of equal educational opportunity related to race, culture, and language make arguments very similar to those we have already discussed. The central idea is that children should have an equal chance to achieve in school, choose and strive for a personally fulfilling future, and develop self-respect, regardless of home culture or language. Sizemore (1979) describes some very large barriers that schools erect for children of color:

> Incredibly, the curriculum of a diverse population is based on the characteristics, life experiences, and culture of one minority: the Anglo-Saxon affluent Protestant group. Characteristically, the monolingual, monocultural and unidimensional curriculum which created cell block classrooms with single age groupings evolved. (p. 341)

Gay (1979) argues that this situation often leads children of color to "experience alienation and isolation in American schools" (p. 327). To provide equal opportunity for children of all American cultural backgrounds, Sizemore (1979) proposes that the classroom should be "multilingual, multicultural, multimodal, and multidimensional in its focus" (p. 348). Such classrooms would support curriculum content drawn from a variety of cultural backgrounds, the development of more than one language, varied instructional styles and systems for grouping students, and evaluative measures that respect differences in cultural background. As Gay points out:

> Children who are secure in their identity, feel good about themselves, and are excited about what is happening in the classroom, are more likely to engage eagerly in learning activities and achieve higher levels of academic performance than those who find the classroom hostile, unfriendly, insensitive, and perpetually unfamiliar. (p. 327)

THEORY AND MULTICULTURAL EDUCATION

If advocates of Multicultural Education champion equal opportunity, choice, and cultural pluralism, what theoretical propositions inform us how this vision can be realized and how schools can help realize it? First, let us define what we mean by theoretical propositions. Writing about theories of cultural pluralism, Newman (1973) says that theory explains "how a phenomenon has arrived historically, how it works or what its meaning is empirically, and, under given circumstances, what one may expect in the future" (p. 50). Writing about theories of gender relations, Tavris and Wade (1984) explain that theory "attempts to account for sex differences"—why they exist and the circumstances under which relationships between men and women change (p. 119).

Advocates of Multicultural Education as it relates to race and ethnicity have written much more about ideology than about theory— more about what ought to be than about why things are as they are and under what conditions things change in the desired direction. However, supporting theories from the fields of sociology and anthropology are usually adopted by educators. Advocates of a Multicultural Education approach to gender, on the other hand, have written more about the theory of how sex roles are learned than about ideology. The two main kinds of theories that support the ideology of Multicultural Education are cultural pluralism theories and cultural transmission theories.

Cultural Pluralism

William Newman (1973) has provided a comprehensive discussion of theories of cultural pluralism and their use by sociologists. We will briefly summarize four main theories and show their relevance to the Multicultural Education approach.

The first theory is assimilation. Newman expresses it with "the formula $A + B + C = A$, where A, B, and C represent different social groups and A represents the dominant group" (p. 53). The theory holds that when minority cultural groups come into contact with a majority cultural group, over time the values and life-styles of the minority groups are replaced by those of the majority group. Newman shows that while some sociological studies support this theory (such as studies of second-generation immigrants), other studies do not (such as studies of third-generation immigrants or of the ethnic resurgency of the 1960s and 1970s). In other words, some degree of cultural assimilation often occurs, but often it is limited and even reverses. Cultural assimilation is not a rule of American life.

According to Multicultural Education advocates, much of schooling has been based on, and has sought to facilitate, the faulty theory of assimilation. "Business as usual" has assumed that the majority culture not only should prevail, but will prevail. It has sought to promote, for example, one language and one dialect, one version of history, one literary tradition, one view of the relationship between people and nature, and so forth. In so doing, "business as usual" has often contradicted reality. For example, for many years, schools, especially in the Southwest, had an English-only policy in an effort to erase the Spanish language and Mexican culture. But rather than dropping Spanish, thousands of children quit (and often were forced out of) school. Spanish has continued to be spoken throughout the Southwest. During the 1970s, bilingual education was increasingly implemented, although there have been heated debates about whether its purpose is primarily to teach English or to teach both languages (Cummins, 1981a, 1986; Fillmore & Valadez, 1985; Krashen, 1981; Skutnabb-Kangas, 1981; Trueba, 1976). In an ethnography of a Chinese-English bilingual program, Guthrie (1985) shows that regardless of school policy, there is both a need and a desire to maintain the Chinese language within the Chinese-American community; assimilationist school practices that deny this reality are misinformed and often place children and teachers in the middle.

Children are often the victims of assimilationist school policies, particularly when "business as usual" teaches children that the home culture is inferior or un-American, when it disrupts a child's ability to function in his or her own community, or when it alienates children and causes them to reject the school. Assimilationist policies can drive a wedge between the child and his or her family, which can interfere with normal socialization. This is particularly a problem when teachers tell language-minority students to refrain from speaking their native language in the home in order to practice English; not only does this impair communication development, but it weakens the family's power to teach the child their values and beliefs. Assimilationist school policies are also harmful when they perpetuate the mistaken idea in the minds of majority-group children that their home culture is the only true American culture and that everyone else wants to or should think, behave, and speak like they do.

Sometimes, children recognize that the school version of reality is incorrect. For example, one of the authors was recently told of an incident in an elementary school. The children were completing some reading exercises that contained content describing a world with definite sex roles. One of the questions read:

> Which of the following gifts would a girl *not* receive at a birthday party?
>   a. A doll
>   b. a toy gun
>   c. a makeup kit
>   d. a tea set

The students replied that the answer that the test developers wanted was "a toy gun" but that this answer was not really true. Unfortunately, children usually do not see through school knowledge that conflicts with what they know. In such cases, they may doubt what they learned at home, try to reconcile conflicting views of reality, or reject the school because the teachers seem stupid.

The second theory Newman (1973) describes is amalgamation, which he represents with the formula $A + B + C = D$, where "D represents an amalgam, a synthesis of these groups into a distinct new group" (p. 63). Newman points out that while many people may have articulated this as the ideal of the melting pot, it describes very little of intergroup relations. One can point to infrequent examples of amalgamation, such as Mexican culture being an amalgam of Spanish and Indian cultures, but such examples are the exception. For cultures to blend, the groups should be of roughly equal status and the people should desire to mix. In the United States, ethnic groups are definitely not all of the same status. Because it has so little relevance for group life in America, amalgamation has little or no relevance to school policy.

The third theory Newman describes is classical cultural pluralism, "expressed in the formula $A + B + C = A + B + C$, where A, B, and C represent different social groups that, over time, maintain their own unique identities" (p. 67). Newman argues that this theory does not explain all of ethnic life in America, but it explains enough that it needs to be taken seriously. Most American cities and many suburban areas contain distinct ethnic enclaves that do not disappear over time. In fact, some become stronger, and some ethnic and religious communities maintain themselves in spite of dispersed membership. For example, a Jewish family that moves to North Dakota immediately joins the only local synagogue and develops ties with the few other Jewish families in town. And the Black community maintains some of its solidarity and cultural distinctiveness, in spite of dispersed membership, by developing Black radio stations, magazines, and newspapers.

Yet, as Newman points out, this theory is inadequate. It fails to account for the development of a shared American culture, for the cultural changes that groups experience over time, and for the varied experiences of different cultural groups. A more accurate theory is modified cultural pluralism: $A + B + C = A_1 + B_1 + C_1$. As Newman illustrates, "An Italian in Italy is different from an Italian-American. . . . A black African is different from an Afro-American" (p. 79). Modified cultural pluralism holds that different ethnic, religious, and racial groups will assimilate into the dominant group to some extent, but that this will vary with the group, and many groups will continue to retain unique cultural characteristics. As a description of group life in America, this theory is more accurate than the preceding three.

Modified cultural pluralism is one of the theories that supports the Multicultural Education approach. The approach advocates that, at the very least, schools should represent cultural pluralism as it actually exists in America. To the extent that there is a shared culture, this should be recognized and taught; but equally important, the cultural diversity that actually exists should also be recognized and taught to all Americans. For example, there is no single American literary tradition, nor has there ever been. Schools that teach that good literature is what White men have written and that White men have been the only authors of good literature are not teaching reality. White male authors may feel that their work is superior to Black female writers, for instance, but Black women tend not to share their perspective (Hull, Scott, & Smith, 1982). Young Americans need to learn diverse perspectives about what constitutes good literature, as well as learning about the literature produced by diverse American literary traditions. This will not exacerbate divisiveness among cultural groups, as critics of Multicultural Education often argue; on the other hand, it may improve relationships by fostering dialogue among groups that will continue to exist regardless of school policies and practices.

This last point is worth emphasizing. Modified cultural pluralism holds that some cultural diversity will continue to exist in a nation the size of the United States, despite the attempts of the dominant group to assimilate people. Forced assimilation will only antagonize groups. If some degree of cultural diversity is natural, then it makes sense that schools embrace it rather than pretending that it is not there or that it is harmful to the country.

You have probably noticed that this discussion has said little about disability or gender. Cultural pluralism theory has some applicability to disability in that America does contain subcultures of deaf, blind, and physically impaired people. Like ethnic groups, these groups share a common American culture, but also maintain some group cohesion and distinctive cultural characteristics, although necessity often plays a larger role than choice in the development of disability cultural groups. But the implications for Multicultural Education are similar. For example, wheelchair sports are highly developed and command fairly large participation. Physical education programs that fail even to alert young people to the existence of wheelchair sports are perpetuating a limited conception of American athletics.

When it comes to gender, cultural pluralism theory has less relevance. One can argue that males and females have distinct cultures; for example, compare the contents of *Ladies Home Journal* with that of *Gentleman's Quarterly*. But feminist advocates of the Multicultural Education approach seek to reduce rather than preserve gender cultural differences, not by assimilating females into the male world, but rather by upholding alternative interests and life-styles that can be chosen by individuals without regard to gender. To provide a theoretical basis for this, we turn to theories of how culture and roles are learned.

Cultural Transmission and Social Learning Theories

The ideology of Multicultural Education highlights cultural diversity and awareness and knowledge about diverse alternatives. It does not advocate that the world is fine as it is and that children should learn about more of it. Rather, it is borne of a concern that society as it exists is unfair and detrimental to many people. Society does not afford equal opportunity to all. Furthermore, people are expected to conform to restricted definitions of what is considered "normal" if they want to succeed. For example, people of all ethnic backgrounds are often expected to display the behavioral and linguistic style of White, middle-class Americans before they will be taken seriously. Women who do not adhere to expected sex roles are labeled aggressive or mannish, while men who do not conform to the he-man image are often viewed as effeminate or sissy. Multicultural Education seeks to have all American children learn knowledge, values, and behavioral patterns that support cultural diversity, flexibility, and choice.

Theories of cultural transmission, social learning, and modeling provide guidance by alerting teachers to how children normally acquire society's values and beliefs. Teachers who want their students to learn values and beliefs for a multicultural society will need to change the content of what is usually transmitted to make it congruent with the ideology of Multicultural Education.

Cultural transmission theory was developed in the field of anthropology, and social learning and modeling theory in the field of psychology. We will first explain how these theories are similar, then discuss their contribution to Multicultural Education.

To anthropologists, cultural transmission refers to the wide variety of ways members of a cultural group transmit their culture to the younger generation. Although some of this transmission takes place in the school, much also takes place in the home, church, and neighborhood.

Social learning theory and modeling theory (used considerably by scholars of sex role socialization) describe principles by which individuals learn particular behavioral patterns. In chapter 3 we described Bandura and Walters's (1963) theory of prejudice formation; their work in social learning theory also has relevance here. Social learning theorists focus on the consequences that follow behavior patterns, and modeling theorists focus on the process of imitating role models. Social learning theory as articulated by Bandura and Walters argues that children learn alternative behavior patterns by observing adults, then learn when to imitate this behavior through reinforcement. For example, girls learn indirect and nonaggressive speech patterns by listening to older females speak; they learn to use such speech patterns themselves when others react favorably to them when they have used such patterns. Sex role theorists also usually discuss cognitive development theory, which we presented in chapter 3; it describes the mental process of constructing stereotypes (Tavris & Wade, 1984). All these theories argue that children are strongly molded and shaped by their environments and that the values, beliefs, and behavioral patterns that young people develop result from the constant press of their social environment.

One implication of these theories is that children learn through a complex variety of messages. Often, when we think of teaching, we think of telling; both anthropologists and psychologists inform us that this is a great oversimplification. For example, Tavris and Wade (1984) describe a host of sources of information about sex roles, including how parents treat each sex, how teachers treat each sex in the classroom, toys given to each sex, messages in children's books, messages in television, sexism in language (e.g., "use of men or mankind to refer to humanity," p. 233), and sex-different styles of speech. Thus, a teacher might tell children that males and females are equal, yet teach children that they are different and that males are more important in a variety of unconscious ways.

As another example, Spindler (1974) describes the process of cultural transmission in eight very different societies. His main point is that although the content and many of the particulars of the transmitting process differ from one society to the next, the general process is similar:

> If a child is told, sees demonstrated, casually observes, imitates, experiments and is corrected, acts appropriately and is rewarded, corrected, and . . . is given an extra boost in learning by dramatized announcements of status-role change, all within a consistent framework of belief and value, he or she cannot help but learn, and learn what adult cultural transmitters want him or her to learn. (p. 300)

What this means for the teacher is that if one wants children to learn to value America's cultural diversity and to value nonsexist options, it is not enough simply to tell children that these should be valued. The whole environment of the school must be teaching this. Consider, for example, a music class in which most of the music the children are taught was written by White men and is embedded within the classical European tradition. The teacher may never say a word about which groups write the best music, but the fact that one music tradition receives the most emphasis teaches children which music is "best." If one wanted children to value diverse music traditions, one would model this by teaching and giving roughly equal emphasis to music written by members of diverse groups.

A second implication of cultural transmission theory has to do with the nature of culture in complex societies. Culture consists of shared understandings and beliefs, but not everyone in society shares identical knowledge and beliefs. Goodenough (1976) points out that "the different ways of doing things family to family and village to village, all become noteworthy" (p. 4). Each society consists of many subsocieties. A child does not simply learn a single, homogeneous American culture. Rather, as Goodenough argues:

> The process of learning a society's culture, or macro-culture, as I would call it, is one of learning a number of different or partially different micro-cultures and their sub-cultural variants, and how to discern the situations in which they are appropriate and the kinds of others to whom to attribute them. (p. 5)

This insight has relevance for the ideal of equal opportunity. For equal opportunity to exist, members of diverse subgroups need to learn the cultures appropriate to functioning successfully in various contexts. It is imperative for members of subordinate cultural groups to learn to function successfully in higher-status groups. For example, children whose home language or dialect is not standard English need to develop competence in standard English, as well as learning which situations require them to use it. Schools that fail to teach members of subordinate groups the language, behavioral patterns, and knowledge of the dominant cultural group are not providing the means for more equal opportunities in society.

But it is also valuable to learn to function successfully in groups other than the dominant one. Banks (1981) points out that it is "very difficult for Anglo-Americans to learn to respond to nonWhites positively and sensitively if they are unaware of the perceptions of their culture that are held by other ethnic groups and of the ways in which the dominant culture evolved and attained the power to shape the United States in its image" (p. 99). To develop cultural sensitivity, Anglo-Americans need to learn the cultures of other American subgroups and should learn them well enough to be able to function appropriately within at least one or two other cultural contexts.

This means that to be successfully educated, it is not enough to learn only the dominant culture. This requires redefining success in schools and codifying cultural diversity into the measures we use to assess school success. For example, science from a multicultural perspective would include scientific theories of Native Americans in addition to those of the European tradition; thus, the successful student of science would have a working knowledge of more than one science tradition. The edge currently enjoyed by White, middle-class children, mastery of whose culture currently constitutes school success, would be shared with other groups.

One can also relate this idea to gender and handicap. Child care, for example, tends to be a female cultural domain, while automobile repair tends to be a male domain. It is not uncommon for men and women to have nonsexist intentions, but end up performing traditional sex roles simply because, in the course of growing up, the woman learned how to change diapers proficiently while the man mastered the fine art of tuning up an engine. Outside school, children often learn sex-specific domains of knowledge; to prepare both sexes for multiple roles, the school would need to make sure that it taught knowledge to both sexes that tends to be learned by only one sex.

With respect to disability, the concept of subsocieties implies that children not only learn to question stereotypes of disabled people, but also learn how to function in disability cultural groups. This could mean becoming proficient in sign language or in wheelchair basketball and learning the norms and perspectives shared by people who use these skills.

A third implication of cultural transmission theory was already stated in chapter 4 and will be briefly mentioned here. This is the concept of cultural compatibility. Educational anthropologists and psychologists have found it difficult for some children to learn what the teacher is trying to teach when the teaching style, communication style, cognitive schemata, or background experience of the teacher is different from that of the child. As anthropologist Solon Kimball (1974) emphasizes:

> New learnings always take place within the perceptive system of the individual being taught. Children from subcultural groupings other than those of the teacher face a difficult problem in adjusting, if they do, to the demands of the teacher and she [or he] in turn, to their ways of behaving and thinking. (p. 82)

A teacher implementing the Multicultural Education approach, like a teacher implementing the Teaching the Exceptional and the Culturally Different approach, would try to make the process as well as the content of learning as compatible as possible with that of the home culture. This means, for example, that Multicultural Education in rural Oregon would not be identical to Multicultural Education in inner-city Chicago, since each would reflect the styles of learning and experiential backgrounds of the children to maximize their ability to learn.

RECOMMENDED PRACTICES

The Multicultural Education approach seeks to reform the entire process of schooling for *all* children. Unlike the Teaching the Exceptional and Culturally Different approach, this approach is not just for certain groups of students. It is for everybody, and it seeks not only to integrate people into our existing society, but to improve society for all. Unlike the Human Relations approach, it does not stop with the improvement of attitudes, but seeks also to develop skills and a strong knowledge base that will support multiculturalism. Unlike the Single-Group Studies approach, it seeks to change more about schooling than the curriculum. We have organized our discussion of recommended practices around the following typical elements of schooling: curriculum, instruction, evaluation, home/community—school relationships, staffing, and extracurricular activities. Recommended Multicultural Education practices are summarized in Table 5–1.

Curriculum

Multicultural Education advocates argue that the curriculum should be reformed so that it regularly presents diverse perspectives, experiences, and contributions, particularly those that tend to be omitted or misrepresented when schools conduct "business as usual." Concepts should be selected and taught to represent diverse cultural groups and both sexes (Baker, 1983; Banks, 1981; Gay, 1975; Gollnick & Chinn, 1986; Grant, 1977; Sadker & Sadker, 1982). As Gay (1975) points out:

> Fragmented and isolated units, courses, and bits of information about ethnic groups interspersed sporadically into school curriculum and instructional programs will not do the job. Nor will additive approaches, wherein school curricula remain basically the same, and ethnic content becomes an appendage. (p. 176)

For example, if one is teaching poetry, one should select poetry written by members of a variety of groups. This not only teaches children that groups in addition to White wealthy men have written poetry; it also enriches the concept of poetry because it enables children to explore various poetic forms, as well as elements that are common to diverse poems. It is further recommended that the contributions and perspectives that a teacher selects depict each group as the group would depict itself and show the group as active and dynamic. This requires that the teacher learn about various groups and become sensitive to aspects of each group's culture that are important to that group. For example, teachers wishing to include Native Americans sometimes choose Sacajawea as a heroine to teach about; but from the Native American perspective, Sequoya would be a preferable historic figure. Sacajawea served White interests in leading Lewis and Clark west, while Sequoya served the interests of the Cherokee by developing an alphabet for encoding the Cherokee language.

A related recommendation is that curricular materials and all visual displays (such as posters) be free of race, gender, and handicap stereotypes and include members of all groups in a positive manner (Grant, 1977; Seaburg, Smith, & Gallaher, 1980). Materials today are improved over those published 2 decades ago in this regard, but teachers still need to examine them closely. For example, recent studies have found that Hispanic Americans, contemporary Native Americans, and Asian-Americans, and particularly the female members of these groups, are omitted or stereotyped; roles for males are still stereotypical, even though roles for females have been broadened (particularly those of White females); and interpretations of history reflect the interests of the wealthy (Anyon, 1979; Butterfield, Demos, Grant, Moy, & Perez, 1979; Grant & Grant, 1981).

Advocates of the Multicultural Education approach recommend that teachers make sure they are teaching *concepts* related to diverse groups, rather than fragments of information (Baker, 1983; Banks, 1981; Gay, 1975). Sometimes, teachers try to represent people of color and women by grafting bits and pieces onto traditional concepts. For example, Cortes (1973) points out that it is not enough to add a few Mexicans to U.S. history that is organized around the idea of manifest destiny and the westward flow of culture. From a Mexican perspective, the U.S. Southwest was gained through conquest, and culture has flowed northward as well as westward.

Diverse materials should be used to present diverse viewpoints. Students should become comfortable with the fact that often there is more than one perspective, and rather than believing only one version, they should learn to expect and seek out multiple versions.

Some advocates recommend that as much emphasis be placed on contemporary culture as on historic culture and that groups be represented as active, real, and dynamic (Gay, 1979). For example, when women are included in history, usually they are White women involved in the suffrage movement. This is only a small fraction of what could be learned about women in social studies. Black women, too, have always actively resisted oppression. Many became involved (both historically and today) in Black women's clubs working to improve social conditions; many have achieved outstanding accomplishments; and many others have been (and still are) brutally victimized (Giddings, 1985). Oversimplified bits of information can be misleading and lead to stereotyping.

All these recommendations should permeate the total curriculum. This means that *all* subject areas should be taught multiculturally all the time. As Foerster (1982) puts it, "Multicultural Education is an orientation which has its inception in the teacher's mind and permeates the entire curriculum . . . on a day-to-day basis" (p. 124).

The language in the curriculum and used by the teacher should be non-sexist. Gollnick, Sadker, and Sadker (1982) point out problems with using masculine nouns and pronouns, such as *caveman, forefathers,* and *he,* to refer to both sexes. When children hear these terms, they usually interpret them literally. When they hear the word *caveman,* they visualize a man. The teacher might protest that words such as *congressman* and *businessman* refer to man and woman alike, but to a child they do not. Not only do the words designate one sex, but real life often confirms this. Thus, girls who hear about congressmen and study mainly or only male members of Congress may never entertain the idea that they could one day serve in Congress themselves.

Advocates often recommend that multicultural curricula endorse bilingual education and a vision of a multilingual society. In an earlier chapter, we discussed approaches to bilingual education that are directed toward those who do not speak English. Bilingual education can also be provided to *all* students in a school. Trueba (1976) advocates that all Americans should become "capable of thinking and feeling in either of two cultural and linguistic systems independently, and of interacting effectively and appropriately with the two linguistic and cultural groups" (p. 14). One of the authors of this book was visiting a bilingual school in New York. He was sitting in the office when some Black students entered and addressed him in Spanish. They were surprised to realize that he (like most Americans) was limited to only one language. This example also illustrates how promoting bilingualism among minority students extends language learning from the once-privileged elite culture of the middle and upper classes to subordinant groups. Some people also recommend that sign language be recognized as a complete, legitimate language, since it is the fourth most commonly used language in the U.S., behind English, Spanish, and German.

Advocates of Multicultural Education, like those of Teaching-the-Culturally-Different, recommend that the curriculum relate to and draw on students' experiential background and the community, and that examples used to explain concepts be based on students' daily life experiences. The curriculum should "bring the community into the schools and. . .bring the school to the community" (Foerster, 1982, p. 125).

Finally, some educators address access to the curriculum, recommending that schools adopt policies to ensure accessibility for all groups. For example, Gollnick and Chinn (1986) recommend that "minority students, as well as white students, . . . make up the college preparatory and general education classes" (p. 277). Stockard et al. (1980) recommend working actively to avoid sex-segregated enrollment in vocational electives such as industrial arts and home economics and in academic courses such as upper-level mathemathics and science. Valverde (1977) points out that programs designed specifically for low-income and minority students, such as bilingual education, sometimes reduce these students' access to the rest of the curriculum by resegregating them within the school. To guard against these forms of segregation within schools, he suggests that schools "move to make the mainstream itself culturally diverse" (p. 200).

Instruction

If the Multicultural Education approach is to work and the curriculum is to be provocative and challenging, teachers will need to be guided by certain instructional principles that are directly connected to the nature and purpose of the multicultural curriculum. Rodgers (1975) tells us that "the instructional program is theoretically and structurally tied to the curriculum and the way in which it is implemented and that the materials and resources play a pivotal role in the implementation" (p. 284). These instructional principles that advocates of Multicultural Education endorse come from their vision of what a school should provide.

One principle is that the student is an innately curious individual, capable of learning complex material and performing at a high skill level. A second principle is that each student has his or her own unique learning style, and teachers should not only build on this when teaching, but also help students "discover their own particular style of learning" so that they can learn more effectively and efficiently (Kendall, 1983, p. 12).

A third principle is that teachers should draw on and make use of the conceptual schemes that students bring to school. For example, Hollins (1982), drawing on the work of Ausubel, argues that students come to school with good conceptual schemes. Rather than replacing these with new ones, the teacher should use and build on the students' own schemes. And since conceptual schemes are channeled through language, utilizing the students' native language helps develop the conceptual schemes that the children bring with them to school. Simply put, we need to start where the students are and use what they already know.

Having high and realistic expectations for all students is a fourth instructional principle of this approach. Bennett (1986) argues that high expectations are a necessary prerequisite for equal education: "If teachers are to provide equal opportunities for learning, their expectations for student success must be positive and equitable" (p. 67). And it is not only the teacher who needs to have high expectations for the students; students also need to have high expectations for themselves.

Fostering cooperation is a fifth principle. In chapter 3, on the Human Relations approach, we discussed the importance of instruction that teaches students to work cooperatively with others. For example, researchers like Cohen (1979) and Forehand and Ragosta (1976) have pointed to the positive effects that small-group cooperative learning can have on the attitudes of students who come from different backgrounds. Bennett (1986), after reviewing research on cooperative learning, says "research results show that student team learning improves both academic achievement and students' interpersonal relationships. All students (including high, average, and low achievers) appear to benefit" (p. 303). Fostering cooperation is particularly important for students with limited English proficiency. As Arias (1986) points out:

> Hispanic students are segregated in schools or classrooms in which children of limited English proficiency are the majority. Linguistic isolation reflects the residential isolation that limits the exposure of some Hispanic students to the native English discourse of peers. Schools frequently exacerbate Hispanic student linguistic isolation by homogeneously grouping students by language ability in classrooms for instructional purposes. (p. 50)

A sixth principle of multicultural instruction is to treat both boys and girls equally and in a nonsexist manner, both consciously and unconsciously. The importance of this principle is found in a comment by Stockard et al. (1980), who argue that "observational studies of classroom interaction show that teachers tend to give boys both more negative and more positive feedback about their actions than they give girls" (p. 13). Teachers do this unconsciously, and it provides boys with more opportunity to learn than girls.

The development and fostering of a positive self-concept, a seventh principle, is just as important to this approach as to the other two approaches—Human Relations and Single-Group Studies—where we have discussed it. Bennett (1986) provides an insightful comment on the importance of self-concept and success in school:

> When a student with low self-esteem enters a classroom, self concept

becomes one of the most challenging individual differences in how he or she will learn. Because students with a negative self-image are not fully able to learn, school becomes an arena for failure that prevents them from achieving the success needed for high self-esteem. (p. 131)

There are probably many other principles of instruction that could be added here. Our purpose has not been to be exhaustive, but to illuminate those instructional principles that are central to the approach.

Evaluation

Evaluation has been addressed less than curriculum and instruction, although those who have addressed it have made several recommendations. One recommendation is that evaluation of achievement reflect the multicultural curriculum. For example, if children are taught a multicultural history curriculum, achievement testing over their mastery of history should not dwell on accomplishments of White wealthy males.

A second and more discussed recommendation concerns standardized testing. Sizemore (1979) points out that standardized achievement and IQ tests are "based on monocultural assumptions and the notion of a single normal curve for all human abilities" (p. 354). Their main purpose is to rank-order students and to sort them into different groups for different and unequal opportunities. She writes, "In a nation of minorities, the preferred minority is still the affluent white Anglo-Saxon Protestant male. The sorting mechanisms continue to work in his favor" (p. 354). For these reasons, she and others argue that standardized tests should not be used. Achievement tests should be based on the curricula the students were actually taught, and they should be used only to improve instruction. Tests to determine eligibility for special education (and especially those used to determine mental retardation) should be culturally sensitive, like the System of Multicultural Pluralistic Assessment developed by Mercer (Mercer & Lewis, 1977).

A third recommendation is that when students are grouped for instruction, grouping plans should serve a varied student population rather than penalizing those who do not fit some notion of "normal." Stainback, Stainback, Courtnage, and Jaben (1985) point out that the age–grade level system, coupled with standardized testing, assumes that all students of the same age should require the same amount of time to learn the same thing; those who deviate are placed in pullout programs such as special education. They recommend that testing and grouping practices should employ criterion-referenced rather than norm-referenced tests, nongraded grouping arrangements, and flexible pacing and time requirements. By expecting and allowing for diversity (which is not to be confused with lowering expectations), and by providing variable ways of evaluating and grouping students, far fewer students will be seen as handicapped.

A fourth recommendation is that evaluation procedures not penalize students by requiring skills that are extraneous to what is being evaluated. This means, for example, that if a science teacher wishes to assess how well students have learned science concepts, the test should not require students to read and write above their skill level; if a student cannot read some of the questions or write well enough to answer questions, the test should be given orally. (This does not mean that no one should be teaching reading and writing skills to the student, only that these skills should not interfere with the student's ability to display what he or she has learned about science.) Time limits should not be placed on tests (unless there is a good reason to do so) if it prevents those who work slowly from completing the test. Children who are fluent in a language other than English should be tested in their native language if their performance in English would not be as good (unless the purpose of the test is to evaluate their mastery of English).

A fifth recommendation is that assessments of students' English language proficiency take into account the different contexts in which school communication takes place and the different factors involved. Personality traits, such as sociability, may affect the rate and proficiency of a student's learning English in peer interaction situations; however, cognitive skills may be more involved in acquiring English proficiency in the classroom context (Fillmore, 1979). Cummins (1981a, 1981b) found that it takes substantially longer for a student to acquire the cognitively demanding English used in academic situations compared to that used in social situations. Teachers have prematurely transitioned students into an all-English curriculum when the students lacked sufficient cognitive and academic language proficiency to achieve. Accurately assessing the language factor in addition to the other factors already discussed is crucial to the educational achievement of language-minority students.

Finally, a sixth recommendation is that educators make sure that the tests they give do not contain sex or race stereotypes or sexist language. For example, Tittle (1973) examined eight major achievement tests and found all but one to use more male than female nouns and pronouns, as well as stereotypical test items (e.g., girls cooked while boys hiked).

Home/Community–School Relationships

Advocates of the Multicultural Education approach encourage schools to maintain a strong relationship with the home and community. They believe that when it comes to the education of their children, parents and community members must be more than mere spectators, simply attending graduation ceremonies, open house, or sporting events. They supported government thinking when it endorsed and required "maximum feasible participation" of community members in federally sponsored programs. They argue that just as citizen participation is fundamental to American democracy, so is it fundamental to school success for people of color and women (Grant, 1979).

According to Reed and Mitchell (1975), most home/community–school relationships are token in nature. They argue that for the most part, few community services to the school exist. Those that do exist—for example, the Parent-Teacher Organization or a fund-raising group to buy an additional computer for the school—are directed by the school and usually do not represent the community as a whole. Furthermore, those efforts are led by a fairly small group who do virtually all of the planning; they see themselves and are seen by school personnel largely as "communication leaks" through which information about the school program is disseminated to the community (p. 190).

Advocates of the Multicultural Education approach want to see the community involved in budgetary procedures, the selection of school personnel, and curriculum development (Montano 1979). One advocate, drawing on his own personal experience, describes the importance of school-community relationships as follows:

> The most productive approach to improving education for minorities has been a school-community partnership. In this partnership, the community's contribution is to define the problem. The school, representing both the dominant culture and the education profession, then contributes to problem solving abilities. The coequality of school and community can strengthen school-community relationships and can reveal problem areas which have escaped previous identification and consequently impeded progress. (Montano, 1979, p. 152)

Advocates of this approach, like advocates of the Human Relations and the Single-Group Studies approaches, also acknowledge the importance of the school recognizing and affirming the home/community cultures of all of its students. They embrace the idea that just as there is no one model American, there is no one model home or community. Homes are as varied and diverse as the people who make up a multicultural community.

Staffing

The Multicultural Education approach is concerned with school-wide as well as classroom practices. One school-wide area of concern is staffing. There are three main recommendations here. One is that staffing patterns reflect cultural diversity and nonsexist roles (Baker, 1983; Gollnick & Chinn, 1986; Stockard et al., 1980). This means that more than a token number of staff members should be of color, that staff members of color should be administrators and teachers as well as aides and custodians, that half of the decision makers should be female, and that teachers should not teach sex-stereotypical subject areas (e.g., there should be female mathematics teachers in addition to male mathematics teachers).

A second recommendation is that staff members have high expectations of students. Gollnick and Chinn (1986) point out that research often shows that teachers base their expectations on student characteristics such as socioeconomic status, language, race, and sex; the Multicultural Education approach recommends hiring teachers who do not stereotype students and who have high expectations of them. Actually, no approach recommends hiring biased teachers, but advocates of this approach have been more outspoken against teacher biases than have many advocates of previous approaches.

A third recommendation is that relations between staff members be collegial and that a cooperative spirit prevail. It is especially important that teachers from various programs and support services be integrated within the mainstream life of the school. Recent research on schools with bilingual education programs reveals that in effective schools, there are few divisions between the bilingual and regular school staff (Carter & Chatfield, 1986).

Extracurricular Activities

A second school-wide area of concern is extracurricular activities. Baker (1983) recommends that schools make sure that athletic programs include minority students and women, and that cheerleading teams include both sexes and minorities. She points out that female students sometimes are not actively encouraged to participate in certain sports and that students from lower socioeconomic backgrounds are often unable to participate in sports such as skiing, requiring access to facilities outside school. Both Baker (1983) and Gollnick and Chinn (1986) recommend that clubs and organizations not perpetuate racial or sex segregation and that positions of student leadership not be dominated by one group. Stockard et al. (1980) point out that "males more often belong to chess, science, and lettermen's clubs and females more often belong to dance teams and aspire to be cheerleaders . . . [and even] in the band, they generally play different instruments" (p. 40). Schools should work actively to avoid segregation and stereotyping in such areas.

Getting Started

John Martin, Marie Sanchez and Ellen Foxley were returning to James Madison Junior High after spending 3 days at the district's multicultural in-service institute. They had been selected by their school principal, Dr. Herman Kempner, because of their interest in the concept and the school's goal for the year of implementing Multicultural Education into the classroom. James Madison Junior High was a newly constructed magnet school not too far from the city's downtown area. As a magnet school, it received a richly diverse student population, which was 8% Asian, 12% Black, 10% Hispanic, 3% Native American, and 67% White. The socioeconomic status of these students was also varied: About 55% came from families that would be considered solid middle-class, and the other 45% represented students who came from the working class. About 18% of the total student population were considered handicapped, or in need of special services. The girls outnumbered the boys by 2% this year; this percentage had fluctuated 1 or 2 percentage points in either direction over the last 5 years.

Kempner, or "Doc," as he was more often called by his colleagues, had made Multicultural Education the school goal partly because of his recent trip to Hawaii and Japan and partly because of the Chernobyl crisis. He believed that technology and the possibility of a nuclear disaster necessitated people working together. He argued that their school's contribution to the problem would be to help students accept and affirm cultural diversity as a fact of life in the United States and to acknowledge that it is a valuable resource that should be preserved and cherished. The school had no particular overt problem between the different race and class groups, nor any overt problem between the handicapped and nonhandicapped students.

John, Marie, and Ellen had all become interested in multicultural education in different but equally fulfilling ways. John had attended an Ivy League college and had become a Teacher Corps intern to avoid conscription. His internship had been in an inner-city school in Los Angeles, and he had surprised himself by really enjoying teaching. At the completion of his internship, he took a job at James Madison, where he has been teaching language arts for the last 16 years. Marie had grown up in a Hispanic barrio in

Austin, Texas. She had attended a local university in Dallas and had fallen in love with the city. She has been teaching mathematics at the junior high school for 5 years. Ellen had been teaching social studies at James Madison for 4 years. She had come to the school after living most of her life in Alaska, where her mother was the principal in a school that had a large enrollment of Eskimo students. She had worked for her mother for 2 years before deciding to see the "lower forty-eight." Early in her teaching career, she had become involved with the women's movement and had helped establish a local NOW chapter.

The workshop had provided those important commodities— time and material resources—for each of the three teachers to develop lesson plans for their classes. Also, it had encouraged and provided time for them to collaborate on developing school-wide implementation plans. They shared these plans with Doc on their first day back and waited for his reaction. The school-wide plans called for each subject-area department to assess how well content about contributions and perspectives of men and women of different cultural groups was integrated into its curriculum and to establish a procedure for improvement where needed. It was suggested that each teacher have the primary responsibility for his or her curriculum but that the process would be less difficult if subject-area colleagues worked together. The school-wide plan also suggested that each teacher assess his or her own teaching style to determine to what extent it meshed with the different learning styles of the students and that the counseling staff help the teachers as needed. Finally, the plans recommended hiring more teachers of color for the core subject areas, because of the 35 core-area teachers, only 2 were Black and 1 was Hispanic.

They waited for Doc's reaction to their proposal. It wasn't long in coming. He said, "How do you think the teachers will respond to these area meetings and work? They have been very slow to start responding to multicultural education as a school goal, other than putting up a few posters here and there."

Ellen replied, "There is one thing I remember my mother saying:'A successful instructional program requires a strong leader.' Doc, you know that unless you really get involved, most of the teachers will write this whole thing off as 'here today, gone tomorrow.' "

Doc sighed and said, "I know you're right. I'll put it on the agenda for this month's staff meeting, and then will really get into it." He then asked, "What are each of you going to do in your own classrooms?"

John replied first, saying that he had already developed several lesson plans. One set of plans for literature required him to change not only which pieces of literature he taught, but also his teaching method. For example, he was going to include Mildred Taylor's, *Roll of Thunder, Hear My Cry*, Scott O'Dell's *Carlotta*, Lawrence Yep's *Dragon Wings*, and Jean Craighead-George's *Julie of the Wolves*.

He also was going to have these books put on tape so that students with reading problems could listen and follow along.

Marie responded that she had come up with a plan to use Emma's and Paul's wheelchairs to help teach circumferences, diameters, and radii. Also, she and John were planning a lesson together that involved mathematics and essay writing. It would require students to measure various dimensions of a building and then refer to those measurements in an essay discussing how architectural facilities could be redesigned to accommodate handicapped individuals.

Ellen said that she was changing her social studies unit on World War II to include the internment of Japanese-Americans on the West Coast; the roles of Black, Hispanic, and Asian-Americans in the war; and the roles of women in the War. Doc complimented the three on their excellent ideas. He asked them to share their ideas with the staff at the next meeting. Also, he asked if they would be willing to be on call to help others get started. The meeting adjourned as the three responded "yes."

CRITIQUE

Some of you may be thinking that this approach solves all the problems not addressed by the other approaches. Others of you may feel dissatisfied with this approach, yet perhaps uncertain about what is dissatisfying to you. Although this approach has been prolifically advocated, it has also been criticized on different grounds and from different perspectives. First we will present criticisms of the goals of the approach from the perspectives of the first three approaches. Next we will present criticisms that support its goals but question its implementation. Finally, we will present criticisms that our fifth approach tries to resolve.

Advocates of the Teaching the Exceptional and the Culturally Different approach see the Multicultural Education approach as misdirected. They believe that American society is essentially good and just and that the worst way to deal with differences in language, culture, or learning styles is to nurture them. For example, Broudy (1975) believes that it will cause social divisiveness and lock some groups out by allowing them to fail to develop knowledge and skills for participation. He notes that "some groups will be encouraged not to participate not only in the culture of this country but also in the intellectual and artistic achievements of the human race" (p. 175). Glazer (1981) argues that "most [immigrant groups] had not come here to maintain foreign language and culture, but with the intention . . . to become Americanized as fast as possible" (p. 33). He extends this argument to all groups, immigrant or not (e.g., Mexican-Americans). Ivie (1979) believes that Multicultural Education sidesteps the problem of how to improve education for children who are failing. He, as well as Broudy and Glazer, argues that it is both undesirable and unrealistic to think that the mainstream will become pluralistic, and that the best thing schools can do is to try to equip those who are poor, minority, and handicapped with the skills and knowledge they will need to get a job and compete for upward mobility in the existing society. For example, they would probably fault John for teaching fewer traditional literary classics in order to include works by authors of color, Marie for taking up mathematics instruction time to discuss building accessibility for the handicapped, and Ellen for cutting back on time spent on political and military aspects of World War II in order to focus more on people of color and women.

Those criticizing the Multicultural Education approach from a Human Relations perspective raise different objections. These critics believe that American society does not promote enough love and interpersonal caring for a fulfilling existence. They believe that as people learn not to stereotype others and learn to communicate with, share with, and care about those with whom they come into contact, eventually other social problems will be solved. They argue that the Multicultural Education approach becomes misdirected when it emphasizes cognitive knowledge about different groups over exploration of interpersonal feelings, and social issues such as power over interpersonal issues. These critics believe that the Multicultural Education approach may give students a broad knowledge base, but that unless interpersonal relationships are stressed and experienced, attitudes and prejudices will not change. The objection is a question of emphasis. Human Relations advocates and Multicultural Education advocates usually do not leave each other in bitter disagreement, but rather move in somewhat different directions.

Advocates of the Single-Group Studies approach usually agree with much of the vision of Multicultural Education, but object that it weakens attention to the particular group they represent. Sometimes, members of diverse groups initially embrace Multicultural Education's rainbow concept, but become disenchanted when their own group continues to receive minimal attention while others receive more. For example, multicultural curriculum materials today usually give good representation to Black men and White women, but barely a nod to Puerto Ricans or Hmong people. In addition, the issue of language, which is a central concern of bilingual educators, often remains peripheral to Multicultural Education. There is no theoretical reason why any particular group or issue should be left out; but the reality is that when attention is divided among a wide variety of groups, each group cannot receive in-depth and comprehensive treatment (at least, not without substantially lengthening the amount of time students go to school).

A related objection of many Single-Group Studies advocates is that they do not see multiple forms of diversity as equally important. Many ethnic studies educators see race as *the* basic form of oppression, while radical feminists insist it is gender, and class analysts argue that it is the economic structure. Studying multiple forms of diversity is seen as superfluous, a waste of time, and weakening the study of that form of diversity of most concern. Ricardo Gomez (chapter 4), for example, would be less than enthusiastic about Ellen's approach to teaching history because it would fail to mine the richness of Mexican-American history to its fullest extent. Ellen would certainly do more than the usual to portray Mexican-Americans as active and visible contributors to American life, but Ricardo would want to focus more intensively on them.

Now for some problems with the implementation of the approach. One problem we have observed is that educators often treat multiple forms of diversity, especially race and gender, as parallel but separate (Grant & Sleeter, 1986). For example, when teaching about Blacks and women, teachers often really teach about Black men and White women. And many teachers deal with race and handicap in isolation of one another without examining how racism leads Whites to label people of color unjustly as handicapped. The approach itself does not call for this to happen, but it seems to happen for a number of reasons. Many educators and scholars simply become interested in one form of oppression (such as sexism) and often do not resolve their own biases related to other forms (such as racism). In addition, integrating race, class, gender, and handicap requires more time and effort because one must learn about multiple forms of diversity.

Another implementation problem is that it requires a reeducation of the educators using the approach. This approach is extremely ambitious. For example, to teach instrumental music from a multicultural perspective, one needs to learn a wide variety of music traditions. Few of us received a multicultural education in our own schooling, so acquiring one now requires considerable commitment, time, and creativity. One cannot halfheartedly do a good job of Multicultural Education. In the vignette, the teachers were able to benefit from the time, materials, and knowledge provided at the in-service institute. They also knew that their colleagues would be unwilling to invest the necessary time and effort in the approach without the principal's strong encouragement.

You have probably noticed that this chapter included only bits and pieces about disability and even less about social class. The mainstreaming movement is only beginning to develop a Multicultural Education approach to disability; in time, we expect to see more in this area. Special educators seem to have moved from focusing almost exclusively on how to teach those viewed as disabled, to wondering how to integrate them socially with their regular education peers, to asking how to make the mainstream itself more pluralistic. Marie's inclusion of people in wheelchairs in her mathematics curriculum is an example.

The small amount of attention given to social class is a more serious problem with this approach. Unfortunately, social class receives only fragmented attention: Many educators who are concerned about race are concerned about class only to the extent that people of color are disproportionately poor; educators interested in gender are concerned about the increased pauperization of women; and Multicultural Education advocates often recommend that children have equal opportunity regardless of social class background. But in the ideal society, if race and gender status differences are eliminated, what about class differences? Multicultural Education advocates do not come right out and say that a classless society is preferable to one stratified by class. Nor do they say that lower-class culture is just as worthy as middle-class culture in the same way they argue that the cultures of Native Americans are as worthy as that of Anglo Americans. They argue that the *people* are as worthy, but do not argue that class *cultures* are equally worthy and desirable. The Multicultural Education approach simply does not say very much about social class, particularly about the extent to which the ideal society should have different social classes. This was evident in the teaching ideas proposed by John, Marie, and Ellen. The Single-Group Studies and the Social Reconstructionist approaches both offer a critique of social class; the Multicultural Education approach is relatively silent about it.

Disaffected Multicultural Education advocates who have moved on to our last approach have leveled another criticism: The Multicultural Education approach directs too much attention to cultural issues and not enough to social structural inequalities and the skills that students will need to challenge these. For example, young people in school may learn nonsexist values and roles and may learn to make choices without relationship to gender. But when they leave school and enter the "real world," which is still sexist, how will they respond? Sociologists often argue that they will rework their beliefs and behaviors to fit the circumstances in which they find themselves. Boys may have received as much reward in a nonsexist school for sewing as for giving orders, but out of school many will have access to rewards for more "masculine" behavior and to roles that require them to give orders, dominate, and compete.

In a similar vein, Suzuki (1984) has warned against "unbridled" focus on ethnicity when the issues of greatest concern to people of color include powerlessness, racism, and poverty. He has expressed concern that multicultural education often becomes too much a celebration of differences without acknowledging the social problems that give rise to some of those differences and without dealing sufficiently with issues of social justice. Ogbu (1978) argues that many features of Black culture, for example, have developed directly in response to powerlessness and economic subordination; overemphasis on the value of cultural diversity without serious examination of injustices in the social structure is misdirected.

TABLE 5–1 *Multicultural Education*

Societal goals:	Promote social structural equality and cultural pluralism (the United States as a "tossed salad")
School goals:	Promote equal opportunity in the school, cultural pluralism and alternative life-styles, respect for those who differ, and support of power equity among groups
Target students:	Everyone
Practices:	
Curriculum	Organize concepts around contributions and perspectives of several different groups; teach critical thinking, analysis of alternative viewpoints; make curriculum relevant to students' experiential backgrounds; promote use of more than one language
Instruction	Build on students' learning styles; adapt to students' skill levels; involve students actively in thinking and analyzing; use cooperative learning
Other aspects of classroom	Decorate classroom to reflect cultural pluralism, nontraditional sex roles, disabled people, and student interests

TABLE 5-1 *continued*

Support services	Help regular classroom adapt to as much diversity as possible
Other school-wide concerns	Involve lower-class and minority parents actively in the school; encourage staffing patterns to include diverse racial, gender, and disability groups, in nontraditional roles; make use of decorations, special events, and school menus that reflect and include diverse groups; use library materials that portray diverse groups in diverse roles; include all student groups in extracurricular activities, and do not reinforce stereotypes; make sure discipline procedures do not penalize any group; make sure building is accessible to disabled people

REFERENCES

Anyon, J. (1979). Ideology and United States history textbooks. *Harvard Educational Review, 49,* 361–386.

Arias, M. B. (1986). The context of education for Hispanic students: An overview. *American Journal of Education, 95,* 26–57.

Baker, G. C. (1983). *Planning and organizing for multicultural instruction.* Reading, MA: Addison-Wesley.

Bandura, A., & Walters, R. H. (1963). *Social learning and personality development.* New York: Holt, Rinehart & Winston.

Banks, J. A. (1981). *Multiethnic education: Theory and practice.* Boston: Allyn and Bacon.

Bennett, C. I. (1986). *Comprehensive multicultural education.* Boston: Allyn and Bacon.

Broudy, H. S. (1975). Cultural pluralism: New wine in old bottles. *Educational Leadership, 33,* 173–175.

Brown v. Board of Education 347 U.S. 483, 493. (1954).

Butterfield, R. A., Demos, E. S., Grant, G. W., Moy, P. S., & Perez, A. L. (1979). A multicultural analysis of a popular basal reading series in the International Year of the Child. *Journal of Negro Education, 47,* 382–389.

Carter, T. P. & Chatfield, M. L. (1986). Effective bilingual schools: Implications for policy and practice. *American Journal of Education, 95,* 26–57.

Cohen, E. (1979). *Status equalization in the desegregated school.* Paper presented at the Annual Meeting of the American Educational Research Association, San Francisco.

Cortes, C. E. (1973). Teaching the Chicano experience. In J. A. Banks (Ed.), *Teaching ethnic studies* (pp. 181–200). Washington, DC: National Council for the Social Studies.

Cummins, J. (1981a). The role of primary language development in promoting educational success for language minority students. In *Schooling and language minority students: A theoretical framework* (pp. 3–49). Los Angeles: California State University Evaluation, Dissemination, and Assessment Center.

Cummins, J. (1981b). The entry and exit fallacy in bilingual education. *Journal for the National Association of Bilingual Education, 4*, 23–60.

Cummins, J. (1986). Empowering minority students: A framework for intervention. *Harvard Educational Review, 56*, 18–35.

Ferguson, A. (1977). Androgyny as an ideal for human development. In M. Vetterling-Braggin, F. A. Elliston, & J. English (Eds.), *Feminism and philosophy* (pp. 45–69). Totowa, NJ: Littlefield, Adams & Co.

Fillmore, L. W. (1979). Individual differences in second language acquisition. In C. Fillmore (Ed.), *Individual differences in language ability and language behavior* (pp. 203–228). New York: Academic Press.

Fillmore, L. W., & Valadez, C. (1985). Teaching bilingual learners. In M. C. Wittrock (Ed.), *Handbook of research on teaching* (pp. 648–685). New York: Macmillan.

Foerster, L. (1982). Moving from ethnic studies to multicultural education. *The Urban Review, 14*, 121–126.

Forehand, G. A. & Ragosta, M. (1976). *A handbook for integrated schooling.* Princeton, NJ: Educational Testing Service.

Gay, G. (1975). Organizing and designing culturally pluralistic curriculum. *Educational Leadership, 33*, 176–183.

Gay, G. (1979). On behalf of children: A curriculum design for multicultural education in the elementary school. *Journal of Negro Education, 48*, 324–340.

Gay, G. (1983). Multiethnic education: Historical developments and future prospects. *Phi Delta Kappan, 64*, 560–563.

Gee, E. G., & Sperry, D. J. (1978). *Education law and the public schools: A compendium.* Boston: Allyn and Bacon.

Gezi, K. (1981). Issues in multicultural education. *Educational Research Quarterly, 6*, 5–14.

Giddings, P. (1985). *When and where I enter: The impact of black women on race and sex in America.* New York: Bantam Books.

Glazer, N. (1981). Pluralism and the new immigrants. *Society, 19*, 31–36.

Gollnick, D. M. (1980). Multicultural education. *Viewpoints in Teaching and Learning, 56*, 1–17.

Gollnick, D. M., & Chinn, P. C. (1986). *Multicultural education in a pluralistic society* (2nd ed.). Columbus, OH: Merrill.

Gollnick, D. M., Sadker, M., & Sadker, D. (1982). Beyond the Dick and Jane syndrome. In M. P. Sadker & D. M. Sadker (Ed.), *Sex equity handbook book for schools* (pp. 60–95). New York: Longman.

Goodenough, W. H. (1976). Multiculturalism as the normal human experience. *Anthropology and Education Quarterly, 7,* 4–6.

Gough, P. (1976). *Sexism: New issue in American education.* Bloomington, IN: Phi Delta Kappa Educational Foundation.

Grant, C. A. (1977). The mediator of culture: A teacher role revisited. *Journal of Research and Development in Education, 11,* 102–117.

Grant, C. A. (1979). *Community participation in education.* Boston: Allyn and Bacon.

Grant, C. A., & Grant, G. W. (1981). A multicultural evaluation of some second and third grade textbook readers—A survey analysis. *Journal of Negro Education, 50,* 63–74.

Grant, C. A., & Sleeter, C. E. (1986). Race, class, and gender in education research: An argument for integrative analysis. *Review of Educational Research, 56,* 195–211.

Guthrie, G. P. (1985). *A school divided.* Hillsdale, NJ: Lawrence Erlbaum.

Hollins, E. R. (1982). Beyond multicultural education. *Negro Educational Review, 33,* 140–145.

Hull, G. T., Scott, P. B., & Smith, B. (Eds.). (1982). *All of the women are white, all of the blacks are men, but some of us are brave.* Old Westbury, NY: Feminist Press.

Hunter, W. (1974). *Multicultural education through competency-based teacher education.* Washington, DC: American Association of Colleges for Teacher Education.

Ivie, S. D. (1979). Multicultural education: Boon or boondoggle? *Journal of Teacher Education, 30,* 23–25.

Kendall, F. E. (1983). *Diversity in the classroom.* New York: Teachers College Press.

Kimball, S. T. (1974). *Culture and the educative process.* New York: Teachers College Press.

Krashen, S. D. (1981). Bilingual education and second language acquisition theory. In *Schooling and language minority students: A theoretical framework* (pp. 51–79). Los Angeles: California State University Evaluation, Dissemination, and Assessment Center.

Mannheim, K. (1956). *Ideology and utopia* (L. Wirth & E. Shils, Trans.). New York: Harcourt Brace Jovanovich.

Mercer, J. R., & Lewis, J. F. (1977). *System of multicultural pluralistic assessment.* New York: Psychological Corporation.

Montano, M. (1979). School and community: Boss-worker or partners? In C. A. Grant (Ed.), *Community participation in education.* Boston: Allyn and Bacon.

National Coalition for Cultural Pluralism. Cited in W. R. Hazard and M. D. Stent (1973), Cultural pluralism and schooling: Some preliminary observations. In M. D. Stent, W. R. Hazard, & H. N. Rivlin, *Cultural pluralism in education* (pp. 13–25). New York: Appleton-Century-Crofts.

Newman, W. N. (1973). *A study of minority groups and social theory.* New York: Harper & Row.

Ogbu, J. U. (1978). *Minority education and caste.* New York: Academic Press.

O'Neill, O. (1977). How do we know when opportunities are equal? In M. Vetterling-Braggin, F. A. Elliston, & J. English (Eds.), *Feminism and philosophy* (pp. 177–189). Totowa, NJ: Littlefield, Adams & Co.

Reed, D. B., & Mitchell, D. E. (1975). The structure of citizen participation: Public decisions for public schools. In D. B. Reed & D. E. Mitchell (Eds.), *Public testimony on public schools.* Berkeley, CA: McCutchen.

Rodgers, F. A. (1975). *Curriculum and instruction in the elementary school.* New York: Macmillan.

Sadker, M., & Sadker, D. (1982). *Sex equity handbook for schools.* New York: Longman.

Sarason, S. B., & Doris, J. (1979). *Educational handicap, public policy, and social history.* New York: The Free Press.

Seaburg, J. J., Smith, J. C., & Gallaher, T. H. (1980). Building a multicultural education media collection. *Viewpoints in Teaching and Learning, 56,* 100–104.

Sizemore, B. A. (1979). The four M curriculum: A way to shape the future. *Journal of Negro Education, 47,* 341–356.

Skutnabb-Kangas, T. (1981). *Bilingualism or not? The education of minorities.* Clevedon, Avon, England: Multilingual Matters.

Spender, D. (1982). *Invisible women: The schooling scandal.* London: Writers and Readers Publishing Cooperative Society.

Spindler, G. D. (1974). The transmission of culture. In G. D. Spindler (Ed.), *Education and cultural process* (pp. 279–310). New York: Holt, Rinehart & Winston.

Stainback, W., Stainback, S., Courtnage, L., & Jaben, T. (1985). Facilitating mainstreaming by modifying the mainstream. *Exceptional Children, 52,* 144–152.

Stent, M., Hazard, W., & Rivlin, H. (1973). *Cultural pluralism in education: A mandate for change.* New York: Appleton-Century Crofts.

Stockard, J., Schmuck, P. A., Kempner, K., Williams, P., Edson, S. K., & Smith, M.A. (1980). *Sex equity in education.* New York: Academic Press.

Suzuki, B. H. (1984). Curriculum transformation for multicultural education. *Education and Urban Society, 16,* 294–322.

Tavris, C., & Wade, C. (1984). *The longest war: Sex differences in perspective* (2nd ed.). New York: Harcourt Brace Jovanovich.

Tittle, C. K. (1973). Women and educational testing. *Phi Delta Kappan, 54,* 118–119.

Trueba, E. T. (1976). Issues and problems in bilingual bicultural education today. *Journal for the National Association of Bilingual Education, 1,* 11–19.

Valverde, L. A. (1977). Multicultural education: Social and educational justice. *Educational Leadership, 35,* 196–201.

Ysseldyke, J. E., Thurlow, M., Graden, J., Wesson, C., & Algozzine, B. (1983). Generalizations from five years of research on assessment and decision making: The University of Minnesota Institute. *Exceptional Education Quarterly, 4,* 75–93.

CHAPTER 6

Education That Is Multicultural
and Social Reconstructionist

You are probably stumbling over the name of our fifth approach—Education That Is Multicultural and Social Reconstructionist—wondering why it contains so many words. Each word contributes. Social reconstructionism is a recognized philosophical orientation toward education. As Brameld (1956) puts it, reconstructionism offers a "critique of modern culture" (p. 37). It holds that "magnificent as their services to society [may] have been in the past, the major institutions and the corresponding social, economic, and other practices that developed during the preceding centuries of the modern era are now incapable of" (pp. 37–38)—and one can end this statement with whatever social issue one is concerned with. To Brameld, the social issues of concern were ending war and economic depression. To advocates of this approach to multicultural education, they are eliminating oppression of one group of people by another.

As Grant (1978) has explained, the expression *Education That Is Multicultural* means that the entire education program is redesigned to reflect the concerns of diverse cultural groups. Rather than being one of several kinds of education, it is a different orientation toward the whole education process.

GOALS

Education That Is Multicultural and Social Reconstructionist deals more directly than the other approaches have with oppression and social structural inequality based on race, social class, gender, and disability. As noted in Table 6–1, it prepares future citizens to reconstruct society so that it better serves the interests of all groups of people and especially those who are of color, poor, female, and/or disabled (see p. 201). This approach is visionary. Although grounded very much in the everyday world of experience, it is not trapped by that world. In fact, it is similar to the view revealed in these words by George Bernard Shaw (1921): "You see things; and you say, 'Why?' But I dream things that never were; and I say, 'Why not?'"

Brameld (1956) describes social reconstructionism as a utopian philosophy. By this he means "any construction of the imagination that extends beyond the here-and-now to become a far-reaching idealization of human, especially cultural, potentialities" (p. 24). He goes on to explain:

> "Utopian" does not here connote a flight from reality into a realm of totally unrealizable, fantastic perfection. The utopian attitude is not that of the impractical daydreamer who cannot bear to face the hard problems of his [or her] own day or his [or her] immediate environment. The vision of utopianism is, rather, a realizable one—a vision of what can be and should be attained in order that man [and woman] may be happier, more rational, more humane than he [or she] has ever been. (pp. 24–25)

Social reconstructionism speaks, in the words of Aronowitz and Giroux (1985), the "language of possibility. In this case, we move to the terrain of hope and agency, to the sphere of struggle and action, one steeped in a vision which chooses life and offers constructive alternatives" (p. 19).

Advocates of this approach do not loudly and clearly articulate one particular vision of the ideal society. They begin by assuming that resources should be distributed much more equally than they are now and that people should not have to adhere to one model of what is considered "normal" or "right" to enjoy their fair share of wealth, power, or happiness. But advocates believe that it would be another form of elitism for a small group of educators to tell other people what the "right" vision of the better society is. Rather, young people, and particularly those who are members of oppressed groups, should understand the nature of oppression in modern society and develop the power and skills to articulate their own goals and vision and to work constructively toward that.

This approach does this by teaching political literacy. As Freire (1985) explains:

> A political illiterate—regardless of whether she or he knows how to read and write—is one who has an ingenuous perception of humanity in its relationships with the world. This person has a naive outlook on social reality, which for this one is a given, that is, social reality is a *fait accompli* rather than something that's still in the making. (p. 103)

Through a process called conscientization, Freire believes that people should learn to question society, see through versions of "truth" that teach people to accept unfairness and inhumanity, and become empowered to envision, define, and work toward a more humane society.

This approach, more than the others, is called different things by different advocates. For example, one may encounter terms such as *emancipatory pedagogy* (Gordon, 1985), *critical teaching* (Shor, 1980), *transformational education* (Giroux, 1981), *multicultural education* (Suzuki, 1984), *antiracist teaching* (Carby, 1982; Mullard, 1980), and *socialist feminism* (Jaggar & Struhl, 1978). Although educators using these different terms do not advocate exactly the same things (one main difference is that some focus mainly on race, others on gender, still others on social class), their basic goals and theoretical assumptions are very similar. The term we use may be longer, but we believe it is also more descriptive of what is meant.

This approach lends itself well to integrating attention to race, social class, gender, and disability. Most advocates do not do this very well, but most recognize the desirability of doing so (although few even mention handicap). In this chapter, gender, race, and social class will be tied together, although you should be aware that sources cited may not have done so.

Advocates of Education That Is Multicultural and Social Reconstructionist, regardless of the term they use for the approach, agree on several theoretical assumptions about the nature of society and the nature of learning.

ASSUMPTIONS AND THEORY

This approach reverses much commonsense thinking about the relationship between individual beliefs and behavior and the larger social order. People often believe that if individuals become more humane, better skilled, more literate, or more civil, society as a whole will become more just. The first two approaches rest heavily on this thinking, and the fourth contains some of it. A fundamental assumption from the field of sociology, however, is that the reverse is true: Individuals shape their beliefs and behavior to fit their niche in the social structure. Try to change individuals and they will quickly return to their old ways if the world they experience remains unchanged. Change their world significantly, and their attitudes, beliefs, and behavior will change accordingly. Of course, that raises the question of who is supposed to change society if it isn't individuals.

The present approach has an answer to that question. We will address it by discussing three interrelated theories on which this approach is based: conflict theory, cognitive development theory, and a sociological theory on culture.

Conflict Theory

Conflict theory, also called critical theory, is a sociological perspective for understanding social behavior. Various versions of conflict theory have been developed by theorists such as Weber (1947, 1968), Marx (1972), and Dahrendorf (1959). Although there are serious disagreements between schools of conflict theory, we will synthesize the main points of agreement.

First, social behavior is organized much more on a group basis than on an individual basis. Weber calls major social groupings "status groups." Collins (1977) explains that "the core of such groups is families and friends, but they may be extended to religious, educational, or ethnic communities" (p. 125). Groupings do not necessarily have definite boundaries; what constitutes a group changes somewhat, depending on the situation. But groupings do follow definite patterns, centering around family, level of wealth, geographic proximity, and religious and cultural ties. As Collins explains, groups are central to human existence because "participation in such cultural groups gives individuals their fundamental sense of identity" (p. 125).

Second, groups struggle with each other for control over resources. Collins notes that power, wealth, and prestige are the main kinds of scarce resources. You can probably think of examples of these in your own community, such as jobs, land, housing, political influence, perhaps even food or water. Groups compete because people are by nature concerned mainly about their own welfare and that of their family, and secondarily about the welfare of others they see as being like themselves. When important resources are in scarce supply, most of us are concerned primarily about attaining these resources for people close to us. People we neither know nor identify with usually occupy much less concern or sympathy, and often none at all.

The more scarce the resource, the more intense the struggle, and the more important group membership becomes. America has an ideology of individual achievement, but for the conflict theorist, this ideology masks reality. The resources a person starts with, the opportunities open to that person, the circumstances in which the person lives, and the way others react to that person all depend to a significant extent on the groups of which that person is a member. For example, writing about gender membership and power, Oakley (1981) writes that "power is unequally distributed in most societies, and depends not only on personal qualities of the individual but on social position. Different people occupy different social positions and men occupy a different position in society from women" (p. 281). A woman may attempt to achieve power within a community, but her individual efforts are shaped partly by her gender: As a mother, her time may be limited by domestic responsibilities; some men in the community may refuse to take orders from her; and her stand on gender-related issues may polarize would-be constituents on the basis of sex. The more influential and coveted the position she seeks, and the more she acts as an advocate for women, the more one is likely to see sex stereotyping and denigration of women to "keep her in her place."

A third idea is that to solidify, extend, and legitimate their control, dominant groups structure social institutions to operate in ways that will maintain or increase their own advantage. But they try to establish and promulgate rules of society in such a way that most people will think the system is fair. For example, in a capitalist economy, people can gain wealth by investing extra money. The investor collects interest, dividends, or profits; the labor necessary for accumulating that money is performed by someone else. The more extra money one has, the wealthier one can become. The secretary who barely earns enough to make ends meet will have little or no capital to invest; the corporate executive will very likely have quite a bit. Yet, most people accept this system as fair because they believe that everyone has an equal opportunity to invest—it just so happens that those who need money the most rarely have any capital to invest.

As another example, Abberley (1987), a sociologist who is disabled, argues that dominant groups oppress disabled people in an effort to control access to jobs for themselves and to convince workers of the rightness of the Protestant work ethic. People are led to believe that normal adults work full-time, which is an advantage to the capitalist; people who do not work full-time are viewed as abnormal, defective. He points out that most concepts of disability are purely biological in nature and that they suggest that defective people cannot be expected to want or have the same advantages as "normal" people. For example, hearing impairment is usually understood as resulting from defects in a person's auditory system without also considering the extent to which the social environment accommodates the hearing impaired. If we view disabled people as biologically defective, we tend to assume that they should be satisfied with less from life. Abberley writes:

> By presenting disadvantage as the consequence of a naturalized "impairment" it legitimizes the failure of welfare facilities and the distribution system in general to provide for social need, that is, it interprets the effects of social maldistribution as the consequence of individual deficiency. (p. 17)

This structuring of social institutions for the benefit of dominant groups results in institutional racism, sexism, and classism. As neo-Marxist sociologists point out, the capitalist economy structures in great wealth differences and enables the class that controls production to maintain and extend its wealth. A few individuals may gain economic mobility, but the lower and working classes as a whole do not. However, because some do become upwardly mobile, and because people seem to act as autonomous individuals, the class system is made to seem fair. Many people do not recognize or understand how the wealthy use their wealth to control the economic and political lives of others. As Apple (1985) puts it, "We castigate a few industrialists and corporations, a small number of figures in government, a vague abstraction called technology, instead of seeing the productive and political apparatus of society as interconnected" (p. 5).

For example, Mitchell (1978) has described four structures in which women are institutionalized into a separate existence from men, an existence that enables men to extend power over women: production, reproduction, sexuality, and socialization of children. Within each of these structures, all of which are interconnected, women's lives are made different from men's. For instance, production refers to a division of labor based on sex. Mitchell points out that in most societies, women's work is different from men's and is connected to women's role as childbearers; furthermore, it is usually valued less than men's work. In industrial societies, as labor moved from the home to the factory, women were increasingly segmented out of the labor force because they were given responsibility for socialization of children, which meant they had to stay home. The fact that child raising, housework, and related jobs (such as teaching) are either unpaid or poorly paid has structured women as a group into an economically and politically oppressed position.

So far, it probably sounds as if social change is almost impossible. But some conflict theorists offer a related theory that provides help:

resistance theory. The main idea behind resistance theory is that people who are oppressed should not just sit back and take it. Although it is not always obvious to people exactly how they are being oppressed, they often act in ways that oppose their oppression.

Opposition can take many different forms. Here we will make a few distinctions. One distinction is between overt behavioral opposition, which is visible to observers, and private, or mental, opposition, which is more difficult for an observer to detect. People often adapt overtly to circumstances they face while privately opposing those circumstances. Theorists such as Anyon (1983), Apple (1985), Genovese (1974), and Giddens (1979) have called this form of opposition *accommodation* or *pragmatic acceptance*. For example, many people who are bilingual accommodate English-only policies by speaking English in public, but privately advocate bilingualism.

Resistance is a term given to overt behavioral opposition. Resistive behavior can be, on the one hand, consciously directed toward extensive and long-term social change or, on the other hand, directed toward making one's own immediate life a little better; or it can be anywhere in between. For example, the 1960s witnessed many instances of Black resistance to racism. Rosa Parks's refusal to give up her seat triggered collective resistance on the part of the Black community in the form of a bus boycott, which became consciously directed toward changing race relations. Collectively, Blacks reduced White control over many areas of their lives through such actions. However, not all resistance to authority is directed consciously toward extensive social change. For example, many Black teenage girls today are having babies partly because they see their own futures as limited because they are poor and because their Blackness is not accepted as equal to Whiteness in society's marketplaces. While society tells them to go to school and not become pregnant until they are married adults, many do not conform to this. Their resistance to dominant social norms can be interpreted as an attempt to create more meaningful lives for themselves, although many members of the Black community view it as harmful to the status of Blacks in the long run. These two examples illustrate quite different forms of resistance to oppression, but what both have in common is the refusal of people to accept restrictions that the social system attempts to impose on their lives and their happiness.

The important point for teachers to realize is that many people are already engaged in some sort of struggle against oppression without necessarily having been taught social theory. Many people, often as part of a group, oppose on a daily basis what they see as unfair authority or restriction imposed by someone else. In school, this may take countless forms, such as girls resisting being viewed as sex objects, students in wheelchairs ganging up against those who tease them, or lower-class students refusing to obey middle-class teachers who look down on them. These naturally occurring examples of resistance are a good place to start teaching about social issues because they are a part of "real-life" issues with which students can identify. After studying an issue, students may decide that their present form of resistance is not as effective as alternative forms. For example, resisting racism by refusing to learn from White teachers is not usually as effective as resisting racism by learning as much academic material as possible to achieve a position of social power. But rather than dismiss or ignore students' opposition to authority, educators can use this as a beginning point for analyzing issues.

Cognitive Development Theory

Education That Is Multicultural and Social Reconstructionist also draws on cognitive development theory, which has been developed by scholars such as Piaget (1952) and Dewey (1938). Cognitive development theory was discussed in chapter 3, so we will not elaborate extensively on it here, although its implications for this approach are somewhat different. According to cognitive development theory, learning is a process of constructing knowledge through the interaction of mind and experience. Knowledge always has a concrete basis, and children need concrete experience in order to develop knowledge. Children develop knowledge by interacting mentally and to some extent physically with people and objects around them. This requires active involvement. Knowledge that is poured into a passive mind is quickly forgotten. As Dewey (1938) remarked, "The educator cannot start with knowledge already organized and proceed to ladle it out in doses" (p. 82). Knowledge that is remembered and used is that which children construct (often with guidance from a teacher, parent, or another child) based on active involvement with materials and events in their environment.

This means that children's understanding of society and of other people is based on the world they experience. If that world is all of one ethnic or racial group, children's comprehension of racism or of other groups is extremely limited. Simply telling children about people or problems beyond their experience may not penetrate their understanding very far. Children need to have direct and active involvement with the group or issue of concern. It also means that if their daily experience contradicts what the teacher tells them, they will probably believe their experience, although they may parrot back what the teacher says. For example, if jobs are hard to find in the children's neighborhood and many people are unemployed, the teacher who tells them that the economy is strong and that anyone who looks can find work will not be believed. These ideas are similar to those discussed in earlier chapters, and they underscore the importance of paying attention to and working with children's experiential backgrounds.

With respect to social action, cognitive development theory has additional implications. Dewey (1938) agreed with Thomas Jefferson's (1779) observation that:

> Even under the best of forms, those entrusted with power have, in time, and by slow operations, perverted it into tyranny; . . .the most effectual means of preventing this would be, to illuminate, as far as predictable, the minds of the people at large. (chap. 79, sec. I)

For Dewey, a democracy requires citizens who are capable of critical thought and collective social action. But these traits are not developed by telling people to think or by explaining the principles of democracy. They are developed by practicing critical thought and social decision making in the school. Dewey saw schools as ideal laboratories for developing an informed and active citizenry because schools are social institutions inhabited by groups of future citizens. The raw material is there. He wrote:

> Most children are naturally "sociable." Isolation is even more irksome to them than to adults. A genuine community life has its ground in this natural sociability. But community life does not organize itself in an enduring way purely spontaneously. It requires thought and planning ahead. (1938, p. 56)

Most schools and classrooms do not practice democracy, nor do they develop students' powers of decision making and collective action. But their potential to do so is an idea attractive to advocates of this approach. Advocates of Education That Is Multicultural and Social Reconstructionist are often drawn to the ideas of Dewey and Piaget because they focus attention on the child's world and because they focus on social action. Advocates are also drawn to these ideas because they suggest equalizing power relations in the classroom.

Democratizing power relationships in the classroom does not necessarily mean turning all power over to the students. As Elshtain (1976) points out, giving students too much power over deciding what to learn and allowing them to dwell excessively on their own experience is not necessarily enlightening because the students by themselves will not necessarily come up with insights about social inequality. The teacher implementing this approach wants students to use experience to gain certain insights about the nature of society. Therefore, the teacher needs to maintain a balance between drawing on the students' world and inviting student decision making, and helping students gain knowledge and ideas that will illuminate not only their own experience, but society in general.

Theory of Culture

The previous chapter described cultural transmission theory as anthropologists have developed it. Many anthropologists, and indeed many advocates of the Multicultural Education approach, believe that behavior is guided mainly by culturally learned ideas and that society is the way it is, in large part, because of our cultural beliefs and values. Change culture, and social institutions will change. Furthermore, many cultural practices are valuable in and of themselves and can be maintained even if the life circumstances of a group change.

Advocates of Education That Is Multicultural and Social Reconstructionist see culture somewhat differently. To them, much of everyday culture is an adaptation to life's circumstances, which have been in part determined by group competition for resources. Certainly, some aspects of culture are passed down from one generation to the next. Language is a good example: Most of us simply learn and use the language developed by our ancestors, although we may make small contributions to this language during our lifetime. But other aspects of culture are created on an ongoing, everyday basis, in much the same way knowledge is constructed. For example, Kanter (1975) has described some differences between male and female cultures in the workplace. Those who hold secretarial jobs, usually women, are rewarded by their employers with little or no career ladder opportunities as well as relatively low salaries. Consequently, women holding such jobs gradually learn to seek some of their rewards for working from co-workers. (Making friends with other secretaries brings satisfaction that routine typing for a small paycheck does not.) In addition, they learn to confine work to working hours, since working overtime will not advance them in a career and may not even bring overtime pay. Such women develop a culture that nurtures relationships and cooperation and that is oriented toward completing assigned work during assigned hours only. On the other hand, the bosses for whom they work, usually men, often have access to a career ladder with increased pay and power. Getting the work done and spending time outside normal work hours on work-related matters pays off more than developing relationships with co-workers. The men, therefore, develop a culture that is somewhat impersonal, intense, and competitive. Both cultures are adaptations to conditions and access to resources, which are based in part on membership in unequal groups.

As this example illustrates, culture represents a group's attempt to interpret, give meaning to, and function within shared circumstances. When this idea is viewed politically, it means that part of the substance of culture results directly from a group's material and political position. Essentially, this means that one should study culture not just to appreciate and admire it, but also to understand the sociopolitical circumstances that helped give rise to it. One should recognize that members of a given group struggle to change their sociopolitical circumstances, which in turn would result in some cultural change. For example, Suzuki (1977) has discussed Japanese-American culture and the implications for educators. He points out that many social scientists have attributed the economic and education success of Japanese-Americans to inherited cultural patterns from Japan: "strong family structure, emphasis on education, Protestant-type work ethic and high achievement motivation—values deeply rooted in the cultural milieu of Meiji-era Japan" (p. 153). Such social scientists assume that culture is an inheritance from previous generations; Japanese-American culture would be a blend of Japanese culture and Anglo culture. Suzuki argues that this view is at best only partially correct.

Japanese-Americans have retained some cultural forms inherited from the Japanese, but what was retained and how it has been changed and redeveloped in the United States has depended strongly on the sociopolitical circumstances that Japanese-Americans have encountered. Suzuki (1977) points out several factors that Japanese-Americans have had to deal with: racism during World War II and the internment camps; the loss of possessions as a result; quotas placed on Japanese immigration, which kept the Japanese-American population very small; and the demand for technical workers immediately after the war. Suzuki (1977) describes how Japanese-Americans tried to reestablish themselves after the war:

> It seemed prudent for them to adopt a low-profile strategy that would not attract too much attention nor elicit adverse reaction. Thus, it is understandable why the Nisei (second-generation) has been stereotyped as quiet, hardworking, non-assertive, dependable and accommodating. (p. 151)

Values and cultural patterns provided some of the substance for interpreting and adapting to the American experience, but sociopolitical factors such as racism and economic circumstances have also been important. Japanese-American culture is continually being re-created as Japanese-Americans confront, interpret, and respond to social conditions. One can apply this example to other groups as well. Culture is continually re-created as people confront their daily environments; inherited patterns of believing and behaving provide themes and forms to help interpret daily life, but culture does not simply flow through passive individuals like water through a pipe.

For this reason, Suzuki (1984) has warned that overemphasis on culture "has led some to pursue ethnicity almost for its own sake, and has led others to believe that multicultural education consists merely of including ethnic content in the curriculum. In the meantime," he continues, "the social realities of racism, sexism, and class inequality are often overlooked or conveniently forgotten" (p. 300). He goes on to point out that ignoring or downplaying the importance of social structure and "the position of an ethnic group in that structure. . .can lead to the mistaken and conservative view that ethnic subcultures are rooted in the past and are static and unchanging" (p. 300).[1]

This does not mean that culture is unimportant. Cultures of diverse groups should be studied. But they, as well as the culture of the dominant group, should be studied not only to help develop appreciation, but also to help understand a group's relationships with other groups, how a group has made sense of its own status, and how it has attempted to compete with other groups. For example, the literature produced by men and women of different ethnic groups tells us something about what it means to be poor, or to live in the barrio or ghetto, or to work in the factory or the home. Literature tells us how people have adjusted their dreams to their conditions, how people have given each other support, how they have resisted oppression. These ideas may not always be stated explicitly, but implicitly they are there and can be examined.

RECOMMENDED PRACTICES

Education That Is Multicultural and Social Reconstructionist has much in common with the Multicultural Education approach, and it also borrows from the other three approaches. However, it is a distinctly different approach. We will first describe and discuss four practices that are unique to it, then briefly discuss practices drawn from previous approaches. Table 6–1 summarizes recommended practices that are specific to this approach, as well as practices it shares with other approaches.

[1]B. H. Suzuki, "Curriculum Transformation for Multicultural Education," Vol. 16 (1984), pp. 294–322. Copyright 1984 by Sage Publications, Inc. Reprinted by permission of Sage Publications, Inc.

Practicing Democracy

Americans believe in the ideals of democracy, which are written into documents such as the Constitution, the Bill of Rights, and the Declaration of Independence. However, advocates of Education That Is Multicultural and Social Reconstructionist point out that most schools do not actively encourage democracy. For example, Banks (1981) points out that there are major "contradictions between the values expressed in our national documents and the ways in which minority groups are treated in the United States" (p. 154). Barbagli and Dei (1977) condemn schools for teaching students to acquiesce to authority rather than exercise it:

> The more hierarchical and rigid these [teacher-pupil] relationships are, and the more they are characterized by the concentration of decisions in the hands of the teacher and by a rigid control on the behavior of the pupils, the more easily will the latter acquire attitudes of docility and submission to authority. (p. 426)

In schools, the practice of democracy often does not go beyond reading the Constitution and learning about the three branches of government in a social studies class. But advocates of Education That Is Multicultural and Social Reconstructionist point out that practicing democracy also means learning to articulate one's interests, openly debate issues with one's peers, organize and work collectively with others, acquire power, exercise power, and so forth. Mann (1974) argues as follows:

> Since political power is a ubiquitous fact of social existence, and since a democracy depends for its vigor and justness upon equitable distribution of power, it is proper that the citizens' schools offer extensive opportunities for learning about how political power operates. (p. 147)

It is not enough just to know that the Constitution exists or that the law says Americans are equal: Citizens need to learn to use these ideas to work for them. This is particularly important for members of oppressed groups. Writing about oppressed ethnic groups, Banks (1981) argues that:

> They must also develop a sense of political efficacy, and be given practice in social action strategies which teaches them how to get power without violence and further exclusion. . . . Opportunities for social action, in which students have experience in obtaining and exercising

power, should be emphasized within a curriculum that is designed to help liberate excluded ethnic groups. (p. 149)

To Freire (1985), this practice would produce women and "men who organize themselves reflectively for action rather than men [and women] who are organized for passivity" (p. 82).

Shor (1980) talks about helping students become subjects rather than objects in the classroom. This means that students should learn to direct much of their learning, and do so responsibly, rather than always being directed by someone else. This does not mean that teachers should abdicate and simply let students do whatever they want. This can result in chaos or "trivial pursuit." It means teachers guiding and directing so that students can grow and develop a sense of responsibility in the way they make decisions.

Many argue that empowering students is the most effective, not to mention ethical, way of dealing with discipline. For example, Van Avery (1975) writes:

> Our society thinks that "more discipline" will make a better world and certainly better schools. But doesn't the cry for discipline really translate to, "Let's try to help people act in a responsible manner"? This society desperately needs people who accept responsibility, not simply accept discipline. (p. 177)

By learning to obey others, young people may learn discipline but not responsibility, since obedience does not require examining situations, thinking through alternative courses of action, or forecasting consequences of various courses of action.

Consider the example of a junior high social studies teacher who has built into his curriculum opportunities for student decision making and student exercise of power, specifically so that his students, who are working class and racially diverse, can practice affecting an institution. After teaching students about various forms of government, he has the class select a form to use to govern the class (usually they select representative democracy). Under his guidance, the class then practices that form for a period of time. He also has the class run school-wide elections: They organize balloting, make campaign posters, plan campaign strategies, and so forth. He provides opportunities for them to select topics to research in small groups and to plan out their research strategies. Again, he guides their thinking so that their decisions are usually workable, and when they are not, students understand why not and what might work better next time.

Practicing democracy also has implications for how teachers interact with the communities they serve. A teacher or a school committed to democracy makes a point of involving parents in deciding on the goals and educational practices of the school. This is particularly important in a lower-class or minority community, where the school often ignores the community or contacts parents mainly when there is a problem.

Analyzing the Circumstances of One's Own Life

Earlier, we discussed the concept of resistance; here we develop its implications. Anyon (1981) explains that people have a practical consciousness that coexists with a theoretical consciousness. Practical consciousness refers to one's commonsense understanding of one's own life, of how "the system" works, and of "everyday attempts to resolve the class, race, gender and other contradictions one faces" (p. 126). Theoretical consciousness refers to dominant social ideologies, explanations that one learns for how the world works that purport the world to be fair and just as it is. These two sets of consciousness do not always mesh; most of us learn to believe a mixture of them. For example, children are taught that America is the golden land of opportunity and that anyone can get ahead by working hard. Yet poor children whose parents work hard for low wages know that this does not necessarily apply to their own families; children of color learn firsthand that racism often thwarts their opportunities. But schools proclaim the dominant ideology, rarely giving much attention to insights that run counter to it that may develop in everyday life.

Advocates of Education That Is Multicultural and Social Reconstructionist recommend that schooling help students analyze their own lives to develop their practical consciousness about real injustices in society and to develop constructive responses. Metcalf and Hunt (1974) believe that this would appeal to most young people, who "are particularly critical of established educational practice" (p. 138). Let us consider some examples.

Freire (1985) has long used this approach to help South American peasants learn to read, having them learn words that will help them examine limitations placed on their own lives, such as vastly unequal land distribution. Most reading texts bear no relationship to their lives, teaching only the dominant group's version of reality; he either does not use these texts or teaches students to question them. Shor (1980) has used this approach in several ways, such as having his students examine hamburgers for nutritional value and then examine who benefits economically when we eat junk food rather than food that is good for us. And based on a study of young women taking business education courses, Valli (1986) suggests that the courses, which were virtually silent about the class and gender oppression experienced by secretaries, should help the young women examine the marginal status of these jobs, as well as ways in which such jobs perpetuate the subordination of working-class women. Or, one could help Hispanic students analyze the impact of current immigration legislation on themselves and their communities, examining its effect on undocumented workers as well as on those who have been citizens for years. Students could survey their neighborhoods for patterns of employment among adults and also for ties, if any, with relatives in Puerto Rico, Mexico, Cuba, and so forth.

So far, this recommendation probably seems most relevant to students who are members of oppressed groups. Advocates of this approach recognize that the dominant, standard curriculum is more congruent with the lives of middle- and upper-middle-class White students than it is with the lives of other students. However, members of advantaged groups can also learn from their own lives how their own privileged position allows them advantages that others cannot afford or gain access to. Furthermore, Metcalf and Hunt (1974) believe that most young people are critical to some extent of the world their elders have created and are open-minded to investigating social problems. They recommend that the curriculum incorporate "a study of an important social movement, rejection by youth, and that this study emphasize examining, testing, and appraising the major beliefs caught up in the movement" (p. 138).

Students should analyze not only their own lives, but also their responses to life circumstances. For example, many children of lower-class parents and many students of color give up and drop out, recognizing that society and the school are strongly biased against them. Although their interpretation of society may be quite correct, their response is not constructive. They are not, according to Hale (1982), seeing school as a place to gain an education for struggle and survival. Dropping out, having babies, taking drugs, and so forth, may be active forms of opposition, but these forms do not empower the young to change the circumstances that they are facing. Criticizing aspects of the student revolt of the 1960s, Aronowitz and Giroux (1985) argue that "if students are to be empowered by school experiences, one of the key elements of their education must be that they acquire mastery of language as well as the capacity to think conceptually and critically" (p. 158). What these authors are stressing is the need for young people to recognize what responses will empower them, which will probably mean using school to develop the skills needed to work for social change and better their own lives.

Developing Social Action Skills

This third recommended practice links the first two: It brings democratic political skills to bear on issues involving race, class, and gender inequalities in students' everyday world. Bennett (1986) defines social action skills as "the knowledge, attitudes, and skills needed to help bring about political, social, and economic changes" (p. 212). She argues that ignoring the fact that some groups "are unable to gain, maintain, and effectively use political power, to ignore this goal, is to make a sham out of the rest of multicultural education" (p. 212).

We should first repeat that advocates do not expect children to reconstruct the world. Rather, they view schools as connected with other institutions in society, either working with most institutions to reinforce inequality or working with opposition movements to institute change. Suzuki (1984) argues that "the schools cannot avoid transmitting values. . . .The only honest position educators can take is to impart values they believe reflect their vision of the highest achievable human ideals"; educators should recognize that "while the schools cannot operate independent of the prevalent culture, they can still play a significant role in the process of social change" (pp. 303–304).[2]

Advocates of this approach view the school as a laboratory or training ground for preparing a socially active citizenry. Bennett (1986) argues that this should begin at the kindergarten level in classrooms operating democratically, as described earlier. This helps students learn to begin to see themselves as powerful agents within a social institution. Elementary school children can begin to examine issues and consider courses of action to take. For example, a reading text by Myers, Banfield, and Colon (1983) features stories that deal with issues of discrimination and oppression, written in terms children can understand. The stories also show people actively working to confront these issues, offering role models of active involvement. Discussion questions invite students to consider similar issues in their own life experiences. Follow-up action projects ask children to investigate, for example, sexist advertising of toys in their own community and to make their findings and feelings known to local advertisers.

Older students can engage in more sophisticated social action projects. Banks (1981) recommends a variety of projects:

> Conducting a survey to determine the kinds of jobs which most minorities have in local hotels, restaurants, and firms, and if necessary, urging local businesses to hire more minorities in top level positions.
> Conducting boycotts of businesses that refuse to hire minorities in top level positions. . . .Conducting a survey to determine what local laws exist (and how they are enforced) regarding open housing, discrimination in public accommodations, etc., and if necessary, developing recommendations regarding changes which should be made in the laws or in the ways in which they should be implemented. Presenting these

[2]B. H. Suzuki, "Curriculum Transformation for Multicultural Education," Vol. 16 (1984), pp. 294–322. Copyright 1984 by Sage Publications, Inc. Reprinted by permission of Sage Publications, Inc.

recommendations to appropriate public officials and pressuring them
to act on the recommendations. (pp. 123–124)

Some advocates recommend that the school work with local community
groups involved in reconstructive action, rather than working in isolation, since this would help young people become involved with real
struggles taking place around them (Aronowitz & Giroux, 1985).

Anyon (1981) explains that the purpose of these kinds of activities
is to politicize students' resistance, to help them turn oppositional
activity into constructive political activity. She explains that these sorts
of activities should also help students develop "a collective self-love of
themselves as a *class* made up of Blacks, Whites, members of both
sexes, and various ethnicities" (p. 129); social action centers around
group change strategies.

Coalescing

One of the main differences between Education That Is Multicultural
and Social Reconstructionist and the Single-Group Studies approach
is that the present approach promotes coalescing across race, class,
and gender lines, as Anyon's statement illustrates. There are some very
good reasons for learning to form coalitions. One is that race, social
class, and gender often should not be treated as separate issues. As
we have pointed out elsewhere, not only do they all involve common
concerns of oppression, but people are all members of a gender *and* a
social class *and* a racial group; separating them is often somewhat
artificial (Grant & Sleeter, 1986).

Another reason advocates call for coalescing is that it makes for
a more powerful group. For example, while the poor may be economically weak as a power base, they gain strength when joined by middle-
class people of color, and additional strength if joined by White women.
Advocates have noted that disenfranchised groups sometimes find
themselves fighting over crumbs, whereas if they worked together, they
might all be able to achieve more.

Furthermore, coalescing guards against a kind of chauvinism that
can result when issues of race, class, and gender are dealt with separately. Giroux (1983) has observed that much neo-Marxist work that
challenges social class contains "reactionary racial and gender views"
which often, "although allegedly committed to emancipatory concerns,
ends up contributing to the reproduction of sexist and racist attitudes
and practices" (p. 287).

Forming coalitions is not easy. Throughout our nation's history,
groups have attempted to coalesce, often fragmenting as a result of

internal competition. For example, Davis (1981) has examined the struggle for suffrage for people of color and women, arguing that White, middle-class women distanced themselves from Black people when they feared that Black men rather than White women would achieve voting rights. Advocates warn that people need to recognize and struggle against all forms of oppression, keeping in mind that the common goal is eliminating oppression rather than simply furthering one's own interests. This involves learning how to handle compromise and how to cooperate with members of diverse groups. It also involves continually examining one's own biases and recognizing sources of one's own advantages. For example, women continue to be divided along race and class lines so long as White, middle-class women refuse to deal with their own racism and classism. Similarly, Blacks, Hispanics, and Asians find themselves divided along gender and class lines to the extent that middle-class males of all colors fail to take seriously the concerns of women and lower-class members of their racial groups.

One promising approach to coalition building is using the school as a base for local social action projects that draw together diverse groups to accomplish something for the community. The school can serve as a coalescing point if community input is regarded seriously and not just as a rubber-stamp PTA. For example, Carter and Chatfield (1986) describe a school that drew students from middle-class Anglo, Mexican migrant, Filipino, and Southeast Asian families. The school became involved with helping a senior citizens' community nearby, and this action helped the school develop cohesion and identification with a common community.

Commonalities with Previous Approaches

Education That Is Multicultural and Social Reconstructionist embraces the recommended practices of the Multicultural Education approach, since the Multicultural Education approach advocates making the school and classroom reflect and celebrate diversity. For both approaches, the curriculum, including materials, visual displays, films, guest speakers, and content taught orally, should regularly represent experiences, perspectives, and contributions of diverse groups and should do so in a conceptual rather than a fragmented way. This should be done all the time, in all subject areas. Nonsexist language should be used, and bilingualism or multilingualism should be endorsed. The curriculum should be equally accessible to all student groups; grouping practices or teaching procedures that enable only certain groups of students access to high-status knowledge or better teaching should be avoided. Teachers should build on students' learning styles rather than assuming that all learn best in the same way, and they should maintain high expectations for all students. Cooperative learning should be used to develop skills and attitudes of cooperation. Sexist teacher behavior should be avoided, and teachers should develop positive self concepts in all students. (Incidentally, educators warn that White male students often find the approach discussed in this chapter threatening to their own self-concepts, and they strongly suggest that teachers work to affirm these students as individuals and include them in social reconstructionist efforts.) Biased evaluation procedures should be avoided; evaluation should be used for improving instruction, not for sorting and ranking students. Home/community–school relationships should be developed, and parents should be actively involved, particularly if they are lower-class and/or minority. Staffing patterns should reflect cultural diversity and offer a variety of role models for males and females of different race and class backgrounds. Finally, extracurricular activities should not perpetuate race and sex stereotypes.

Education That Is Multicultural and Social Reconstructionist shares with Single-Group Studies its social issues emphasis, its concern with representing the interests of oppressed groups, and its desire to mobilize young people to work actively for social justice. It shares with the Human Relations approach an interest in developing cooperation among students and a concern for developing student self-concept. It also shares a desire to eliminate stereotyping, but does not view as particularly effective lessons about stereotyping or attempts to deal with stereotyping without changing the social sources of stereotypes. As with Teaching the Exceptional and Culturally Different, this approach agrees that teaching should start where students are, relate to their experiential backgrounds, build on the language and learning style they bring from home, and develop more effectively students' mastery of basic skills; but it diverges from that approach in its long-term purpose.

Putting It into Action

Elizabeth Harvey was having mixed emotions about her upcoming 40th birthday. She was happy and also unhappy to be celebrating the big four-0, but she also felt special being part of a select group of people—the Baby Boomers—who were celebrating this birthday and having it recognized across the country. Liz had been very politically active in the sixties, participating in numerous peace marches and civil rights demonstrations. She had even passed out flowers in Central Park. All of this seemed so long ago, yet also like it was only yesterday. Her reminiscing was interrupted by the sound of a distant bell that was telling her that her ninth-grade U.S. history class would convene in 3 minutes. She quickly washed and stored her coffee cup, gathered up her papers, and headed out of the teachers' lounge and up the stairs to greet her class.

The class was composed of 28 students: 13 were White, 8 were Black, 6 were Hispanic (3 Mexican-American, 2 Puerto Ricans, and 1 Guatemalan refugee), and 1 was a Native American (Winnebago tribe). The socioeconomic status of the students was working- and lower-class. The students were typical of those found in the majority of the classrooms. Their achievement level and reading scores spanned a wide range: 10 of the students were reading on or above grade level, 12 were reading between one and two grades below grade level, and 6 were reading at the sixth-grade level. This class was typical of the classes Liz had taught at O'Henry during her 7 years of teaching there.

Directly across the hall from Liz, Erick Cosby taught general science. He and Liz were the same age and often joked about their big four-0 birthdays. Erick had grown up in Nashville, Tennessee, and had come to Central City after spending 2 years in the army, including 9 months in Vietnam. The student composition of Erick's class was very similar to that of Liz's class, only he had two White students in wheelchairs, eight Hispanics, six Blacks, and two Hmong.

Next door to Liz's room was Ross Wisser's room. Ross had been teaching English at O'Henry for the last 20 years. He was divorced, lived alone, and was a sports enthusiast. He spent most of his free time following Central City's four major sports teams. He often team-taught with Liz and Erick because he liked their style and liked teaming up on some units or assignments.

Since Liz, Ross, and Erick taught the same classes of students, they often worked together to plan activities and assignments that would combine English, social studies, and science. Presently, Erick's classes were studying health, Liz's classes were studying city government and local agencies, and Ross's classes were studying general composition. The philosophy and style of teaching of all three were geared to challenge and involve the students as much as possible in curriculum planning and instructional processes and to have activities and experiences that would take into account the students' home background and place in the economic structure, as well as any so-called learning or physical disability. All three also believed that if their students were going to succeed in life, they needed to know how the system worked and have the skills and knowledge necessary to take charge of their own lives.

Earlier that day, during their planning period, Erick had persuaded Liz and Ross to use County Hospital as their theme of study. He argued that the recent controversy about closing the facility was receiving a good deal of media coverage. The mayor's office and city council were locked in dispute over whether to close the hospital and have its services picked up by the other hospitals in the area, renovate it so that the community could keep its *own* hospital, or build a new hospital more toward the center of town. He maintained that this lively debate would be excellent for Liz's unit. The students could learn not only about the different branches of city government and the way laws are passed, but also how the members of the council, the mayor, and the different factions within the council bargain and compromise to get their way. The students could also study how people often vote along racial lines and how the benefits and rewards that a councilperson's district will receive often give direction to the way he or she votes.

Erick added, "You know, there is considerable debate as to which companies will get the contract for either the renovation or new construction, and one aspect of the debate centers upon the minority representation of the companies bidding for the contract." He suggested that Ross have the students write letters to the newspaper expressing their views on the subject, as well as interview people in the neighborhood. He also suggested that the students put out their own newspaper about the topic. Ross added that he could borrow a mini camera TV so that the students could learn to do "real live" TV interviews.

Erick said that he would ask the students to contact doctors and other health personnel to get their views on the role of science in this decision-making process, investigating any medical factors that are for or against the proposed plans. He added, "Results of their work could be printed in the newspaper they will print. What the students learn from this may not influence the way things go at City Hall on this issue, but it may influence what goes on in City Hall and in the students' lives on future issues."

Liz and Ross quickly agreed, telling Erick it was a super idea and now they should begin to get down to details. Liz suggested that they reserve the little theater for the next day and bring all three classes together to see what the students think of the idea and, if they like it, to begin to organize around the three subjects. She said, "We can explain what each student's requirements are, as well as give them the opportunity to work in areas of their own interest."

"One requirement," said Ross, "is to get them to work together in groups, but to make certain that they are integrated across race, gender, and class. Also, we don't usually have a problem with the handicapped students fitting in, but let's make certain they are really a part of the groups."

Liz said, "I believe it is important that we guide the class in a way that they learn how the system works and how they can make it work for them."

Erick said, "Anywhere you go in this world, there are people making decisions that will affect your life. You need to know and understand this and learn to become a part of that process. Otherwise, they will make many of your life decisions for you."

The final bell now sounded, and it was time for Liz to start her U.S. history class. She completed greeting her class, and as she moved to close the door to her room, she guardedly called out to Erick, who was doing the same thing across the hall, "Happy four-0, ol' buddy!" Erick pushed the button on his wheelchair, turning himself into direct view of Liz, and said, "The same to you, ol' buddy. Let's go and see what they think about the new unit and get ready for our joint meeting tomorrow."

CRITIQUE

We opened this chapter by noting that this approach is called different things by different people and that most advocates are still working on integrating race, social class, and gender. This point represents a difficulty that the approach currently faces and will reflect how we critique it.

In a review of the literature on multicultural education, we found fewer works discussing this approach than any other (Sleeter & Grant, 1987). Actually, advocates come to this approach from a variety of camps. Some have come from the Multicultural Education approach; some have come from Black studies, women's studies, Asian-American studies, or some other single-group studies; some have come from bilingual education after rejecting the remedial/compensatory model that many programs follow; some are disaffected neo-Marxists who see social class critiques as too limited; some are social reconstructionists who have only begun to apply this philosophy to race, class, and gender (and who perhaps had applied it mainly to peace education, world hunger, or ecology). As a result, the literature developing the approach is rather scattered, and advocates often do not recognize or dialogue with each other. Earlier we noted that coalition building is not easy; it is also not automatic among advocates of this approach.

This means that the educator who wants to learn about the approach may become frustrated attempting to do so, partly because material is housed under different titles and partly because it is not abundant. In addition, there is relatively little material giving teachers specific guidance in what to do. We located some well-developed theoretical material (though little that integrated race, class, and gender) and two very specific teaching guides (Myers, et al 1983; Schneidewind & Davidson, 1983) but very little connecting theory with practice in an open-ended fashion that would guide a teacher in developing his or her own plan of action.

As a result, one finds very few explicit critiques of this approach. The philosophy of social reconstructionism has been critiqued, as have specific writings developing ideas in this approach; but the approach itself is rarely the subject of thoughtful critique. We suspect it is more often simply ignored by those who view it as too radical to bother with. Therefore, we have had to fashion this critique ourselves. We will first raise four general problems with the approach, then objections from each of the other four approaches.

One problem is with the role of the school in building a "new social order" (Counts, 1982). Counts asks if the school dare do this; skeptics ask if it can. There is good reason to question whether it can. Schools are instruments of society, charged with the mission of preparing the young to take their place in society. As chapter 1 explained, schools do a good job of reproducing the existing society. Expecting them to do otherwise may be unrealistic. Advocates of this approach usually counter, as Suzuki did earlier in this chapter, that schools *alone* cannot change society, but they can collaborate with other institutions in doing so, and that since teachers cannot avoid taking a stance toward society, the issue is *what* stance one will take. We think it is an open question as to how much impact schools can have on social change: This approach or variations of it has not been implemented enough for anyone to know what results it can have.

A second problem discussed by Duck (1980) involves a contradiction between having students think for themselves and persuading them to think like the teacher. The approach does advocate taking seriously what students think, but students often do not recognize as problems what the teacher sees as problems, nor do students always agree with interpretations or solutions the teacher may promote. This situation is due in large part to students' lack of experience or exposure, as well as to vested interests they may have in the status quo. Duck warns that teachers can become extremists who do not tolerate students' views. This is an issue that reconstructionist educators face, and most recognize a tension here.

In the vignette, Erick, Liz, and Ross will have to face this issue if some of their students decide that the County Hospital should be closed and the people it now serves should make do with other medical facilities. Without necessarily stating it to their students, they believe that closing the hospital will hurt low-income people and that this is unfair, and they feel that taxpayers should be willing to support services for low-income citizens. In setting up the unit, they will need to decide how much coverage to give to arguments in favor of closing it and how to respond to students who agree with those arguments.

A third problem is in the implementation more than the approach itself. It is quite possible for an educator to sensitize students to social issues, but then leave them hanging, frustrated, feeling there is not much they can do about them. Shor (1980) has noted that critical teaching can blow up in a teacher's face if the teacher has not thought carefully how students may be feeling and has not planned for constructive release of energy. For example, if students recognize problems inherent in capitalism, what can they do short of tearing down our whole economic structure (which a class of students is powerless to do and for which they probably don't have a full-blown alternative system and a strategy for getting it instituted)? There are constructive actions one can take toward much more circumscribed problems, such as dealing with provision of medical care for the poor in one's own community, but the teacher needs to be ready to deal with this. This is why the unit described in the vignette focused on a specific local issue and on the local politics deciding that issue. But at the same time, Erick, Liz, and Ross would want students to see how this issue is connected to larger race and class struggles, rather than viewing it simply as an isolated local problem.

A fourth problem is how to build the coalitions that this approach advocates. Little has been written or studied about how coalitions among diverse groups can be built. How one brings together labor unions, middle-class Mexican-Americans, and Southeast Asian refugees, for example, is a challenge; helping them recognize and identify with common ground is not an easy task.

Now for criticisms from the vantage point of the other approaches. The main objections raised by advocates of Teaching the Exceptional and the Culturally Different are that this approach seeks too much (and too unrealistic) change and diverts lower-class students and students of color from what they really need. Many educators do not see society as fundamentally flawed and believe that this approach expands problems such as racism disproportionately. (Those who say this, from our experience, are usually middle-class or above and White). They, as well as others who may agree with the magnitude of society's problems, argue that it gets students away from mastery of the skills and knowledge they will need to "make it." A principal of an urban high school recently told us how important he thought it was that his students acquire skills to get a job or go to college, to have a productive role in a society stacked against them; he cautioned that education approaches such as the one described in this chapter would take time away from that, as well as encouraging students to expect social changes that will not be forthcoming.

Human Relations educators fear that this approach will aggravate conflict and tension between people, escalating rather than reducing problems. Whereas the approach values cooperation, Human Relations educators are concerned that too much open discussion of past and present injustices will fuel fires of hate and distrust and that social action projects will promote confrontation. They fear that acts taken in the name of reconstruction will promote anarchy rather than fashioning a better society.

Advocates of Teaching the Exceptional and the Culturally Different as well as Human Relations advocates take issue with a fundamental premise of social reconstructionism: that the mainstream of society needs serious restructuring to be minimally fair to all Americans. Single-Group Studies and Multicultural Education advocates agree with that premise; their objections center around strategy rather than goal. Advocates of Single-Group Studies feel that the present approach bogs down in building coalitions across groups, to the extent that efforts toward change become ineffective. For example, while bilingual educators share some similar concerns with sex-equity advocates, there are also major differences of priority between the two groups. Joining forces might make for a stronger front, but hashing out a mutually agreeable common agenda can consume much of the energy of both groups. Historically, coalitions, if they are formed at all, have been fragile. Thus, groups with partially overlapping concerns may wish each other well, but choose not to try to work together.

Finally, Multicultural Education advocates generally embrace the intent of this approach, but view its feasibility with skepticism. To advocates of Education That Is Multicultural and Social Reconstructionist, the Multicultural Education approach is too limited and usually not aggressive enough. But to many "business as usual" educators, the Multicultural Education approach is radical. Multicultural Education advocates know that it is hard to get teachers and administrators seriously interested in implementing that approach. Education That Is Multicultural and Social Reconstructionist would be even harder to sell, more controversial, more different from "business as usual." We have also observed a certain amount of elitism among some social reconstructionists who see themselves as "correct" and Multicultural Education advocates as too accommodating. This is especially true in England, with the debate between the antiracist and multicultural advocates. This attitude of elitism fosters distrust between the two approaches, which compounds disputes over goals, assumptions, and strategies.

Our last chapter explains which approach we favor and why. Most of the objections raised about the different approaches center on differences in priorities, assumptions, and perspectives. It cannot be proved that one is right and the rest are wrong. Our own choice results from our own study of society, our own interactions with people, and our own convictions about what actions will go the farthest toward improving society. If you disagree with us or with your colleagues, we encourage open dialogue, since this is an excellent stimulus to further learning and growth.

TABLE 6–1 *Education That Is Multicultural and Social Reconstructionist*

Societal goals:	Promote social structural equality and cultural pluralism
School goal:	Prepare citizens to work actively toward social structural equality; promote cultural pluralism and alternative life-styles; promote equal opportunity in the school
Target students:	Everyone
Practices: Curriculum	Organize content around current social issues involving racism, classism, sexism, handicapism; organize concepts around experiences and perspectives of several different American groups; use students' life experiences as starting point for analyzing oppression; teach critical thinking skills, analysis of alternative viewpoints; teach social action skills, empowerment skills
Instruction	Involve students actively in democratic decision making; build on students' learning styles; adapt to students' skill levels; use cooperative learning
Other aspects of classroom	Decorate room to reflect social action themes, cultural diversity, student interests; avoid testing and grouping procedures that designate some students as failures
Support services	Help regular classroom adapt to as much diversity as possible
Other school-wide concerns	Involve students in democratic decision making about substantive school-wide concerns; involve lower-class and minority parents actively in the school; involve school in local community action projects; make sure that staffing patterns include diverse racial, gender, and disability groups in nontraditional roles; use decorations, special events, school menus to reflect and include diverse groups; use library materials that portray diverse groups in diverse roles; make sure that extracurricular activities include all student groups and do not reinforce stereotypes; use discipline procedures that do not penalize any one group; make sure building is accessible to disabled people

REFERENCES

Abberley, P. (1987). The concept of oppression and the development of a social theory of disability. *Disability, Handicap, and Society, 2,* 5–20.

Anyon, J. (1981). Elementary schooling and distinctions of social class. *Interchange, 12,* 118–132.

Anyon, J. (1983). Intersections of gender and class: Accommodation and resistance by working class and affluent females to contradictory sex-role. In S. Walker & L. Barton (Eds.), *Gender, class and education* (pp. 19–38). Barcombe, England: Falmer Press.

Apple, M. W. (1985). *Education and power* (Ark ed.). Boston: Routledge & Kegan Paul.

Aronowitz, S., & Giroux, H. A. (1985). *Education under siege.* South Hadley, MA: Bergin and Garvey.

Banks, J. A. (1981). *Multiethnic education: Theory and practice.* Boston: Allyn and Bacon.

Barbagli, M., & Dei, M. (1977). Specialization into apathy and political subordination. In J. Karabel & A. H. Halsey (Eds.), *Power and ideology in education* (pp. 423–431). New York: Oxford University Press.

Bennett, C. I. (1986). *Comprehensive multicultural education.* Boston: Allyn and Bacon.

Brameld, T. (1956). *Toward a reconstructed philosophy of education.* New York: Holt, Rinehart & Winston.

Carby, H. (1982). Schooling in Babylon. In Centre for Contemporary Cultural Studies, *The empire strikes back: Race and racism in 70's Britain* (pp. 183–211). Wolfeboro, NH: Longwood Publishing Group.

Carter, T. P., & Chatfield, M. L. (1986). Effective bilingual schools: Implications for policy and practice. *American Journal of Education, 95,* 26–57.

Collins, R. (1977). Functional and conflict theories of educational stratification. In J. Karabel & A. H. Halsey (Eds.), *Power and ideology in education* (pp. 118–136). New York: Oxford University Press.

Counts, G. (1982). *Dare the school build a new social order?* New York: John Day.

Dahrendorf, R. (1959). *Class and class conflict in industrial society.* Stanford: Stanford University Press.

Davis, A. Y. (1981). *Women, race, and class.* New York: Random House.

Dewey, J. (1938). *Experience and education.* New York: Macmillan.

Duck, L. (1980). *Teaching with charisma.* Boston: Allyn and Bacon.

Elshtain, J. B. (1976). The social relations of the classroom: A moral and political perspective. *Telos, 27,* 97–110.

Freire, P. (1985). *The politics of education: Culture, power, and liberation* (D. Macedo, Trans.) South Hadley, MA: Bergin and Garvey.

Genovese, E. (1974). *Roll, Jordan, roll: The world the slaves made.* New York: Pantheon Books.

Giddens, A. (1979). *Central problems in social theory.* Berkeley: University of California Press.

Giroux, H. A. (1981). *Ideology, culture and the process of schooling.* Barcombe, England: Falmer Press.

Giroux, H. A. (1983). Theories of reproduction and resistance in the new sociology of education: A critical analysis. *Harvard Educational Review, 53,* 257–293.

Gordon, B. M. (1985). Toward emancipation in citizenship education: The case of African-American cultural knowledge. *Theory and Research in Social Education, 12,* 1–23.

Grant, C. A. (1978). Education that is multicultural—Isn't that what we mean? *Journal of Teacher Education, 29,* 45–49.

Grant, C. A., & Sleeter, C. E. (1986). Race, class and gender in educational research: An argument for integrative analysis. *Review of Educational Research, 56,* 195–211.

Hale, J. E. (1982). *Black children, their roots, culture, and learning styles.* Provo, UT: Brigham Young University.

Jaggar, A. M., & Struhl, P. R. (1978). *Feminist/frameworks.* New York: McGraw-Hill.

Jefferson, T. (1779). *A bill for the more general diffusion of knowledge.* Report of the Revisors, State of Virginia.

Kanter, R. M. (1975). Women and the structure of organization: Exploration in theory and behavior. In M. Millman & R. M. Kanter (Eds.), *Another voice* (pp. 34–75). Garden City, NY: Anchor-Doubleday.

Mann, J. (1974). Political power and the high school curriculum. In E. W. Eisner & E. Vallance (Eds.), *Conflicting conceptions of curriculum* (pp. 147–153). Berkeley, CA: McCutchan.

Marx, K. (1972). *Capital* (Book 1). London: J. M. Bent.

Metcalf, L. E., & Hunt, M. P. (1974). Relevance and the curriculum. In E. W. Eisner & E. Vallance (Eds.), *Conflicting conceptions of curriculum* (pp. 136–146). Berkeley, CA: McCutchan.

Mitchell, C. (1978). Woman's estate. In A. M. Jaggar & P. R. Struhl (Eds.), *Feminist frameworks* (pp. 130–141). New York: McGraw-Hill.

Mullard, C. (1980). *Racism in society and schools: History, policy, and practice.* Occasional Paper No. 1, Centre for Multicultural Education, University of London, Institute of Education.

Myers, R. A., Banfield, B., & Colon, J. J. (1983). *Embers: Stories for a changing world.* Westbury, NY: Feminist Press, and New York: Council on Interracial Books for Children.

Oakley, A. (1981). *Subject women.* New York: Pantheon Books.

Piaget, J. (1952). *The language and thought of the child.* London: Routledge & Kegan Paul.

Schneidewind, N., & Davidson, E. (1983). *Open minds to equality.* Englewood Cliffs, NJ: Prentice-Hall.

Shaw, G. B. (1921). *Back to Methuselah,* Pt. I, Act I.

Shor, I. (1980). *Critical teaching and everyday life.* Boston: South End Press.

Sleeter, C. E., & Grant, C. A. (1987). An analysis of multicultural education in the U.S.A. *Harvard Educational Review, 57,* 421–444.

Suzuki, B. H. (1977). The Japanese-American experience. In M. J. Gold, C. A. Grant, and H. N. Rivlin (Eds.), *In praise of diversity: A resource book for multicultural education* (pp. 139–162). Washington, DC: Teacher Corps.

Suzuki, B. H. (1984). Curriculum transformation for multicultural education. *Education and Urban Society, 16,* 294–322.

Valli, L. (1986). *Becoming clerical workers.* London: Routledge & Kegan Paul.

Van Avery, D. (1975). The humanitarian approach. *Phi Delta Kappan, 57,* 177–178.

Weber, M. (1947). *The theory of social and economic organization.* A. M. Henderson & T. Parsons (Trans.), T. Parsons (Ed.), Glencoe, IL: Free Press.

Weber, M. (1968). *Economy and society.* New York: The Bedminster Press.

CHAPTER 7

Our Choice: Education That Is Multicultural and Social Reconstructionist

By now you probably have a sense as to which approach to multicultural education you prefer. We have tried to present and critique the approaches thoroughly and objectively enough to help you make your own choices. But at the same time, we cannot remain neutral and detached. We do have a strong sense as to which approach goes the farthest toward better schooling as well as a better society. Furthermore, based on our own experience in schools, our research on schools, and our long-standing study of multicultural education, we feel we have an obligation to share our recommendation.

Our thinking is based largely on social conditions that persist and that limit and often damage or destroy the lives of many people. A significant segment of American society has always been poor, and the size of this group in recent years has been growing rather than diminishing. Globally, poverty and hunger are more the norm than is the wealth so many of us take for granted. Racism in the United States is still in many ways as intact as it was decades ago, and as the population of color in the United States grows, one can predict a certain amount of increased competition among racial groups. The family structure in the United States continues to change as more women enter the work force, but family role changes and cooperative networks are not emerging on a large scale. For example, rather than involving husbands and the extended family more actively in child care, many families simply reduce time spent on child care when the mother takes on additional roles. These are some of the trends and persistent problems that concern us.

People tend to live in small, rather insulated worlds with others who share their advantages or disadvantages. Consequently, the educator who is experiencing a relatively comfortable and privileged life may have difficulty fully appreciating and understanding the very real problems faced, for example, by the Mexican-American father searching desperately for work, the single mother wondering how to make ends meet, or the laid-off worker who feels powerless as the local factories close down. But these problems exist, and they are part of the very fabric of American society. There may be periodic improvements of a superficial nature, and these may be widely publicized, but the character and magnitude of the problems have not changed much in the past 2 or 3 decades.

Let us return to the hypothetical class of students with whom we opened the first chapter. How should they be taught? Before proceeding with "business as usual" or with any of the approaches to multicultural education, the teacher should consider these students in relationship to the society in which they live today and will live as adults. As they grow up, what is in store for them? Which approach to education might make a genuine difference?

Half of the students are girls, half are boys. If present trends continue, virtually all of them will attempt to join the labor force as adults, although many of the girls will be only minimally prepared to do so. The girls may be only dimly aware of this, but most of them will wind up with two careers: child raising/housekeeping and holding down a low-paying job. Many of the girls will be heads of households fighting to stay above the poverty line; the Black girls who find themselves as heads of households will have better than a 50-50 chance of living in poverty. Many of the boys, though economically better off, will find themselves alienated from their children, in some cases even feared by their children. Many will find themselves trapped in jobs they dislike but must keep for the sake of their roles as breadwinners. Some will become angry and resentful of their wives and beat them. Some of the girls will have babies at a young age, and some can look forward to being battered wives. Some of the students already know these things because their parents experience them. But most believe that adulthood holds a happy marriage with clearly divided responsibilities and a comfortable income.

Our first approach—Teaching the Exceptional and the Culturally Different—which is an improvement over "business as usual," would address the situation by equipping the girls better to compete with the boys in male-dominated areas, especially in fields requiring mathematics, science, and computers. This will help a few girls, maybe 1 or 2 of the 15. However, it does not address the dual career that most women must occupy, which causes many not to consider full-time, demanding professions that conflict with domestic responsibilities. It also does not help homemakers to receive a full reward for their work. Nor does it address the low pay of jobs that women dominate; moving women out of secretarial work into the sciences, for example, does nothing to raise the pay of secretaries; it only increases the competition for more lucrative jobs.

Our second approach—Human Relations—would help build better cross-sex understanding, which one would hope would lead to better communication and more respect between the sexes. But again, economic problems and role responsibilities would tend to remain intact, which would tend to disrupt relationships among men and women. Women's studies (part of our third approach, Single-Group Studies) would help the students examine sexism and mobilize them (mainly the girls) to challenge it. Although this has greater potential than the preceding approach (and certainly greater potential than "business as usual") for preparing students to recognize and struggle against institutional sexism, it is limited. Women's studies focuses on a single form of human diversity and does not necessarily attend to issues such as poverty (which is also a very important problem) or racism, which the girls of color will face. It also often excludes men, unintentionally presenting sexism as a problem only for women.

Our fourth approach—Multicultural Education—would address sexism by promoting nonsexist role and job choice and by giving as much attention to the female experience as to the male experience in the curriculum. It would also include experiences of women of color as well as White women, and of poor as well as middle-class women. It would attempt to eliminate a sexist division of labor in the home and encourage the young to choose careers without reference to masculine versus feminine roles. But the biggest limitation of this approach is that it does not prepare students to take steps to change "rules of the game" that structure sexism into society. We will illustrate this point with three structures that help perpetuate sexism.

First, many careers, particularly those with the greatest pay, do not lend themselves well to maintaining an active role in parenting. An episode on the TV sit-com "Family Ties" illustrated this well. Mr. Keaton was promoted to a better-paying job with more responsibilities, but he found that it increasingly took him away from home. He had to choose between advancing his career and actively parenting. He resolved the dilemma by returning to his old job. However, the job he gave up still existed and would pull someone else away from the family;

the dilemma of having to choose between a career and active involvement at home was simply waiting for someone else. The very existence of careers that greatly reduce available hours for parenting is one structure that helps maintain sexism, since such careers automatically exclude their holders from active parenting and since women are assumed to have primary responsibility for child care. Men greatly outnumber women in such careers, and their wives end up with most of the parenting responsibility.

A second structural "rule of the game" that reinforces sexism is the nuclear family, in which the woman's primary role is child care and the man's is breadwinner. Even if young people start married life believing they will share roles, they often divide roles by sex owing to a lack of alternatives. For example, when children are young either one parent stays home part of the day or the family pays for day care, which can cost as much as or more than many women make at work. Thus, the woman usually stays home. The extended family, familiar to many people of color, can provide more alternatives because more adults are in the home who can share roles, lessening the need to shift domestic work to one adult. Although the extended family is growing in popularity, the nuclear family is offered as the norm and is legitimated in the structure of houses and in the tax structure. To encourage and support greater role flexibility, one would want to legitimate the extended family as well as the nuclear family, in addition to encouraging attitudes that support nonsexist role sharing.

A third structural problem is the institution of domestic help. Many career-oriented people who can afford it hire domestic help to do the jobs that husband and wife do not have time for, or they make use of services such as day care. In and of themselves, these are good options, but these jobs pay very poorly and are usually filled by women, often women of color. Furthermore, jobs such as "cleaning lady" rarely provide benefits such as health insurance or retirement pay. These are more "rules of the game" that society accepts and plays by that continue to trap many women.

Our final approach—Education That Is Multicultural and Social Reconstructionist—would help students examine these sorts of issues and begin to think of ways of challenging them. In so doing, it offers several advantages. First, it speaks to issues that currently impact on many of the students and eventually will impact on all of them. For example, students who may see little relevance in studying economics see considerable relevance when economics is used to help them understand changes in the availability of jobs locally or reduced availability of government loans for college. Second, it encourages students to take an active stance, to take charge over their lives. It helps them connect what they are doing now with their future lives as adults, but in a way that does not fit them into the status quo with all its problems, but teaches them to challenge it. Finally, it helps them learn to work collectively to speak out, be heard, and effect change. Furthermore, unlike Single-Group Studies, this last approach attempts to join the White girls with the girls and boys of color, and the middle-class with the lower-class students, in an examination of common or related concerns.

Three of the students in our hypothetical class are Hispanic. If present trends continue, and especially if schools continue with "business as usual," one and possibly two of the three will not graduate from high school. They will leave mainly to help take care of the family but also because many will experience alienation in school. Culturally, the school will connect only partially with their own life experiences, and most, if not all, of the teachers and authority figures will be White. As teenagers, all three may have to look for jobs, but at least one will not find a job. Unable to find a job and alienated from school, one of these students may choose to join a gang, because gangs can sometimes offer a source of identity, an underground economy and source of income, and a means of controlling something, even if it is only a city block. As adults, the family income of these three Hispanic students will average only about 75% of the family income of their White peers. One will probably live in poverty, and the other two will live in the lower middle class. All three will continually feel caught in a cultural tug-of-war that will probably intensify. As the Hispanic population becomes the largest American racial minority group, Mexican culture will gain a firmer foothold. Whites will probably continue to respond by asserting the primacy of English and the legitimacy of Anglo-American culture. About 4.5 million American students speak Spanish at home, and language policy will increasingly be a source of tension. The Hispanic students will feel, for example, somewhat alienated from mainstream media, which renders Hispanics almost invisible except in advertisements for Mexican food, in which viewers may be invited to "feel a little Mexican" tonight. Lack of representation will be a problem in many other areas as well, such as in political decision making. Moreover, the Hispanic students as adults may find themselves competing with their former Black classmates for control over elective inner-city offices.

Teaching the Culturally Different deals with these issues mainly by trying to get Hispanics through school (which is important), helping them learn English, and preparing them better to compete for jobs. But this approach does not deal with the cultural tug-of-war, except by acknowledging that it is okay to be Hispanic as long as one can also function effectively in an Anglo world. It ignores White racism entirely; in fact, it denies it. The Human Relations approach helps all the students learn not to stereotype Hispanics, and it develops more positive attitudes about Hispanic culture. But it does not deal with poverty and political powerlessness; it only teaches that these problems will be resolved if people communicate better and appreciate each other more. Chicano studies would offer the Hispanic students a chance to develop group solidarity with other Mexican-Americans. It would offer a source of identification with school and a counter to cultural alienation, since Chicano studies embraces Hispanic culture and concerns. It would also offer a forum for examining the life circumstances and needs of Hispanics. However, the Single-Group Studies approach, in the form of Chicano studies, could subordinate and ignore Hispanic women, would not help Hispanics work with other oppressed groups, and may even aggravate cross-group conflict.

The Multicultural Education approach would make Hispanic culture and concerns an integral part of the curriculum, along with those of other groups. It would help Hispanic students succeed in school by building on their learning styles and experiential backgrounds. It would offer all the students role models of successful Hispanic men and women and would encourage bilingualism as a norm. However, it would not offer a plan for attacking poverty and unemployment, nor would it necessarily help build the political skills and group solidarity that Hispanics need.

Education That Is Multicultural and Social Reconstructionist offers a more direct response to these concerns, in addition to other features of the Multicultural Education approach. For example, Hispanics have a pressing need to gain representation in decision-making roles in many institutions. Although Hispanics are developing more political clout at the local level in areas where the Hispanic population is large, they are still virtually powerless in most states and at the national level. Two issues directly affecting Hispanics are periodically debated and voted on at the national level: language policy and immigration policy. As the Hispanic population in the United States grows, as the Mexican economy continues to suffer, and as Central America continues to be a hotbed of political unrest, these two issues will probably take on greater urgency. Our last approach does not teach a certain stance on these issues so much as it encourages young people, including (and in this case especially) Hispanics, to learn how to research the issues, mobilize, articulate a stand, gain access to the media, use the legal system, and so forth.

A final example relates to the issue of unemployment. It is not enough to equip people better to compete for jobs when there are not enough jobs to go around and when existing jobs are not amply available in minority neighborhoods. Youth of color should learn to seek jobs more effectively, interview skillfully, complete school, and so forth. But future citizens should also begin to examine the job structure itself and consider improvements. For example, students could research the availability of jobs in Black, Hispanic, and White neighborhoods. They could find out why businesses tend not to locate in lower-class neighborhoods, and they could study ways of attracting business. Students could find out how to assess hiring discrimination and how to fight it effectively. They could analyze wage structure in relationship to cost of living to understand the extent to which local employers tacitly support near-poverty existence by keeping wages low; and then they could find out how to change this.

It may sound as though we are writing a social studies curriculum, but we are not. The topics we have suggested lend themselves to reading (one can learn reading skills by reading about virtually any topic), writing, mathematics skills, learning to use the scientific method, some science topics, art, and music (here we are referring to the content of song lyrics), as well as social studies.

We could continue with examples from the hypothetical class, but we suspect that our point has been made. However, there is one group whose presence and probable discomfort we would like to acknowledge: that of the White, middle-class or upper-class male. This would constitute about eight members of our hypothetical class and a sizable portion of the readers of this book. We could start cataloging the problems this group will face after schooling—indeed there are problems. But this group will tend to have greater access to resources and more power than any other group. How does Education That Is Multicultural and Social Reconstructionist regard him? Mainly as a necessary ally. There are and always have been White males who have joined the struggle against oppression and who have worked *with* (rather than dominated) members of subordinate groups. Their presence and help is necessary partly *because* of, rather than in spite of, their membership in dominant race, class, and gender groups. At the classroom level, White male students are often willing to join with others as long as they feel valued and a genuine ethos of cooperation is fostered. As they become adults, they will be offered advantages not available to their classmates; they will need to decide whether to use their privileged status for their own benefit or for the benefit of others.

Which approach is the best one is a value decision that the individual educator must make. This book has outlined goals, assumptions, underlying values, and practices of five ways of approaching diversity in the classroom. One cannot choose not to choose, because to accept the status quo is also to make a choice. We hope that this book has helped the educator in that process.

INDEX